Arriflex 16 SR3: The Book

Jon Fauer

illustrations by Mary Mortimer

ISBN 0-936763-02-7

Manuscript written with Microsoft Word 7.0
Typography using
Adobe Pagemaker, Adobe Photoshop
Corel Photo-Paint

Printed in the United States of America

Published by:
Arriflex Corporation
617 Route 303
Blauvelt, NY 10913
(914) 353-1400
Fax: (914) 425-1250

Foreword

As our "tools of the trade" are becoming ever more versatile and useful, they are undoubtedly also getting more varied and complex. Learning and retaining all the facts and features of these advanced camera systems is essential if one expects to explore their full range of creative possibilities and the efficiency they can bring to a wide spectrum of production environments.

While we as the manufacturer can provide you with the technical support and information necessary to introduce our products to the market, only a working, creative person, applying the technology to the film making process with all its variables, can convey and teach the fine points about these subjects with authority.

We are fortunate to have accomplished professionals of all ranks in our industry who are willing to share their valuable experience. Jon Fauer is one of those. While building an illustrious career as a cinematographer, Jon has always stayed "on top" of technological advancements in all areas even remotely connected with our industry, and he has always freely shared his knowledge with all who could benefit.

This store of knowledge combined with the creative mind seems to occasionally require an outlet, which we were of course willing to provide to Jon in the form of a major project.

Jon met the challenge with characteristic enthusiasm, and we are proud and happy to be able to offer you his most comprehensive volume on camera systems yet: *The Arriflex 16 SR3 from Concept to Setup to Maintenance.*

Unlike with his previous, successful works on the *Arriflex 16SR* and the *Arriflex 35 Book*, this time we also produced a detailed series of films covering all subject matters referred to in this book. The films were shot in Super 16 with SR3' s, and are available in VHS format video cassettes.

In closing, I want to express our sincere thanks to Jon for his friendship and support, and congratulate him for this truly impressive and important work, which will benefit many. I also want to thank all who generously contributed their time and knowledge to a project they can all be proud of.

Volker W. Bahnemann
President
Arriflex Corporation

Film Series

Arriflex 16 SR3 Camera System

This book is accompanied by three VHS video tapes (all shot with Arriflex 16 SR3 cameras in Super16), demonstrating and expanding on many of the procedures described here. The tapes feature real crews in real situations, and supplement the text as a complete resource on the 16 SR3 Camera System, available for reference and review. The tapes cover the following topics:

I. Arriflex 16 SR3: Intro

A day in the life of the 16 SR3 camera system across North America: on location, in studios, hand-held, remote controlled, underwater and in the air. (8 min.)

II. Arriflex 16 SR3: Camera Prep

A detailed exploration of the 16 SR3 camera presented by real camera assistants during a rental-house checkout. (Approx. 45 min.) Topics include:

Basics of Camera Checkout
Camera Cases
3 Ways to Mount the Camera
Power Sources, Cables
On-Board Batteries
Powering Up the Camera
Main Camera Display
The 6 LCD Display Modes
Default Camera Speeds
Regular16 or Super16 Format
Fiber Optic Viewing Screen
Viewing Screen Focus
Setting Diopter
Timing Test
ARRIGLOW and Lightmeter
Adjusting Mirror Shutter Angle
Video Assist
24V to 12V DC Converter
Anti-Flicker Processor
Frame Store
Adjustment of Video Assist
Mounting Lens and Rods
Matteboxes
PL to Bayonet Adapter
16 SR3 vs Highspeed 16 SR3
Eyepiece and Finder Extender
Orienting and Adjusting Finder
Eyepiece Heater
Attaching Magazines
Scratch Test
Checking and Setting Up Lens
Lens Care
Checking the Gate
Loading Mags in Changing Tent
Loading Mags in Darkroom
AC Kits, Tips and Tools
Wrapping Up

III. Arriflex 16 SR3: Camera Setup

The next step: on the job. On the set of "Dr. Quinn Medicine Woman," in the Mojave Desert for a car commercial, and on location with a variety of different shoots. A tour of advanced features and accessories. (Approx. 60 min.)

Beginning of Day Setup
"Building" the Camera
User tips
Advanced Features
The System
ARRIHEAD 2
Camera Trucks
Review: Main Camera Display
Setting the 6 Modes
Remote Control Unit (RCU)
Laptop Camera Controller (LCC)
Iris Control Unit (ICU)
RCU + ICU
Speed - Aperture Ramps
Lens Control System (LCS)
Color-Coding and Labeling Cables
Shared Accessories
16 SR3, 535, 535A and 435
External Sync Unit (ESU)
Video Anti-Flicker
Using Framestore
Non-Linear Postproduction
Timecode Theory
Electronic Slates
Jam-syncing the Camera
Timecode on the 16 SR3

Additional tapes are planned, including:

IV. Arriflex Camera Care

Cleaning up at the end of the day. Service and maintenance procedures, presented by Arriflex Service Technicians. (Approx. 45 min.)

Dealing with equipment after a day at the beach
How to cope with sand, salt, wind, and water
Converting the 16 SR3 from Regular to Super16
Assembling the Video Elbow
16 SR3 Magazine Care
Removing the 16 SR3 Magazine Throat Assembly
Checking 16 SR3 Magazine Take-Up Tension
Adjusting 16 SR3 Take-Up Tension
Checking flange focal depth
Checking lenses on an MTF Collimator

The Arriflex 16 SR3 Camera System tapes are available wherever this book is sold, or directly from Arriflex Corporation.

Contents

Arriflex 16 SR3: The Book

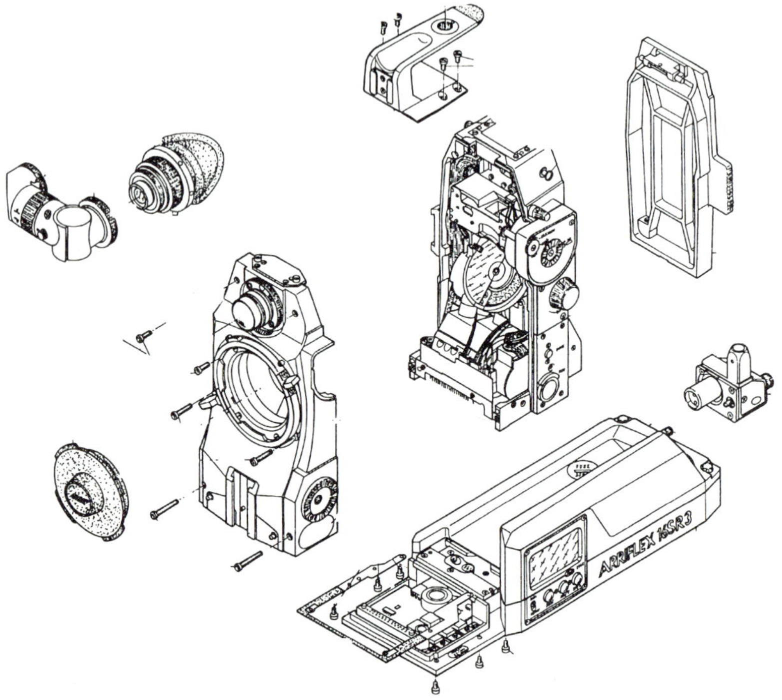

Exploded Camera Views in this book courtesy of Arnold & Richter (ARRI) for illustrative purposes only. See "Do not Attempt" in next section, pg. 22.

Introduction

Sorry this book took so long to arrive. It's been a long time since the **16 SR1**, **SR2**, and **35 BL/35-3** books came out.

The success of the previous manuals took us totally by surprise, thanks to the overwhelming generosity and support of so many readers. The books were an assembly of notes taken down over the years, using a particular camera system, written from a particular point of view. The systems happened to be my own, and they were subjected to over a million feet of film running through their gates each year. I don't work for Arriflex. I'm a freelance Director of Photography. Perhaps there is just enough healthy criticism and anecdotal cynicism to maintain credibility, which may reassure readers that this book is not going to be a company advertisement. Fortunately, my friends at Arriflex have been not only tolerant, but also very supportive.

When I traded in my BL for a 535, it came with the best manual ARRI had ever done. I wondered whether a book would even be necessary. But I kept on keeping notes, which soon filled up an entire laptop computer hard drive. Just when I thought it was safe to come out with a 535 book, the 435 started accelerating its way toward an earlier delivery date than expected. Since the two cameras are part of the same advanced system, I decided to hold off on that book until I had used a 435.

There was another surprise. Sixteen millimeter shooting experienced a major resurgence. Several factors caused this.

Slow speed film stocks were manufactured virtually free of grain, with enhanced resolution and color. HDTV had everyone scrambling, without a clue as to final format standards. The answer was to originate in the medium Europeans had been using for quite some time: Super16. It could be transferred to any videotape format worldwide. It could be screened in standard or widescreen format. It looked cheaper on spreadsheets.

Of course, studio accountants didn't plan on the Directors of Photography quadrupling their lighting budgets to accommodate the slower speed films. The faster 16mm film stocks look grainier than their 35mm counterparts, which is why many cinematographers shoot with the slower emulsions in 16mm.

Anyway, a record number of TV series were shot using the new Arriflex 16SR3 cameras, and a record number of cameras were sold. I received lots of requests to do a 16SR3 book. But I hadn't used the camera, and hadn't shot anything in 16mm since **Tales From the Darkside** a number of years ago. I didn't really want to write a manual without having thoroughly used the camera. Although it wouldn't have been too difficult, I didn't want to inflict on the industry a regurgitated manufacturer's instruction manual without tips and advice from actual on-location use.

Then Volker Bahnemann, president of Arriflex Corporation, got the idea to do a book and series of instructional films on the 16 SR3 Camera System. Arriflex lent me 2 complete SR3 packages, which I brought everywhere for 9 months in 1995. Whenever we were shooting (usually 35mm commercials) in an interesting place, Jonathan Ercole and I stayed a few extra days to find and film another crew using SR3 cameras. We filmed Bill Bennett in the Mojave Desert shooting a car commercial in the rain. Wolfgang Bayer in Jackson Hole, Wyoming. Ozzie Smith at the Paramount Ranch shooting the series **Dr. Quinn, Medicine Woman.** Pat Longman shooting aerials in Miami. Nick Smeloff at Denver International Airport and Vail, Colorado. And many others.

It felt good going back to my "beginnings." I hadn't really done documentary style shooting since the National Geographic, ABC Sports and Mel London days. The freedom of mobility, using a lightweight equipment package that fit in the back of a car, made for a very enjoyable and interesting project. My wife Noemi and daughter Marlena deserve a special thanks for putting up with me during this project, although I'm sure they found my absence and preoccupation less interesting.

Credits

There are many people to thank for their contribution to this book and its accompanying films. A special note of gratitude is due Volker Bahnemann, president of Arriflex Corporation, who inspired, initiated, and guided the project. He spent many hours, along with Juergen Schwinzer and Franz Wieser, on the creative and production process. I am also indebted to the following who helped write, corrected and proofed the manuscripts: Russell Guenther, Bill Russell, Denny Clairmont, Marge Ruhlmann, and Jonathan Ercole, who also starred in the films.

As always, Mary Mortimer did a superb job on the drawings.

Once again, the entire staff of Arriflex Corporation and Camera Service Center were more than generous in their support, technical advice and patience: Wolfgang Reigl, Cristy Cobb, Roger Reddy, George Schmidt, Laura Stagg, Wolfgang Schmid, Karin Wollin, Joe Sheehan, Frank Karlsson, Charlie Tammaro, Tibor Sands, Jerry Wiener, Hardwrick Johnson, Waverly Taliaferro, and to all the other folks at Arriflex for providing and shipping twenty to forty cases of brand new camera equipment around the country for the 16 SR3 films over the course of an entire year.

Since the credits of the accompanying films fly by so quickly, it is only fitting that the names linger here:

Jonathan Ercole, Anne Gwynn, Jonathan Burkhart, Don Blackburn, William F. Bennett, Jeff Laszlo, Mike Denecke, Roland "Ozzie" Smith, Jeff Norvett, Jim Pfeiffer, Rusty Geller, Alisa Faloona, Dean Mitchell, Geoff Patterson, George Peters, "Tiny" Mike Lehan, Monica Fernandez, Dean Goldsmith, Camera Car Industries, Alan Pedelford, Dominick Mandy, Darius Carter, Jeremy Schmidt, Robert Burns, David Allegra (The Art Director), Paul Yardley, Gaylin Schmidt, Gary Shlifer, Bruce King, Florida Grip Service Inc., John Leeward Movie Tech USA, Michael Clayton, Frank Lemaire, Al Guthery, International Helicopter Service, Jim Dirker, Aircam National Helicopter Service, Bill Jones, Chalk's International Airlines, Roni Edwards, Ronald Haaland, Debbie at Fisher Production Services, Fernando Santo, Anne Bobroff Boie, Michael Bole, Michael Kushner,

Dean Schneider, Eric Altman, Film/Video Equipment Co., Darick D'Ercole, Steve Braun, Gary Hebert, Lee Barbour, Doug Hawryluk, Robert “Frog” Matthews , Dianna Barrett, Frank Fox, Steve "Tunes" Lorton, Vail Assoc, Kristi Brown, Joe Smith, Chris Sandoski, Angie Tetrault, Dave McHugh, Eric Replinger, Nick Smeloff, Future Media, Promethius Patient, Toby Ross, Alex Perera, Miami Seaquarium, John Liberti , Dr. Quinn Medicine Woman—CBS Entertainment, George Stephenson, Jack Regis, Peter Norkus, Bill Loranger, Peter Kowalski, Robert Smith, Lightsmith Electric & Grip Co., Keith Schnell, Reel Things, Dave MacEachen, Angus McNevin, Kent Harvey, John Carlson, Deborah White, Cody Sloan, Dan Melfi, Denver International Airport, David Henry, Cine Video Tech Miami, Pat Longman, Ron Winter, Pennzoil Products, Richard J. Westman, Eisaman, Johns & Laws Advertising, Mark Geffen, Avid Technologies, Michael Phillips, Dana Ruzicka, Dana Music, Howard Phillips, The Edit House, Dana Bromley, South Bay Studios, Dan Sabovitch, Debbi Roth, East Kern Airport District / Mojave Airport, Mark Polyocan, Richard Dare, Stewart Oppenheimer, Steve Seng, Jonathan Giles, The Tape House, Tape House Digital, Karen Stewart, Sarah Sorgie, Angelique Thermes, Peter Heady, Kevin Brown, Cari Chadwick, Patrick Ferguson, Ezekiel Springer, Carl Mandelbaum, Photomag, Cathy Almeda, Biltmore Hotel, Paul Krumper, Wolfgang Bayer, Tristan Bayer, Julia Nielson, Lynn Toll, Mary Alice Foughner, Synergy Films, John Vincent, Tom Lappin, Peter Anway, Tom Johnson, Birns & Sawyer, Alan Albert, Clairmont Camera, Otto Nemenz, Alex Wengert, Karl Kresser, Otto Nemenz International, Michael E. Johnson, Bob Woolman, Eastman Kodak Company, Wilson Chao, Cambridge Television Productions, Larry Blume, John Denis, Denise Rocchietti, Terri Brook, GLG, Felix Andrew, Mike Lonsdale, Steve Ramsey, Steve Baker, Peter Caldwell, Garrett Boehling, Chris Rosen, Dominic Rom, Tim Spitzer, Michael Layton, Joe Mongi, Jay Rice, Jim Mann ,Duart Film/Video, Manhattan Transfer, Sally Savoca, Dave Corbett, Pete Romano, Hydroflex, Bill Turner, Jeff Giordano, Century Precision Optics, Elsie Gaffney, Millie Rodriguez, Taylor & Taylor Insurance, Jim Meade, Tom Boehlens , Steve Manios, Jr., Cartoni USA, Eric Falkenberg, Bob Carr, Mark Henderson , Frank Hatch, Sachtler Corp. of America, Larry Barton, Cinematography Electronics, Howard Preston, Preston Cinema Systems.

My apologies to anyone I omitted.

The World's Worst Assistant

The World's Worst Assistant—a mythological character of monumental ineptitude—was born on a particularly difficult shoot in the Caribbean. Conditions were not friendly to people or cameras: sand, salt water, wind, heat, bugs. We had dug a large hole in the beach to get a low angle. Water was filling the hole faster than we could bail.

As the water reached high-tide level and tempers achieved similar heights—especially mine— using my equipment, against all better judgment never to bring ones own new package on tropical beach jobs—it was at that moment when Scott Rathner, our excellent camera assistant, wondered how the world's worst assistant would cope in such a dreadful situation. "I'd like to change my airplane reservation right now to an aisle seat," he called out to the already-harassed AD. "And while you're at it," Scott added, "can you change my hotel room so I can have a king size bed?"

Since then, the exploits of the World's Worst Assistant have become legendary. Many of the tales have been true, unfortunately. We never cease to be amazed at what really goes on out there. The assistant who tried to loosen a stuck lens with a huge hammer. The production assistant who left the camera truck parked unattended in the world's worst neighborhood to make a phone call—surprised when the entire package had been stolen by the time he returned. The assistant who put film in the gate—emulsion side in.

You've probably worked with Arriflex 16 SR Cameras for the last twenty years. No doubt, you've already used the third generation 16 SR3. But, since every reader of this book will have a different level of expertise, this manual assumes the worst, and is written for The World's Worst Assistant.

The World's Worst Assistant has just made a bold career move from shepherd to camera assistant. They've just opened a new rental house in Ulan Bator, and we are introducing him to an Arriflex 16 SR3 for the first time. He has not read any of our previous books. We apologize to other readers who recognize familiar sections, but we had to repeat certain important facts and procedures.

Disclaimer

Because the World's Worst Assistant is reading this, the usual disclaimer must be made. Some of the modifications, accessories and procedures described in this book have not been tested or approved by Arnold & Richter (ARRI) or Arriflex Corporation, and may void the warranty on the camera. Taking the camera apart without knowing what you're doing definitely voids the warranty. Shooting film tests is recommended whenever there is ever any doubt about anything. Although we have made every attempt to check the facts and techniques described in this text, there lurks the possibility of error, for which we apologize, but are not responsible or liable. Please let us know for future editions or update notices.

Do Not Attempt

As always, upon the advice of those long-suffering service technicians who have seen everything, a word of warning. This book contains several exploded views of the internal workings of the camera. Unfortunately, the World's Worst Assistant has attempted to dissect his camera exactly as depicted, with regrettable results. Also, some advanced service procedures are shown here. But, if you don't know what you are doing, do NOT take anything apart. I am obliged to add a final note of admonition. Like they say in the car commercials, "do not attempt."

Conventions

Certain conventions are used in this book. Reference to a clock face are made for circular positions, such as 3 o'clock for something 90° from the top, when facing the object.

Measurements are shown both in Metric and English where I remembered. It is funny how often we use mixed measurements in film. For example: Load a 1000 **foot** magazine with 35**mm** film, set the 85**mm** lens to a distance of 10 **feet**, and attach a 6.6 **inch** by 6.6 **inch** mattebox with a 138**mm** round filter in the 6 **inch** round rear filter holder adapter, on the 17 inch long 19mm rods.

"K" numbers in the text are ARRI (Munich) part numbers; "300000" series numbers are Arriflex (USA) part numbers.

Arriflex 16 SR3 Camera Views

Front

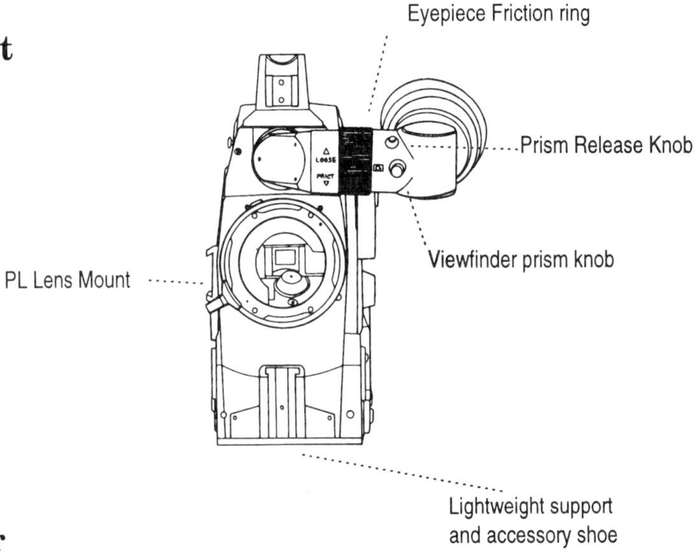

Rear

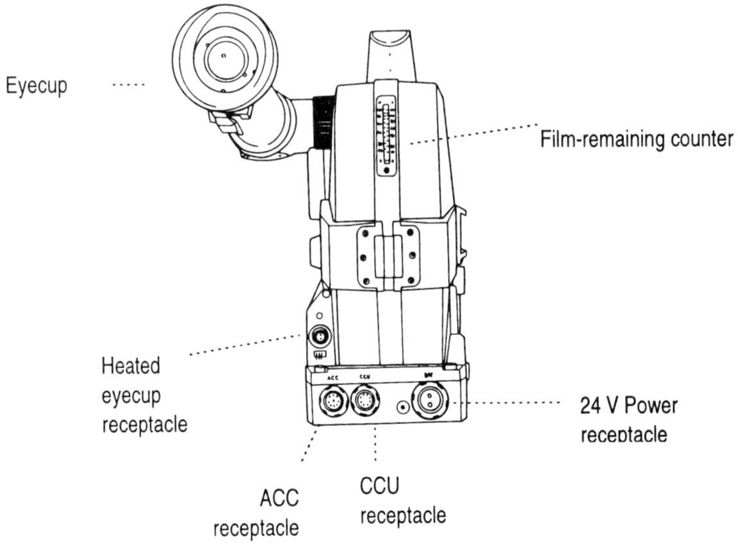

Camera Left

(Magazine Take-Up Side)

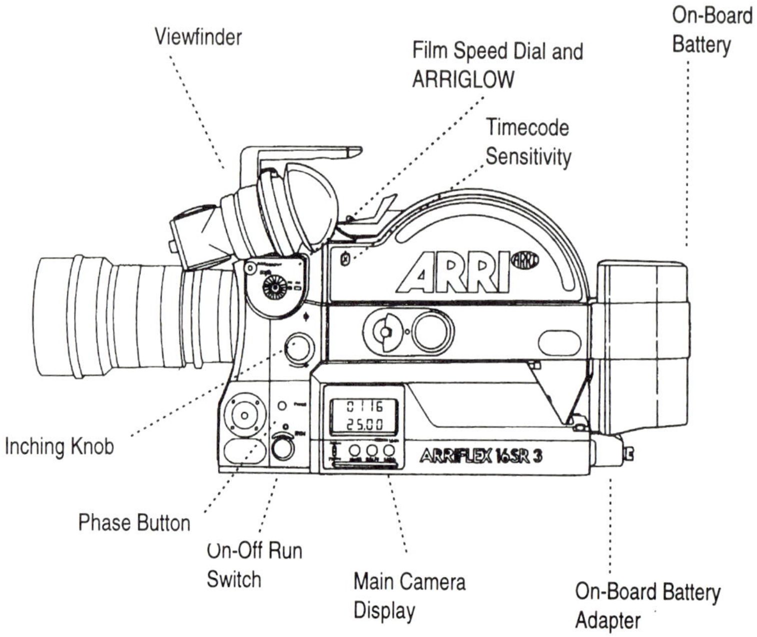

Camera Right

(Magazine Feed Side)

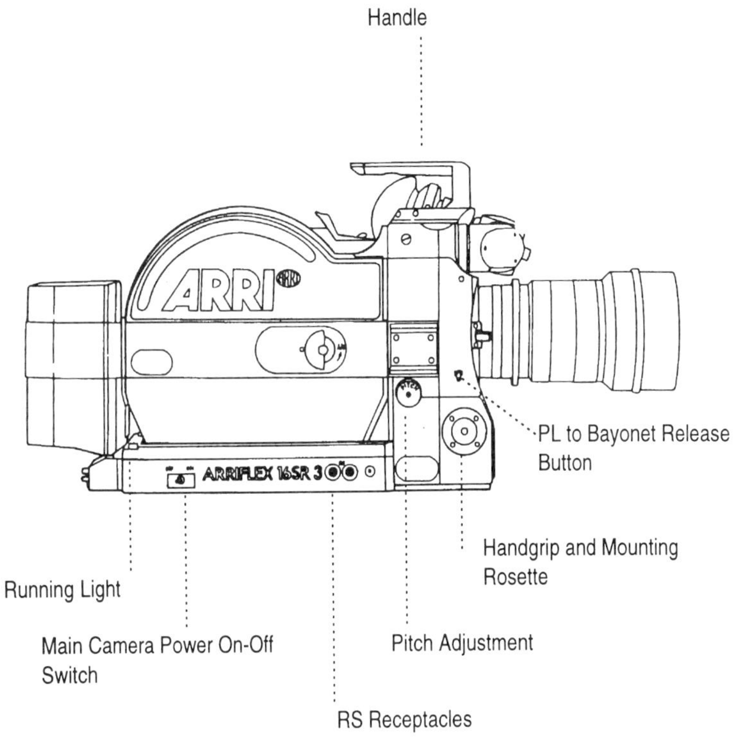

Top

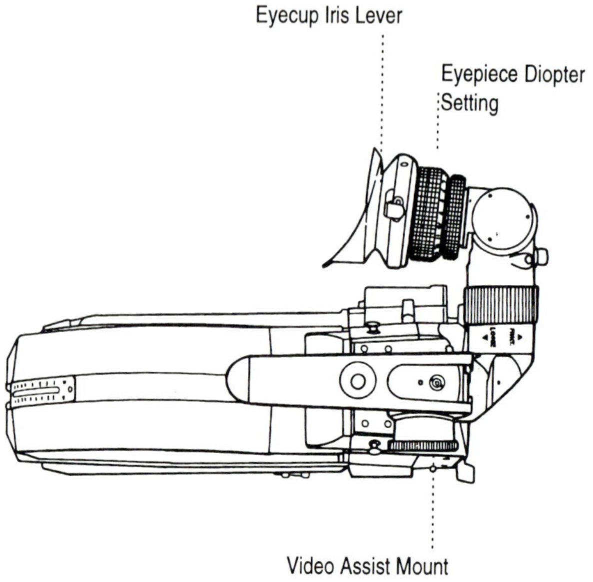
Eyecup Iris Lever
Eyepiece Diopter Setting
Video Assist Mount

Bottom

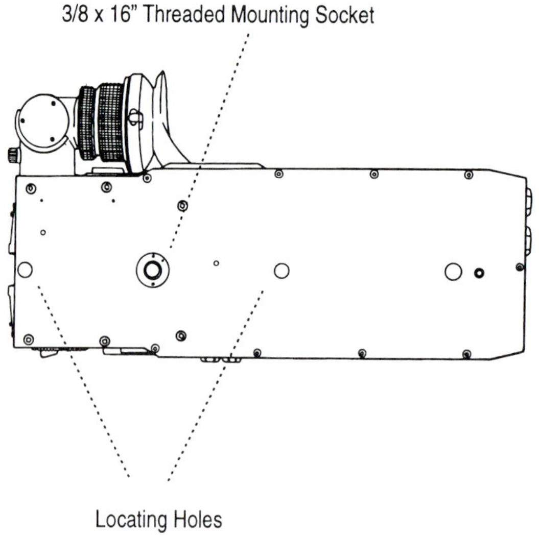
3/8 x 16" Threaded Mounting Socket
Locating Holes

Camera Checkout

A good way to introduce the Arriflex 16 SR3 camera is to describe a checkout at a rental house.

Before almost any film job, it is both customary and prudent to do a "camera checkout." Whether you're working with a rental house or a privately owned camera, it is foolhardy to venture off without first checking out the camera.

The checkout lets you:

- become re-acquainted with the camera
- make sure you have everything needed
- make sure everything fits and works properly
- pack and customize for the job

The Arriflex 16 SR3 is versatile, and can be configured in many ways. We'll go through two popular modes: studio and documentary mode.

Since no two productions are the same, your equipment inventory could fall somewhere in between the two extremes illustrated here.

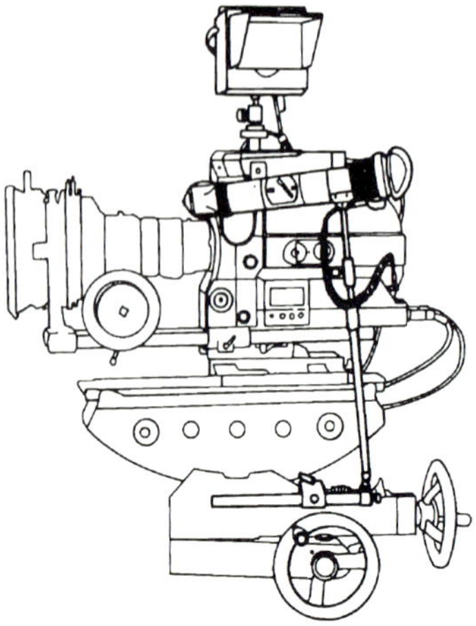

Studio Configuration

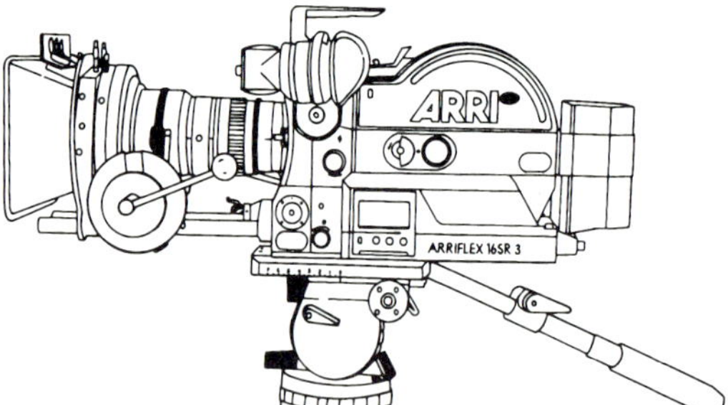

Documentary Configuration

Studio Mode

For lack of a better word, "Studio Mode" might be a camera package to be used on a television movie, a series, or a music video. It's possible you will never even be inside a studio. I guess I call it Studio Mode because some of the accessories involved take on that name: Studio Follow Focus, Studio Mattebox...

Most Rental House studio packages in the United States come in cases made of a laminate over plywood, with metal corners. The cases are extremely durable, and stack well on carts.

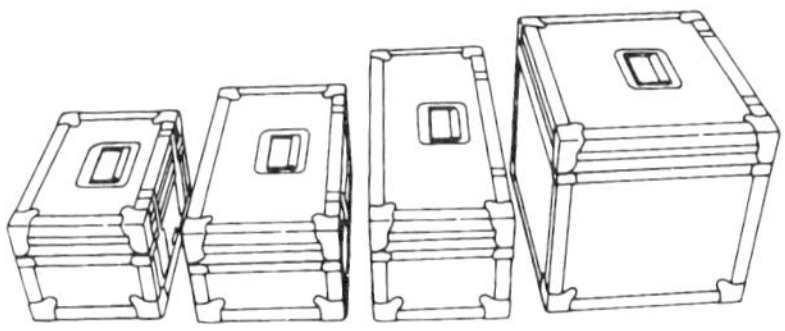

Although a number of companies build this style case, A&J Manufacturing of Los Angeles made the ones pictured here, which we used for the nine months of filming **16 SR3 INTRO.** They survived admirably. For those of you who must order quickly, here are some A&J case numbers:

16 SR3 Camera Case	N16-294
SR Magazine (3) Case	N16-107
ARRIHEAD II Case	F89-115
Lens Case	F89-116

However, it does not cost anything extra to customize to your own particular requirements.

European cases usually have similar layouts, but the exterior is made of rippled, rigidised aluminum. They are much lighter. You save a fortune shipping them, and they are almost as durable. For some strange reason, no one makes them in the United States. See the Appendix for manufacturers in Canada and England.

Camera Body Case

The camera usually rides with the baseplate attached. Video can also ride on the body—but I suggest you detach it before shipping, because it can be knocked out of alignment.

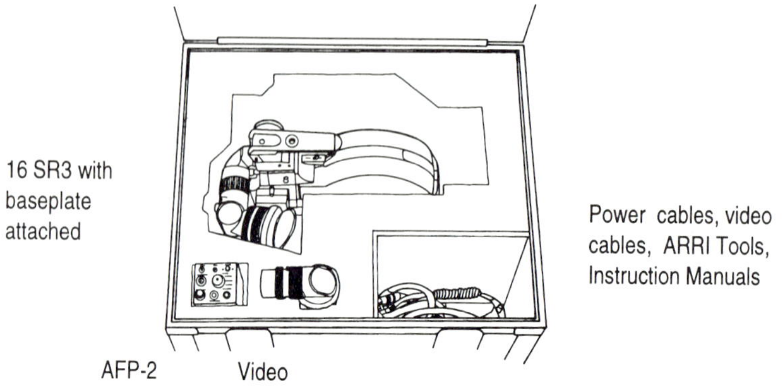

Case for 3 x 400' magazines

Standing the magazines upright will prevent coning of the film. Do not ship mags over long distances with film loaded: the movement and vibration could cause scratches to the emulsion. Also, the spindle might bend.

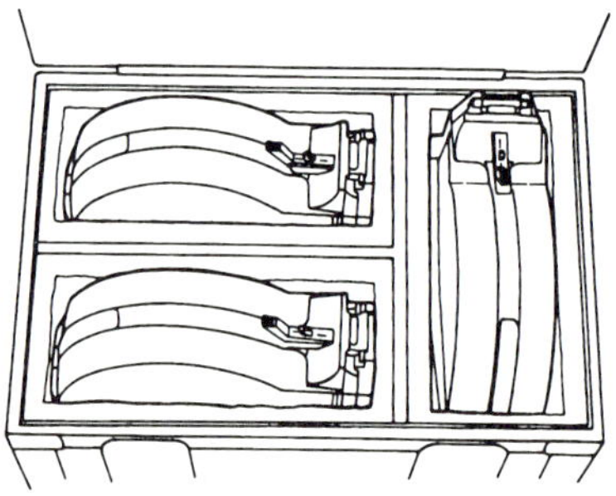

Lens Case

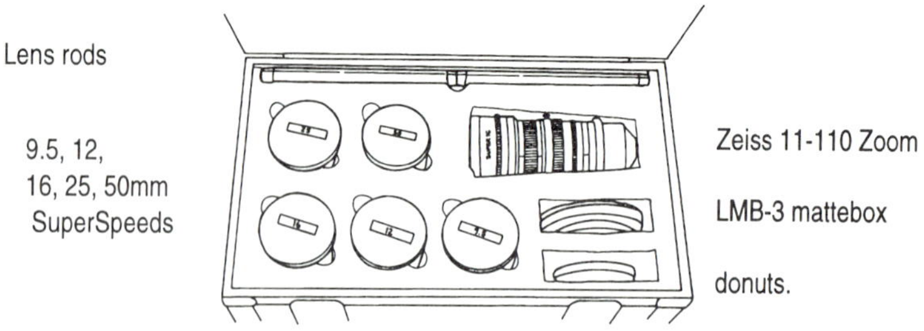

Use 3 or 4 pound density foam in lens cases—not the rigid type. Make sure you have over an inch between lens and case.

AKS Case

The AKS (All Kinds of Stuff) Case holds 4x4 Studio Mattebox, Follow Focus, Battery Charger, Batteries, more Mattebox Donuts, and more Lens Rods.

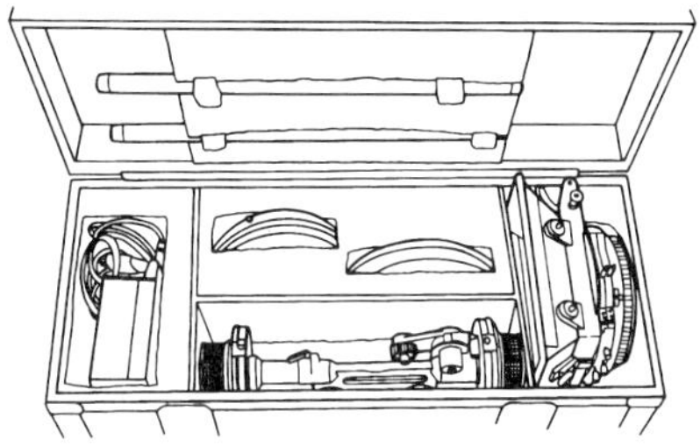

This kind of case typically has big, open compartments, which can allow the various pieces of equipment to rattle around, hitting each other, causing burrs and dings, especially on smooth, round objects like rods that should be treated better.

Since each job goes out with a different number and variety of accessories, it would be impossible for rental houses to have each piece of equipment in its own custom swaddled foam cut-out compartment.

Wrap Loose Parts

You can help prolong the life of the equipment by adding your own pieces of foam rubber between the individual pieces of equipment, preventing metal-to-metal contact—thereby earning the unqualified respect of rental house managers and heartfelt thanks from the crew who use the package next.

Electronic Accessory Case

Electronic Accessory Case holds a Mac Powerbook, which runs ARRI's LCC program. It also holds lens light, on-board 4" video monitor, ESU, RCU-1, cables, more cables, and even more cables. There's also a compartment for instruction manuals. We find we need to carry more of them around as things become more complex.

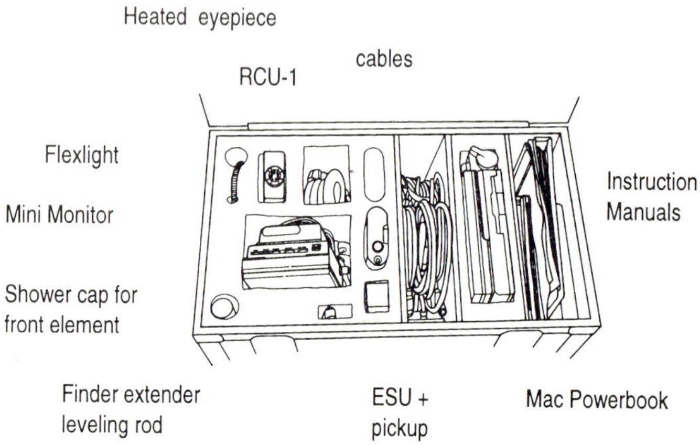

Fluid Head Case

This one is for a Sachtler Studio 7+7 (Video 30) with modified sliding top plate (made by Moviecam) to allow extended range of travel for quick release receptacle.

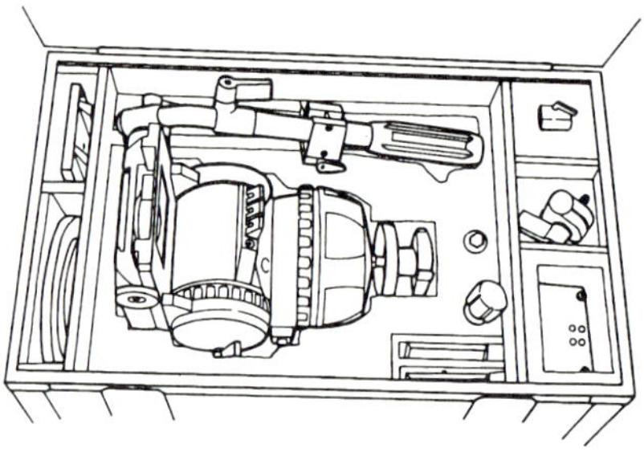

ARRIHEAD Case

Notice the compartment for our "head saver"— a 1" block of wood which we put below the dolly arm to prevent it from lowering so far that the ARRIHEAD wheels hit the chassis, and are seriously damaged. See page 163.

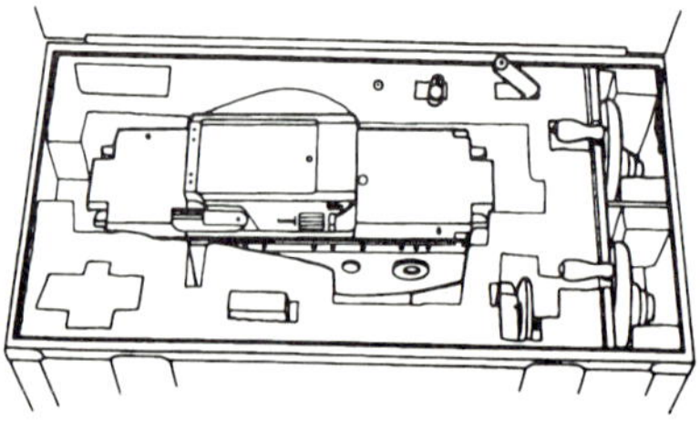

Mounting the Camera—Studio Mode

The bottom of the 16 SR3 camera has one threaded mounting hole in its base, tapped 3/8" - 16 (3/8" diameter, 16 threads to the inch), and two unthreaded locating holes.

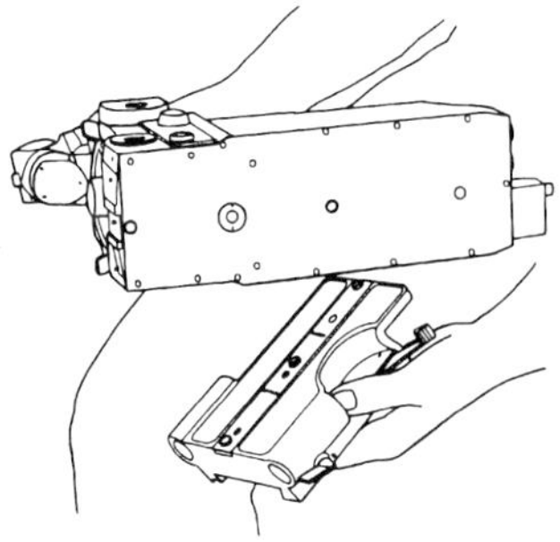

Usually a baseplate rides on the camera. It looks like this:

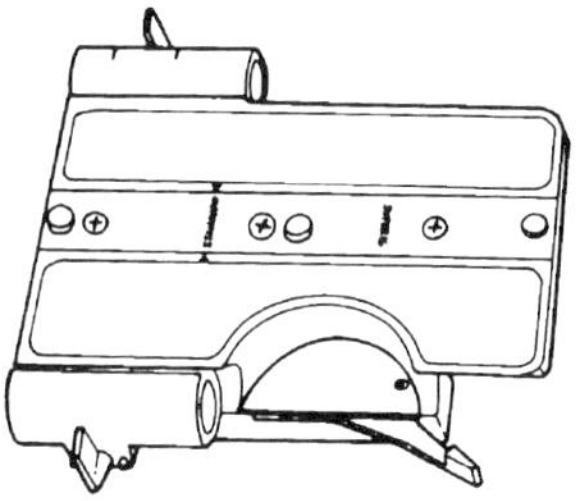

There are a number of baseplates in use. Arriflex catalogs call them bridge-plates. I'm not sure why.

The new style accommodates Super16 and Standard (Regular16.)

The old style doesn't have a Super16 position, but there is a modification kit (Arriflex part 339077).

35mm format baseplates do not fit on the 16 SR3.

The new baseplates are labeled BP-6 (they use 19mm support rods) and BP-7 (15mm—old style rods).

Rods for 16mm shooting typically are 17", 13" and 9 ½" long—the length being determined by the lens you're using. At this point you should be aware that there are two rod diameters in use. For many years ARRI standardized the 15mm diameter rod. However, with the third generation cameras (535, 535B, 435 and 16 SR3), they introduced a thicker, sturdier 19mm rod. Rod size is usually determined by the rental house.

Various rod adapters can be obtained. Chrosziel makes an adapter to mount 15mm accessories on 19mm rods. Preston Cinema Systems makes a bushing to enable using 19mm accessories on 15mm rods.

New style baseplates can be set for Standard 16 or Super16 formats. Be sure yours is set for the format you're using. To change the settings, see the Super16 chapter.

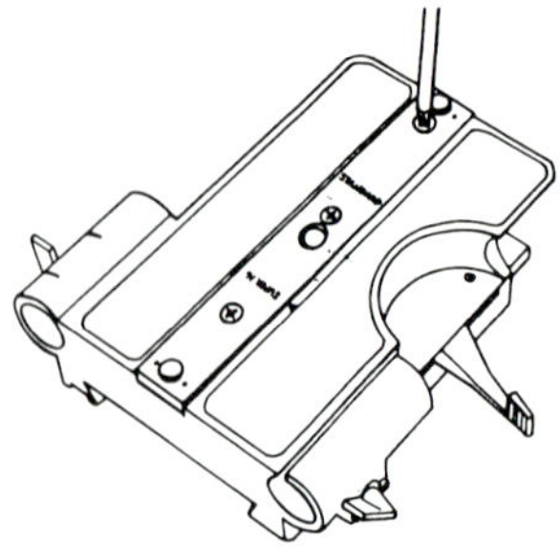

Attach the baseplate (bridge-plate) to the camera. Use a large flathead screwdriver—small ones will burr up the bolt. Sears makes a nice one that's short enough to fit in your tool pouch.

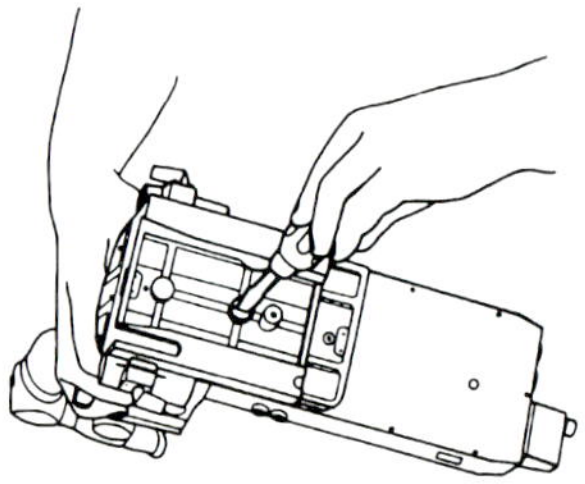

There are basically two ways to mount an Arriflex camera to a head:

ARRI Dovetail
or
Quick Release

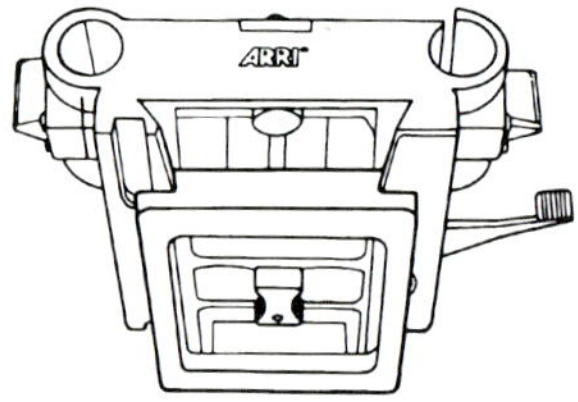

(Quick Release is also called European style, Euro Style, Sachtler Style, Wedge Plate, or Touch 'n Go.)

New style Arriflex baseplates work either way: a Quick Release Adapter slides into the dovetail.

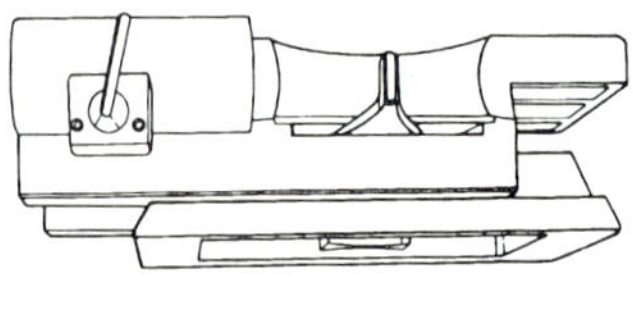

I highly recommend the Quick Release — it's a lot faster and easier to use.

Attaching Quick Release Adapter

First you need a Quick Release Adapter. It usually comes with the ARRI Geared Head, but can be ordered as a spare part (K4.43045.0)

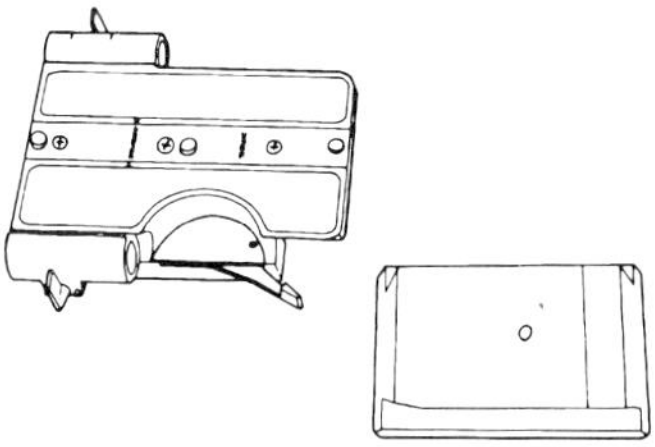

If the Quick Release Adapter is not already mounted in the baseplate, line it up so the ridge on top faces away from the rod holes.

Pull the locking lever back Slide the Quick Release adapter on from the back, all the way forward until it clicks in place.

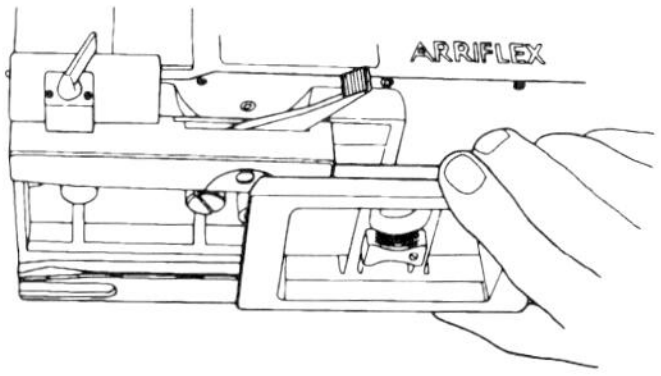

Remember, the ridge on top of the adapter plate faces the rear.

If it doesn't click into place... (sometimes it gets sticky from dirt or gunk) ...pull the plunger away from the camera, slide forward, and feel the plunger engage in the hole.

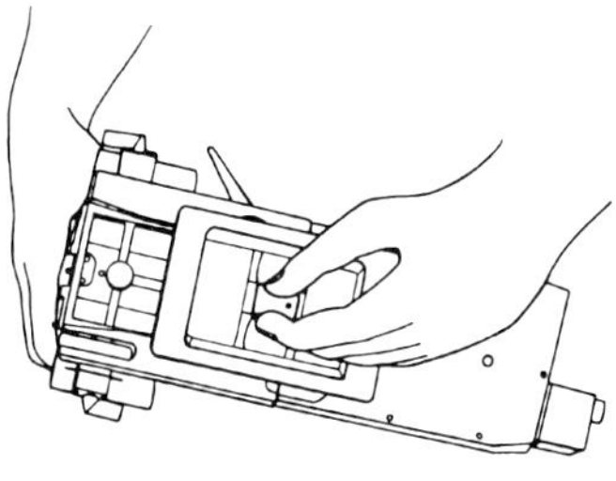

To remove the Touch 'n Go adapter, reverse the procedure—pull up on the plunger.

Tighten the dovetail lock.

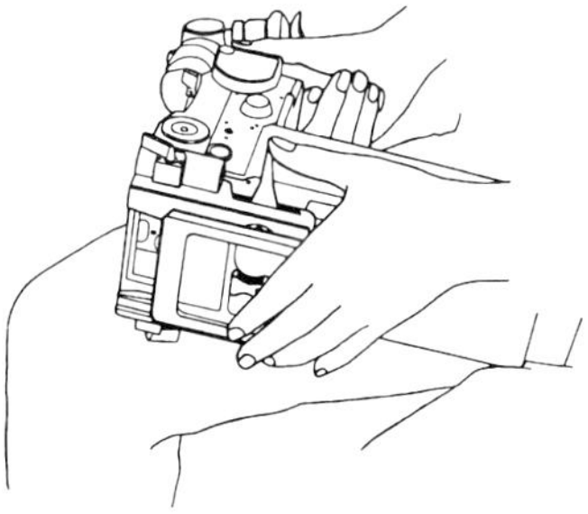

Although ARRI supplies only one size of Quick Release Adapter, you should be aware that there are two sizes of Quick Release plates and mounting systems in use:

Large 4 ¾ " x 3 ¼ " (120mm length)
Small 3 1/8 " x 2 ½ " (80mm length)

The large Quick Release receptacle is found on most heads favored in 35mm format shooting:

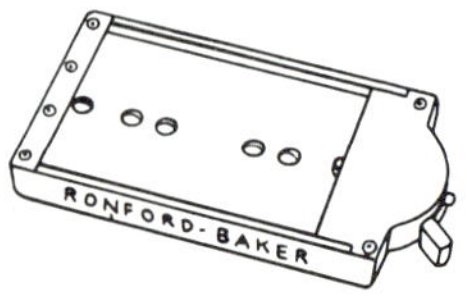

ARRIHEAD
Cartoni C40
O'Connor 25-75 (w. Euro plate)
Sachtler Studio and 30

Most heads popular in 16mm shooting use the small size:

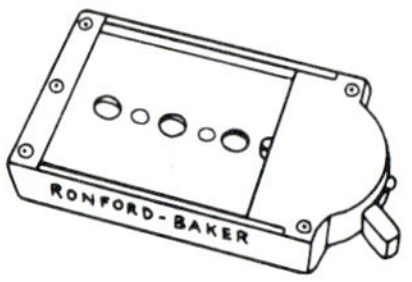

Cartoni C20 and Beta
Sachtler Panoramas,
Horizon II, 18, 20, and 25

Ronford makes receptacles for both, which is invaluable for converting from one size to the other, and for mounting to non Quick Release accessories.

To use an ARRI baseplate on one of the smaller receptacles, have a little quick release adapter milled for you by your favorite machinist.

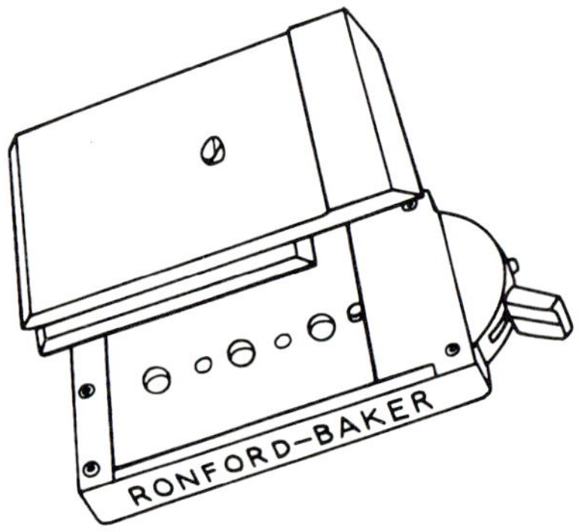

Mount the Camera on the Head

Make sure the Quick Release Receptacle is ready to accept the camera.

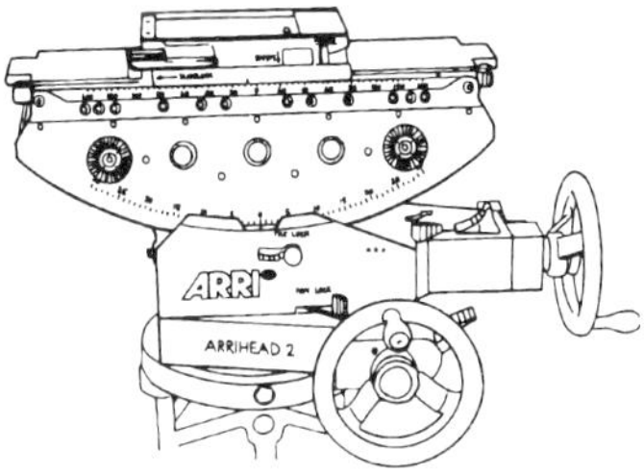

The round release-pin should be sticking up, and on most heads, the release lever should be forward or to the left.

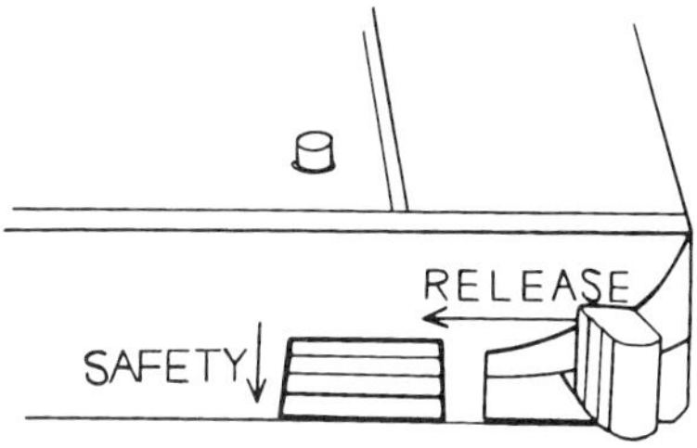

Insert the camera's quick release plate into the receptacle of the head.

The front end goes in first

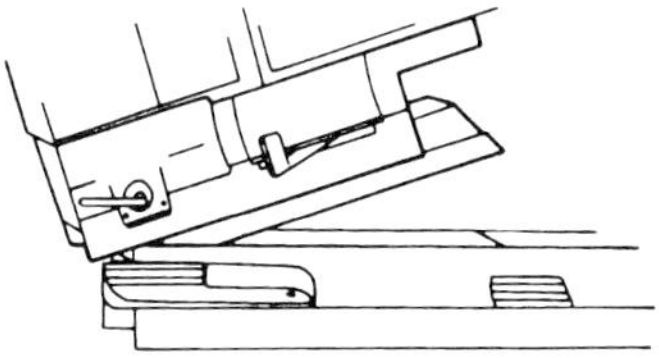

Push down at the back end.

You should hear a satisfying click, telling you the camera has engaged.

Always try pulling up, to ensure the camera is firmly locked.

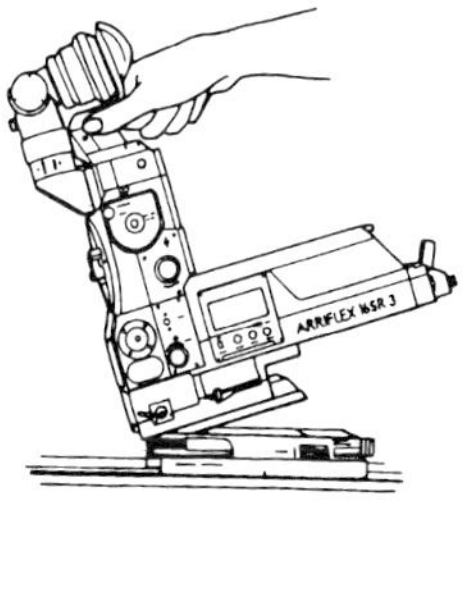

To remove the camera, there is usually a safety lock. On the ARRIHEAD2 , push the safety lock in, slide the release lever in back to the left, and lift the camera out.

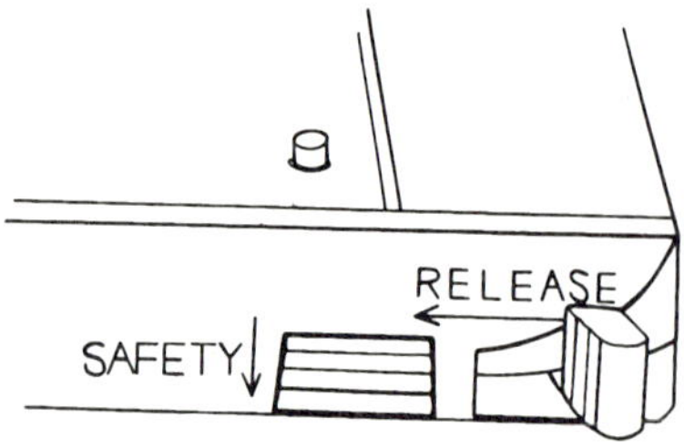

On the Sachtler Head pictured at right, pull down on the safety latch, and slide the release to the left.

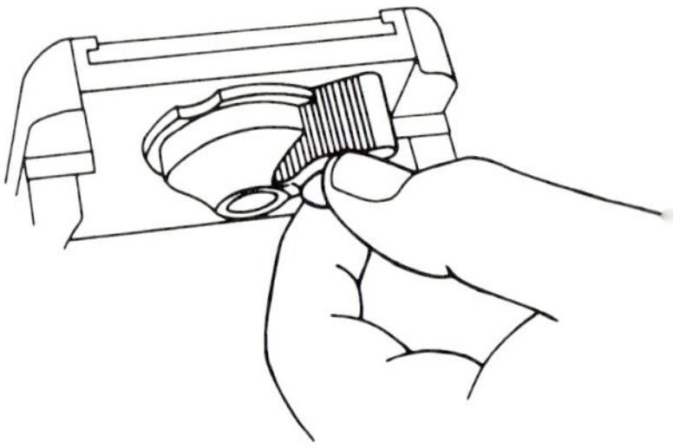

Most other heads have similar systems.

Sliding Baseplate - Dovetail Mount

The other way to mount the camera is with a dovetail sliding balance plate (ARRI part K4.35338.0)

To mount a camera fitted with a dovetail baseplate (bridgeplate), push the right edge against the spring-loaded safety catch of the sliding balance plate. Slide forward, and lock with the locking lever. To remove, push the catch down with your finger as you slide the plate back.

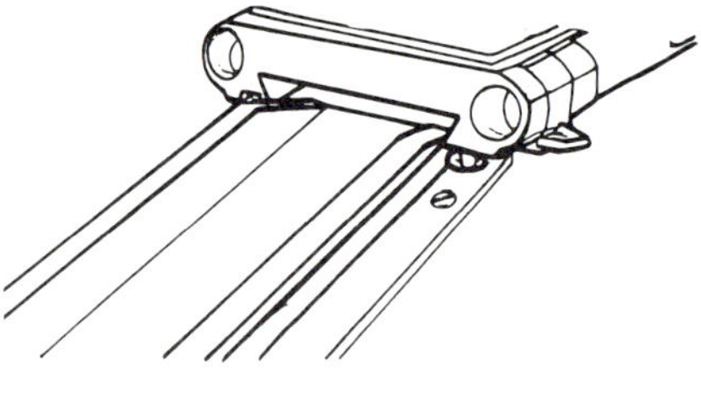

Documentary mode

On most documentaries, you have to travel fast and light. You and your equipment will be subjected to all kinds of weather and human conditions. Packing for this type of production requires a different strategy, as shown by these King Pelican Cases, from Pelican Products. Inside dimensions of King Pelicans: 22" long x 17"wide x 8" deep. The entire package fits in the back of a Geo Metro or on the back of an elephant.

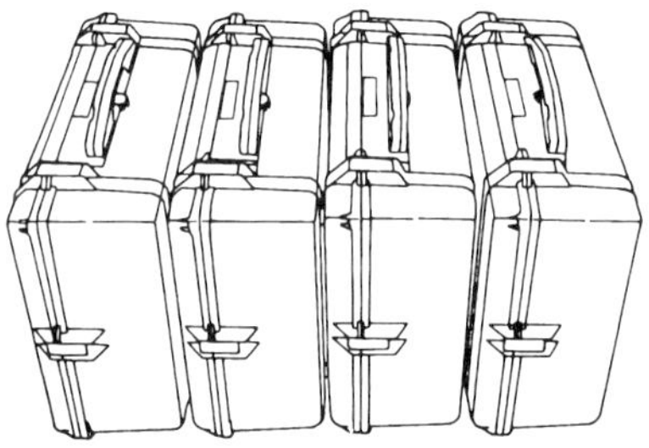

Although your mileage may vary, and your cases could be totally different, the overall difference is that this type of package tends to favor more handheld shooting, with lighter and smaller accessories.

Complete Camera Case

The camera body travels with all the accessories needed to shoot: lens, on-board battery, magazine, handgrip, lens shade.

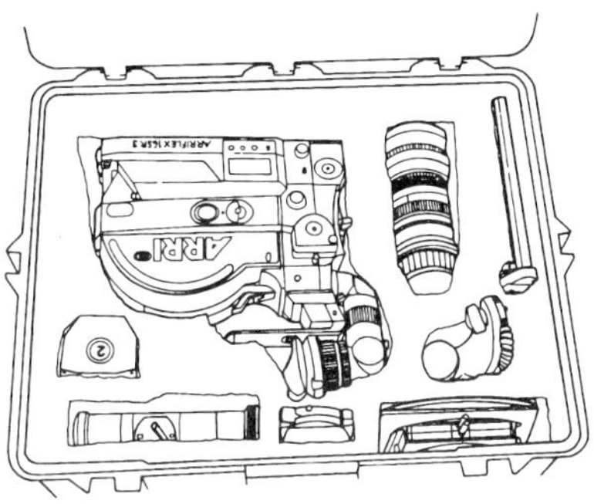

Attache Case

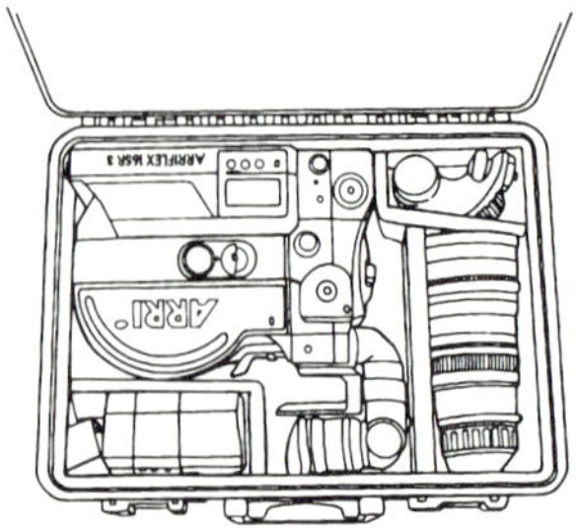

If you want to hand-carry a ready-to-shoot package in a waterproof attaché case, like the yellow one in the **INTRO** film, call Satter Inc to find your closest dealer for a Tundra Sea King SK518 Case. Inside dimensions are 17.8"w x 12.8"h x 5.1"d, and it comes in black, gray or yellow.

Magazine & AKS Case

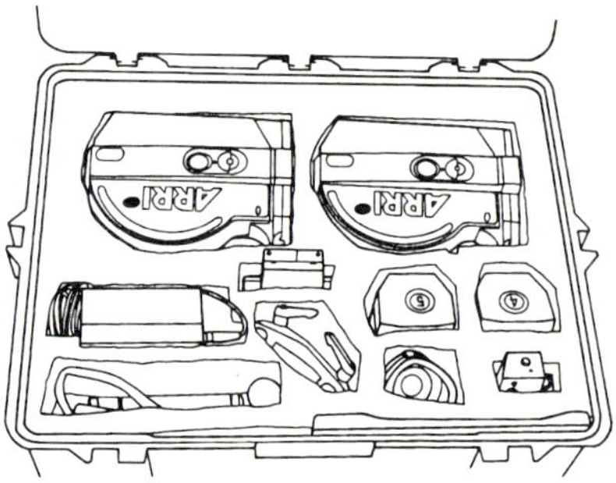

A second case holds magazines, extra batteries, charger, zoom motor, finder extender and other accessories.

Lens Case

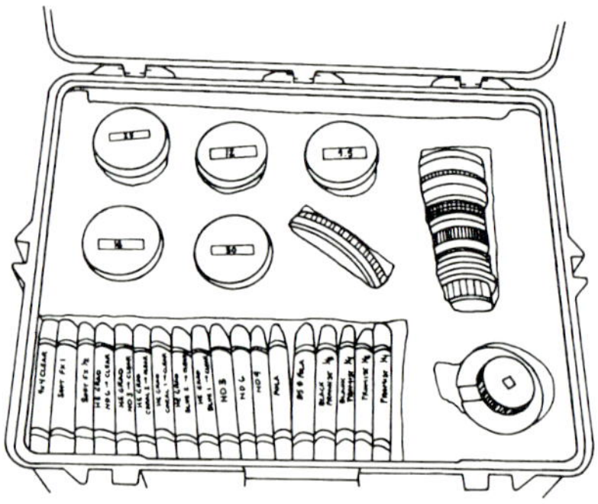

Lenses, lightweight follow focus and filters go in the third case.

A fourth case without foam is great for film and supplies.

Mounting the Camera—Doc Mode

One of the big differences between studio and documentary mode is what goes on the bottom. On a documentary style shoot, you want to move as quickly as possible from handheld to tripod and back again.

Quick Release Plates

You probably won't use the baseplate, except for long telephoto lenses. Your best bet is to mount a small Quick Release Plate directly to the camera's base.

As you have seen, there are two sizes of Quick Release Plates:

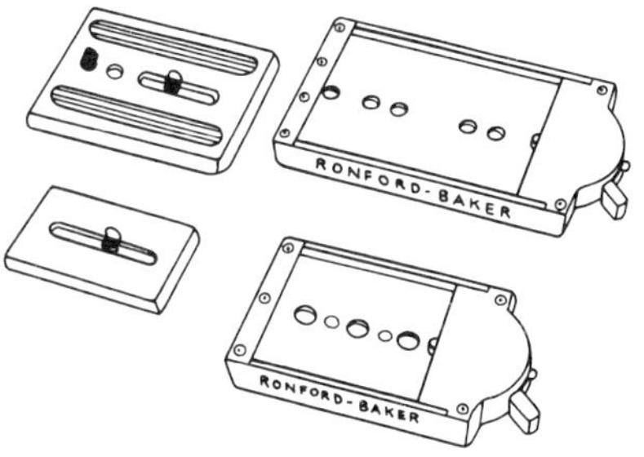

Large 120mm long
Sachtler part #3051
Cartoni part #K-512

Small 80mm long
Sachtler part #1064
Cartoni part #B-511

Most Quick Release Plates have rubber cushions to provide a better grip to the camera's bottom. If your plate looks like the small one above, add a piece of gaffer's or camera tape to the top of the plate. This will prevent the camera from twisting on a slippery metal-to-metal contact.

The quick release receptacles are handy accessories for any job—to mount the camera anywhere. It is also useful to bolt one to any work surface where the camera will remain unattended to prevent accidental spills.

Most of the lighter 16mm (and Video) fluid heads use the smaller plate. Heavier heads, especially those for 35mm format shooting, use the larger plate.

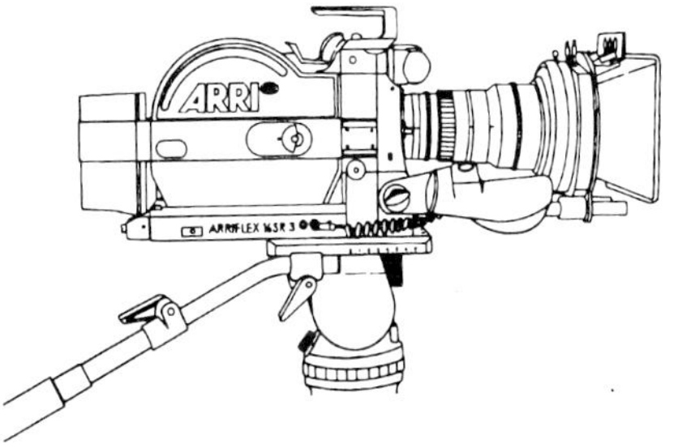

The smaller Quick Release plate is better for handheld shooting because it won't dig into your shoulder.

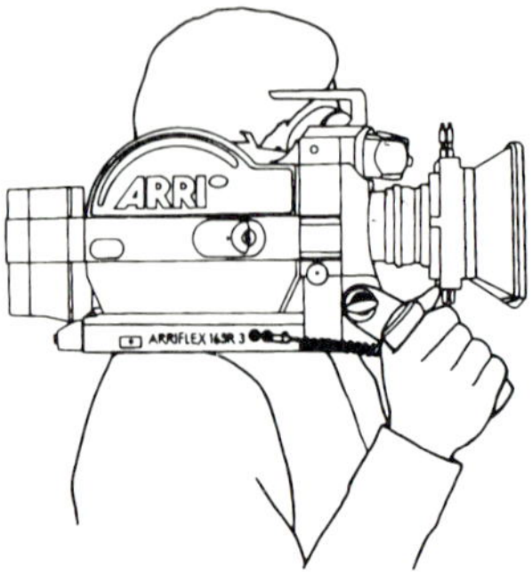

Mounting Depth

As with all 16 SR cameras, the 3/8" x 16 tripod mounting hole is shallow. If you screw a mounting bolt in too deep, too hard, it could cause internal damage to circuit boards in rare instances.

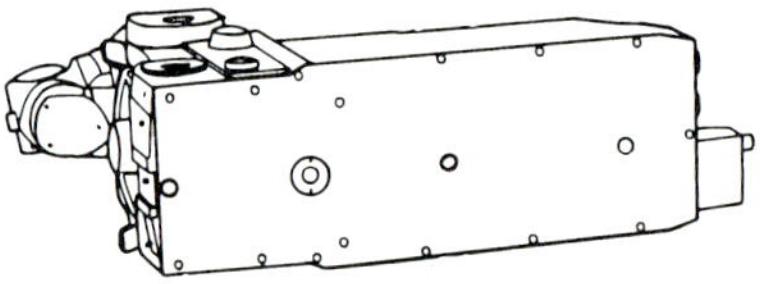

It is helpful to carry several different lengths of 3/8" - 16 bolts for mounting or emergency purposes. Also, get spacing washers with 3/8" holes. Most good hardware stores have them. The part of the mounting bolt that threads into the camera must be **7mm or shorter.**

Attach Handgrip

Attach the handgrip to the camera right side. The shiny knurled spacer ring can be rotated to bevel the grip towards or away from the camera body. Tighten the grip. Plug the 3 pin male Fischer connector into either of the two "RS" (Remote Start) female receptacles on the camera.

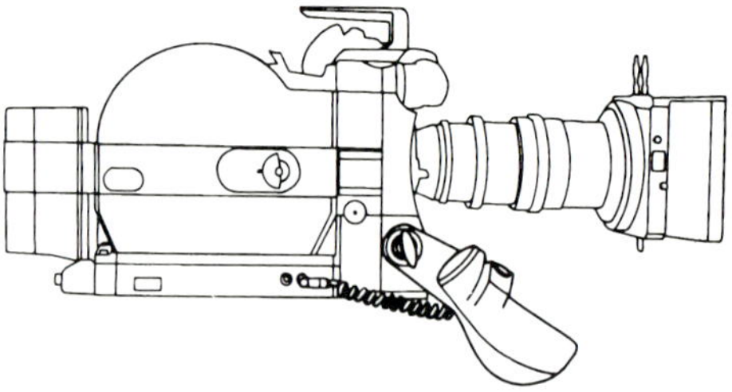

With the camera's main power switch on, you can start the camera by momentarily pressing the green handgrip button. Press again to turn the camera off.

Handgrips from older 16 SR cameras will fit. The older switch will not function, because it makes continuous on/off contact as opposed to the SR3, 535A, 535B and 435 which are momentary. Personally, I find the older style handgrip more comfortable—but that is why there are so many different styles of ski poles and tennis racquets.

Shoulder Pads

The camera's flat base allows you to customize hand-held configurations.

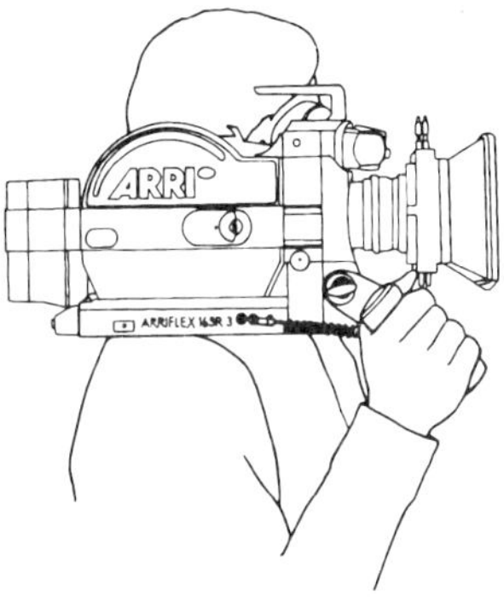

Arriflex makes a flat shoulder pad that fits the length of the base. It screws into the 3/8 x 16" mounting hole.

I like a piece of thin neoprene velcroed to the rear of the base. It should be attached far enough to the rear that it does not interfere with the quick release plate.

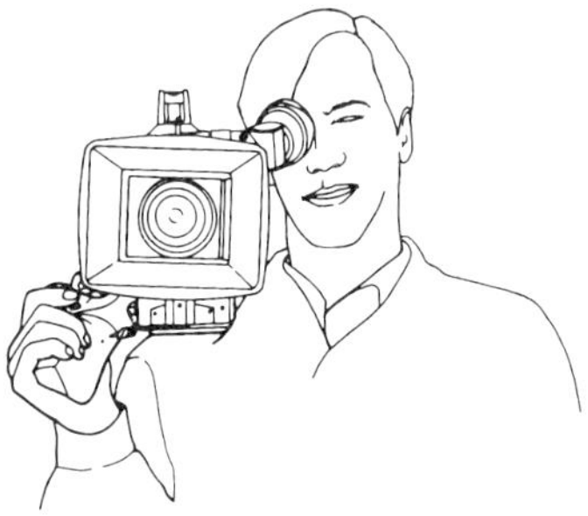

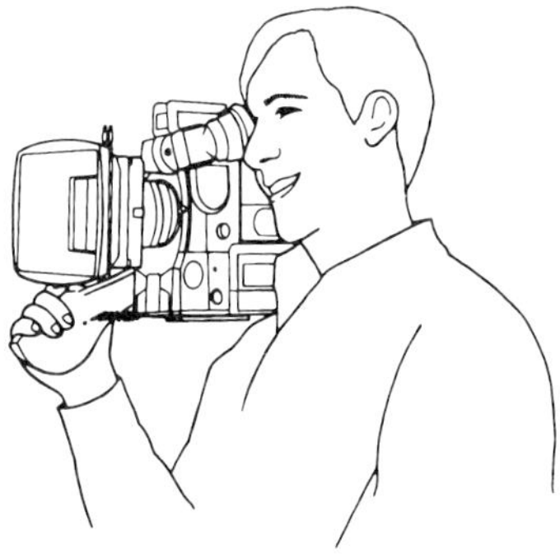

Shoulder Mounts

Although this might be called a studio accessory, the S3 Shoulder Set crosses over into the documentary and music video arena for prolonged hand-held shooting.

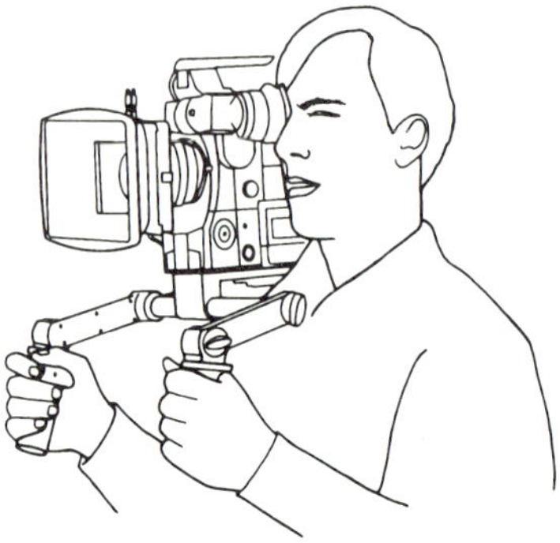

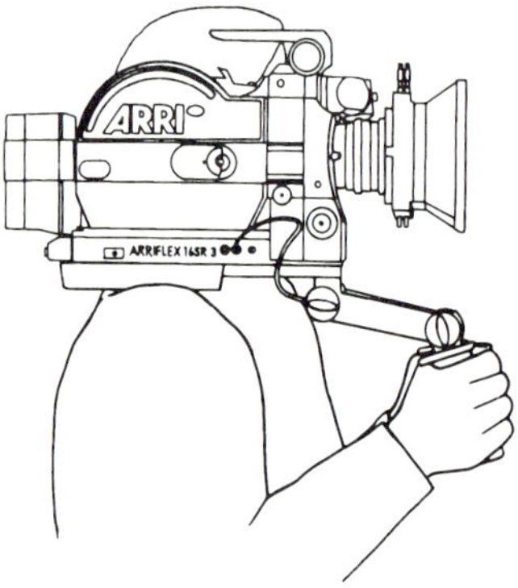

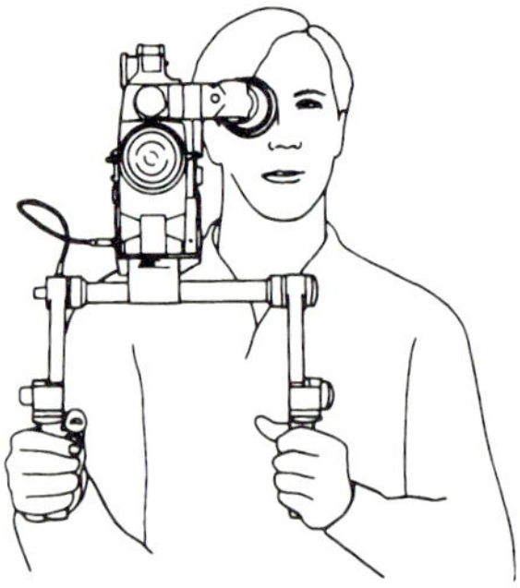

The Checkout Begins: Checklist

From here on, whether it's a documentary or full blown feature, the checkout procedure is the same.

The camera body is sitting before you, mounted to a head

Run down this check list. While you're assembling the camera, check all the things that could possibly be wrong. You should assume the worst, and do it yourself. Murphy's Law lurks everywhere.

Check the Front

- ❑ PL Mount
- ❑ Fiber Screen seated and clean
- ❑ Set diopter
- ❑ Check framing
- ❑ Check viewfinder
- ❑ Eyepiece and Eyecup
- ❑ Finder Extender and Finder Tension
- ❑ Finder Extender Leveler

Check the Rear

- ❑ Remove aperture cover or magazine
- ❑ Check the Gate from Rear
- ❑ Plug in Battery
- ❑ Charge Batteries
- ❑ Power up Camera and Check Status Light
- ❑ Check Camera Speed
- ❑ Check Main LCD Display and the 6 Modes
- ❑ Check Shutter Angle
- ❑ Attach Magazine
- ❑ Check for Scratches
- ❑ Attach Rods, Lens, Follow Focus, Mattebox

Check Optics

- ❑ Check Viewing Screen Depth
- ❑ Check lenses
- ❑ Set up your lenses
- ❑ Check ARRIGLOW
- ❑ Check Light Meter
- ❑ Check Video Assist
- ❑ Mini Monitor

Check Advanced Accessories

- ❑ Timecode
- ❑ LCC
- ❑ RCU
- ❑ ICU
- ❑ LCS
- ❑ ESU
- ❑ Identify, color-code and label cables

Pack Up

- ❑ Load Magazines
- ❑ Pack cases
- ❑ Label contents of cases on camera tape

The Viewing System

Check the Front

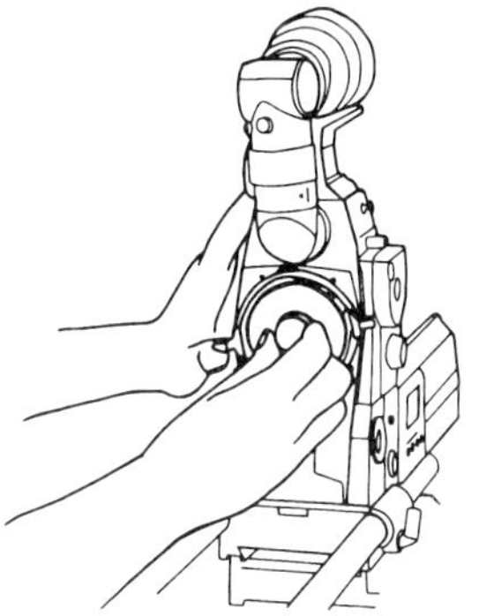

One of the first things you should do is "check under the hood." I've seen cameras so abused in shipping that the fiber screen had been shaken loose from its mount, and the mirror shutter had shattered.

So, the first thing to do: check that the fiber screen is in place—clean and ready to go.

Turn the PL mount counter-clockwise to open. (To remember which way, think "clock to lock"— clockwise locks the mount. It's easy to forget when you're rushing to shoot a sunset and the director is screaming to hurry up.)

Pull the lens cavity cap straight out.

Look at the fiber screen *(above the mirror shutter).* The shiny stainless fiber screen holder should be flush against the black guide rails.

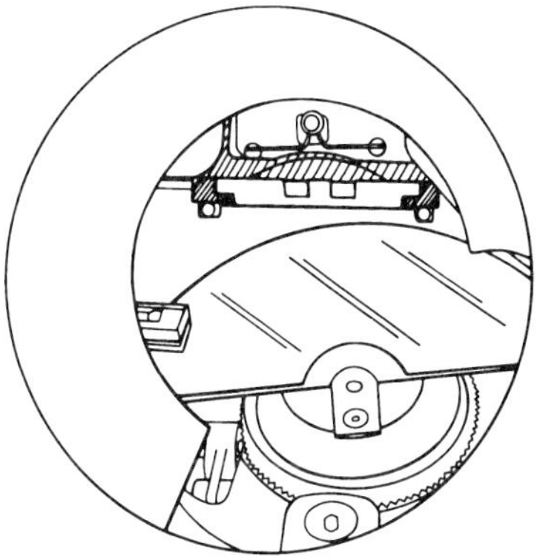

If not, clear the mirror shutter. Turn the manual inching knob *(camera right, above PHASE button)* in the direction of the arrow (counter-clockwise).

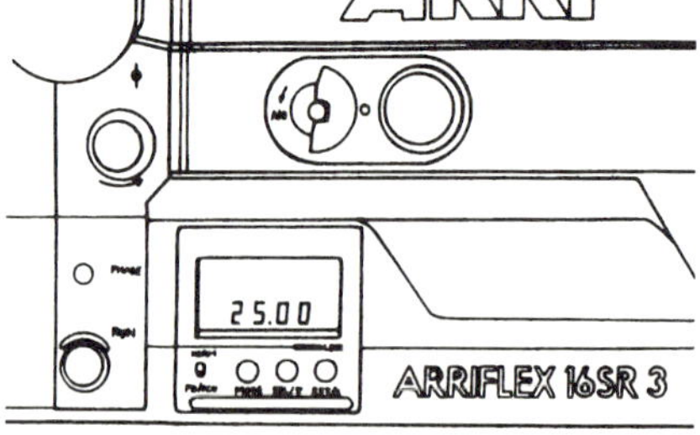

The mirror portion of the shutter should be at the bottom of its rotation, so you should be able to see the open aperture.

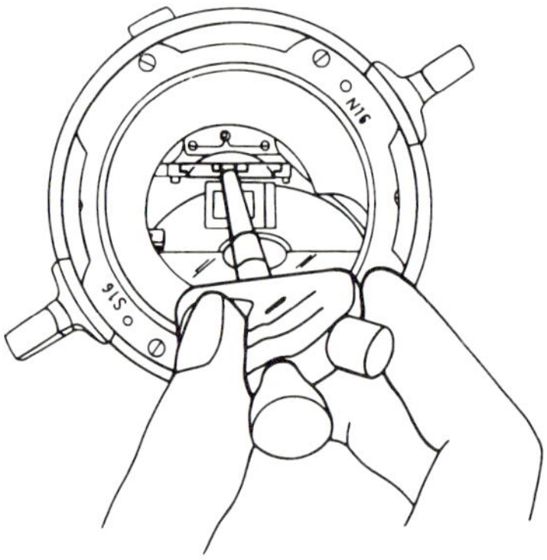

Carefully and gently push on the stainless steel rim of the fiber screen with a plastic skewer or wooden stick. If the fiber screen were loose, it would click back into position, held in place by spring tension.

DO NOT USE ANY METAL OBJECTS! You'll scratch and burr up the parts.

DO NOT USE YOUR FINGERS. Although some ARRI manuals tell you to check the seating by pushing with your fingers, I don't recommend sticking your craft-service donut-sticky fingers anywhere inside the camera cavity. There is too great a risk of touching the mirror. And even if you washed your fingers with the diligence of a surgeon, the oils in your skin can eventually eat away at even the best of steels.

But if you must use your finger, wrap it first in a lens tissue or Kimwipe.

Rotate the mirror shutter back into the viewing position.

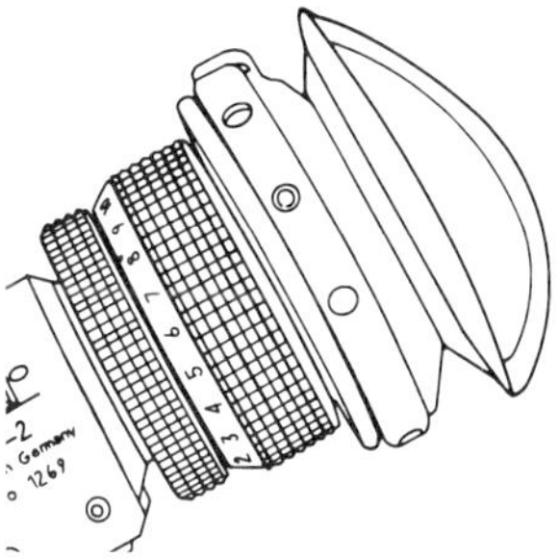

Look through the eyepiece. Turn the diopter adjustment ring until the markings on the fiber optic viewing screen are sharp. If the screen looks dirty, or if the cross-hair does not look centered—you should remove the viewing screen to clean it.

If you see dirt sharply in focus after “throwing” the fiber screen out of focus, it usually means that one or more of the optical elements of the eyepiece are dusty, and should be cleaned.

Removing the Fiber Screen

Before you pull the fiber screen, clear the mirror shutter out of the way again, so you won't accidentally scratch it.

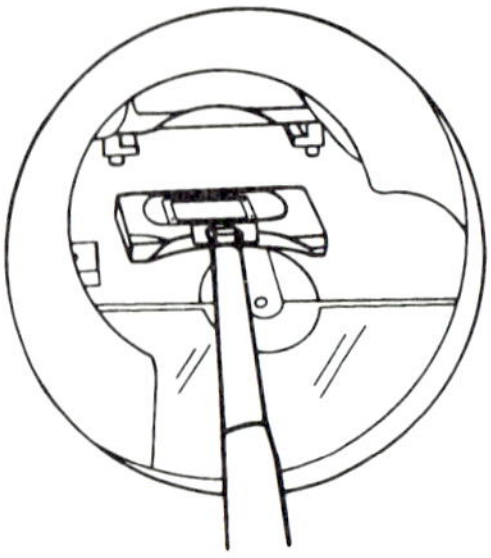

Pull the fiber screen if it looks dirty, needs changing or checking.

The only proper tool to use is the Hirschmann Forceps, at around $10.50, perhaps the cheapest item sold by Arriflex (# 05.07238.0).

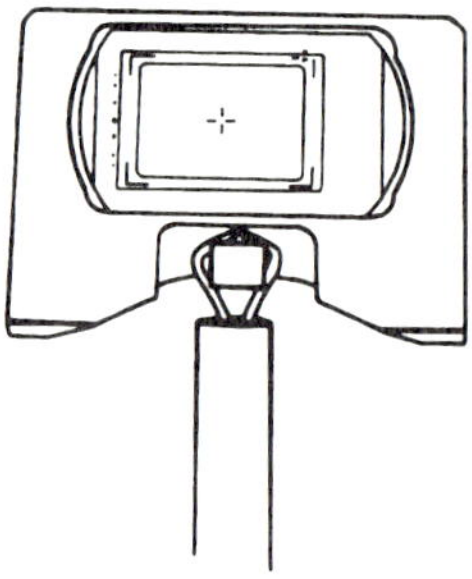

In emergency, you can use "Spring-loaded grabbers for electronic test probes," available from Jensen Tools and other electronics suppliers at twice the price.

Don't use anything else—especially not pliers or tweezers.

Grab the "T" handle of the fiber screen carrying tray with the Hirschmann Forceps. Make sure the carrying tray is clamped firmly, and will not slip off. Gently pull the tray out toward you.

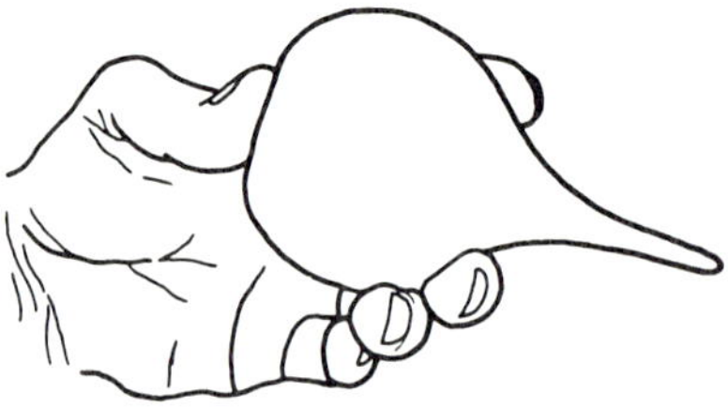

Clean it with an air bulb syringe. Do NOT use Dust-Off on the viewing screen: it will leave a faint chemical residue. Pure compressed air is OK.

If the screen is really dirty, you may clean it with a mild lens fluid. I suggest Panchro Mirror Cleaner. (See Supplies & Resources)

Sometimes there are black spots on the screen. These are "dead fibers." They cannot be cleaned off.

DO NOT BLOW ANY AIR INTO THE LENS CAVITY WITH THE SCREEN REMOVED. You will blow the light-meter needle off its pins.

When putting the screen back in place, be sure it goes in all the way until it clicks in place. Otherwise, you will have a framing error, as mentioned earlier. It only goes in one way: chrome side of holder up; black, ridged side down.

The fiber optic screen provides a brighter image than a conventional groundglass. This is particularly helpful when shooting under low light conditions, with SuperSpeed lenses, or stopped down for exterior scenes with heavy ND filtration.

You might experience some "ghosting" when shooting close-up or macro scenes of bright objects. It then becomes difficult to find an exact focus point. To help focus, close down the aperture slightly, focus, then reset your aperture for correct exposure.

In the 16 SR3 viewing system, there is extra area around the outermost frame line that aids in framing.

The 16 SR3 has an aperture plate that converts from Regular to Super16. We'll discuss it further in the Super16 section. The Regular16 aperture basically works as a mask, exposing less picture area.

Shoot S16 (even when framing Standard 16)

My suggestion is to always leave the aperture set to Super16, and always use single perf film. (Double perf film in a Super16 gate can cause flares in some situations.)

I suggest using the 1.66(S16) - TV 1.33 viewing screen when framing a show for standard TV. That way, you have the luxury of later repositioning the frame if ever there is a need—a dreaded scratch, for example, or an extra on the edge of frame whom the producer or client absolutely hates. Even more important, the negative will be ready for HDTV when it becomes available, thus insuring a more valuable future for your production.

Always instruct the lab which format you are using. For example, if you are framing for standard TV, and exposing the entire Super16 frame, write on the purchase order: **"Shot in Super16 format, transfer Normal TV 1.33:1 centered."**

If you're shooting and framing for Super16, write: **"Shot in Super16, transfer 1.66:1 centered with black letterbox top and bottom."**

Other than the aperture bar, there are no aperture masks, as the 35mm cameras have. Be aware of this as you're shooting with the different formats. A quick way to check the relation of the frame lines with the aperture is to inch the mirror shutter halfway across the aperture area. Aim the eyepiece toward a bright light. Look into the front. You'll see whether the frame lines are even with the edge of the aperture. Keep looking while manually inching the mirror shutter around.

Framing Chart

It is a good idea to shoot a test of the framing. Put a showcard on the wall. Sight through the lens, and mark the four outer corners. Use a straight-edge to connect the four points. Draw the rectangle. Then use triangles, cut from tape, to indicate the outer edges. Have a print or transfer made. You'll see how your frame lines match the lab or video facility. They often don't.

16 SR3 Viewing Screens

1.37

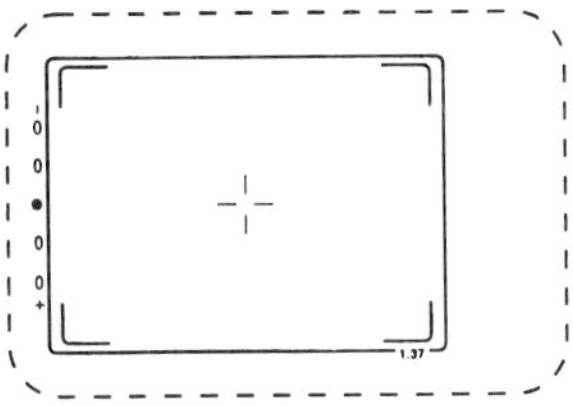

K2.41290.0 303310

1.85 (S16) - TV 1.33/1.78

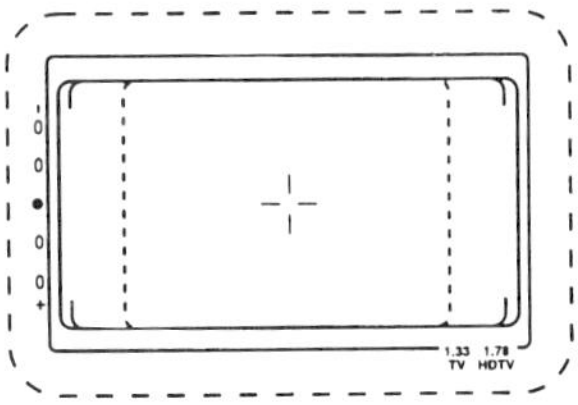

K2.47036.0 303350

1.37 - TV 1.33

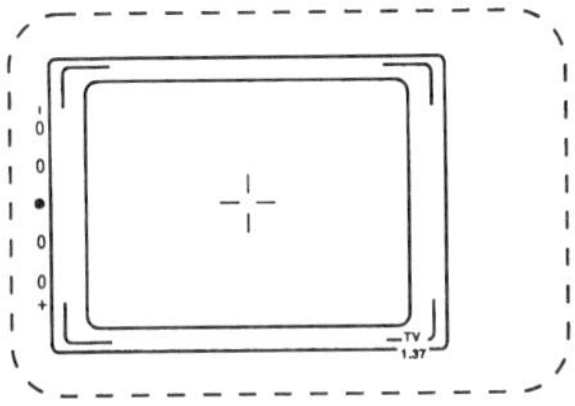

K4.46996.0

TV 1.33

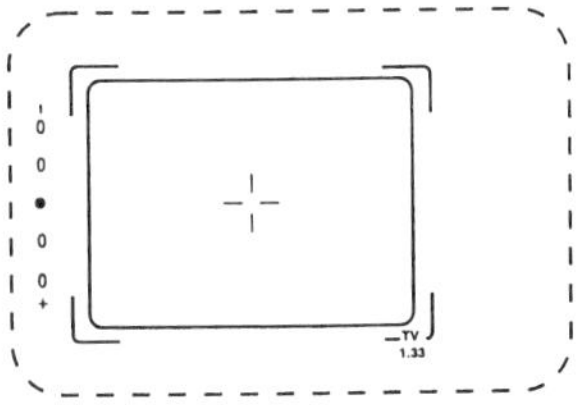

K4.45868.0 303300

1.66 (S16)

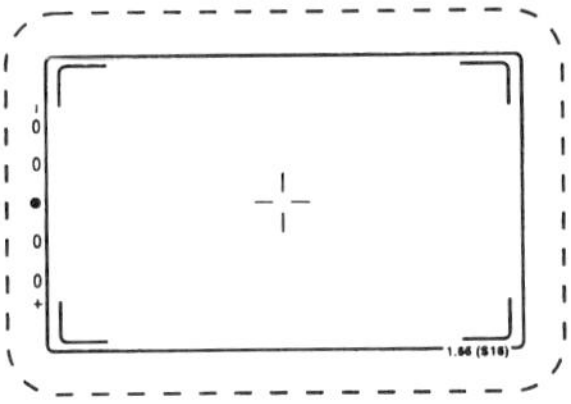

K2.41289.0 303320

1.66 (S16) - TV 1.33

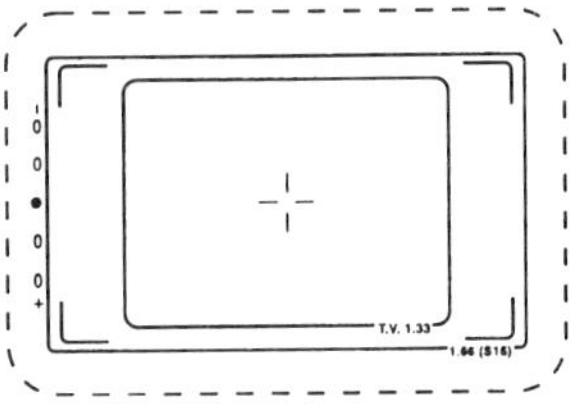

K2.46436.0 303305

HDTV 1.78 - TV 1.33

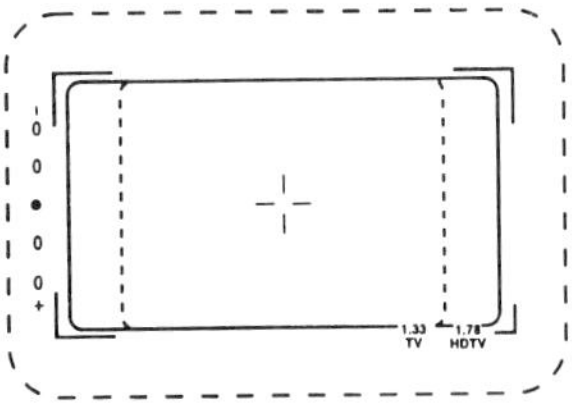

K2.41283.0 303330

1.85 (S16)

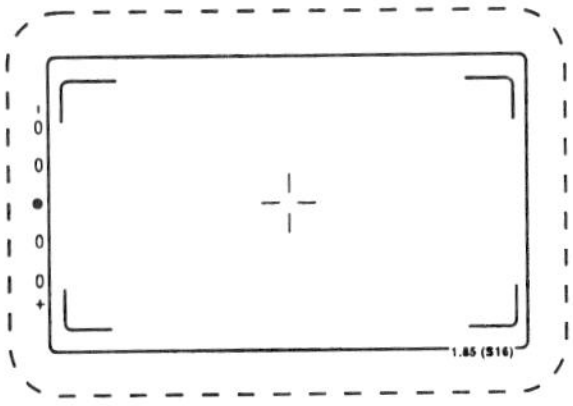

K2.47027.0 303340

Note: "K" =factory numbers
303=Arriflex USA numbers

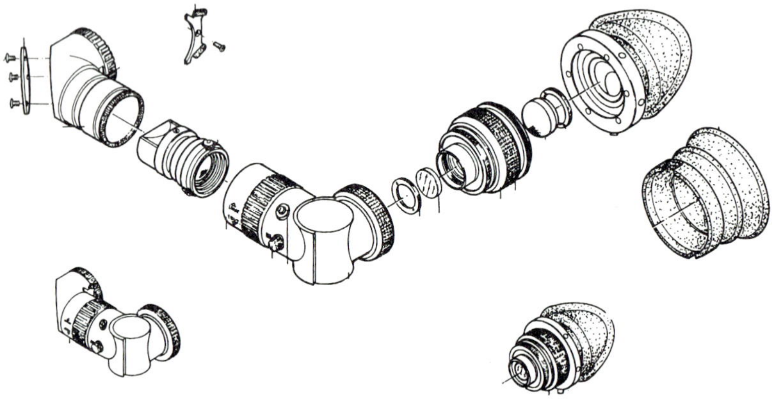

Exploded View of Viewfinder Assembly

Viewfinder System

As with previous 16 SR cameras, the swingover viewfinder system of the 16 SR3 is symmetrical. Magnification of the finder assembly is 10X.

It swings 95° to either side of the camera, so you can shoot from either side.

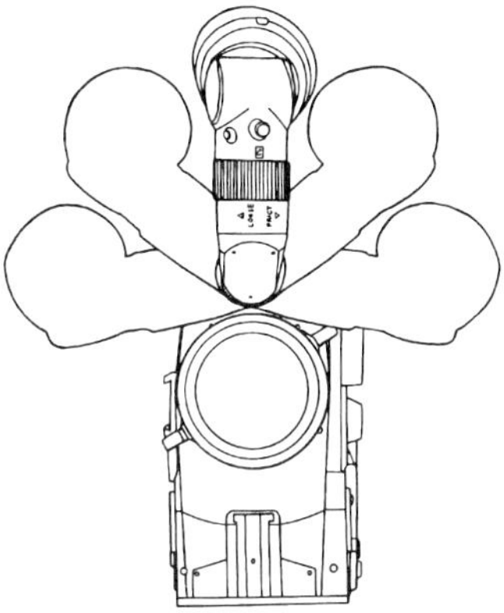

The finder rotates 360° parallel to the camera.

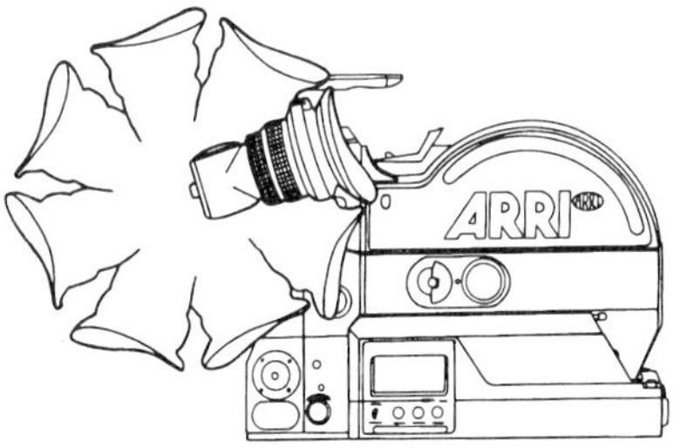

And it pivots 25° out from the side of the camera.

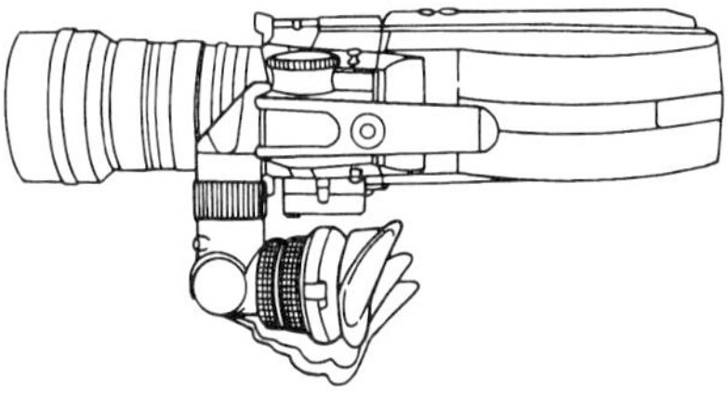

The viewing system, combined with the fiber optic screen, provides what looks to me as the brightest image of any 16mm camera.

The mirror stops in the viewing position. The image will almost always appear upright and correct left-to-right.

You can manually adjust the horizon of the viewfinder prism for contorted viewing positions and when using the finder extender.

Eyepiece and Eyepiece Heater

The optical coating of the eyepiece is soft. Do not wipe with a lens tissue or chamois. This could scratch the element.

Instead, blow dirt and dust away with Dust-Off or an air syringe. If the element is dirty or smudged, use lens cleaning fluid applied first to the tissue. We like Panchro fluid.

If your eyepiece fogs up in damp or cold climates, use the heated eyecup (HE-3). Start on the HI setting. Switching to low while shooting is usually more comfortable. Turn it off when not in use, because it draws a fair amount of current.

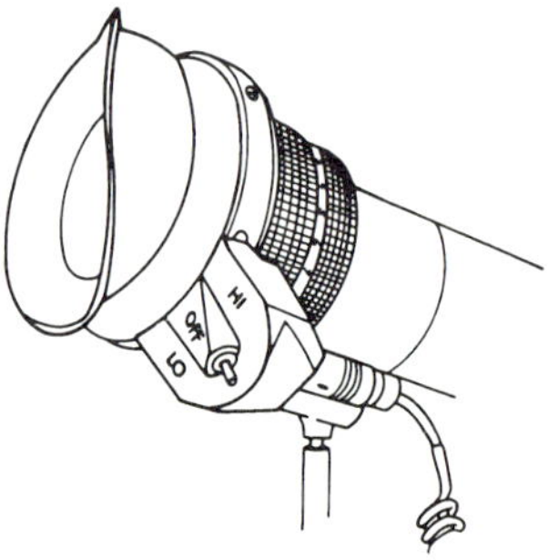

To attach the heated eyecup, swap it with the regular one. Plug in the coiled cable (KC-27): the straight end goes into the eyecup; the offset plug goes into the camera, at the rear left side, above the red running light.

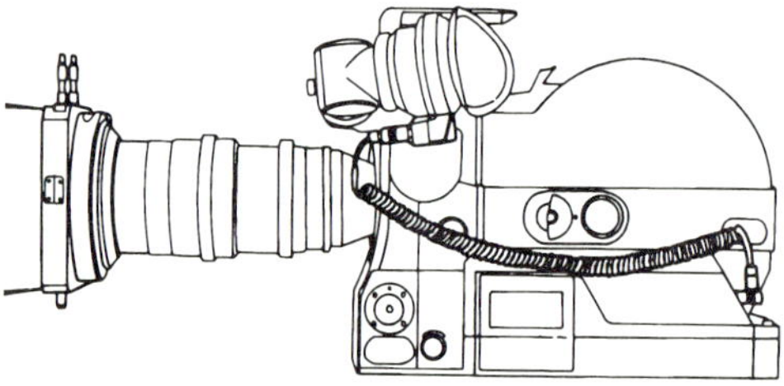

The green light above the receptacle on the camera is illuminated when the eyecup is drawing power. It turns off when the eyecup reaches temperature.

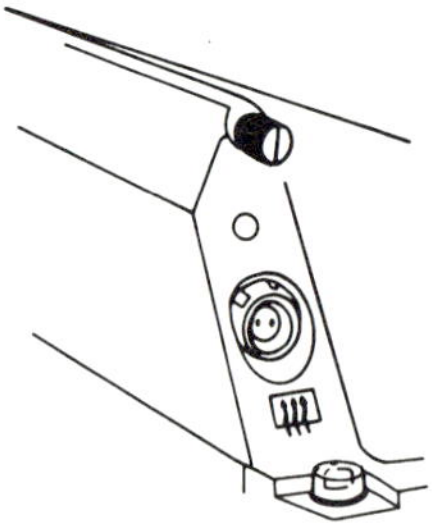

Do NOT breathe on the eyepiece element instead of using lens fluid and lens tissue. The acids in your breath are corrosive enough to eventually eat through the coating.

Eyecup

A combination chamois/foam eyecup cushion will also help eyepiece fogging problem. The chamois breathes. These cushions are available from most rental houses.

There are two styles of rubber eyecups that come with the camera: a bellows style, and traditional ARRI contoured one. I prefer the contoured one: less chance of light leak.

To swap the eyecups, pull the eyecup assembly straight back, away from the finder.

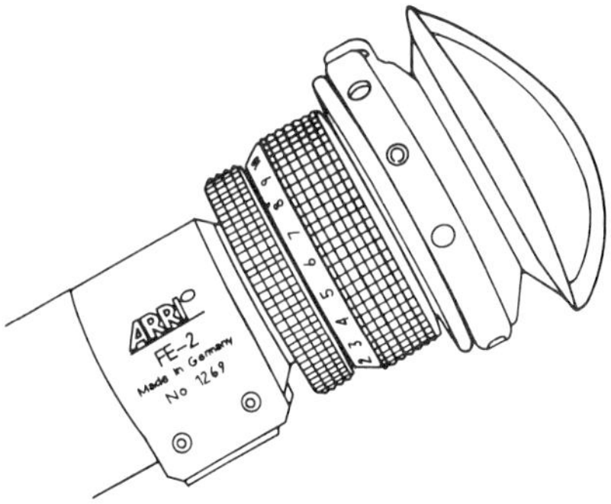

Loosen the 6 black flathead screws around the circumference of the outer metal ring. Do not remove the 4 tiny Phillips head screws on the opposite side—the side you look through—those hold the light-trap iris leaves in place.

After removing the 6 flathead screws, separate the black metal retaining ring from the rubber eyecup.

Replace the eyecup, and reposition the metal housing. It's tricky finding the tiny screw holes.

Unlike previous model cameras, you will not damage internal wires of the heated eyecup assembly by doing this swap.

Isopropyl alcohol is a good solvent to clean the rubber eyecup. You can get individually foil-wrapped isopropyl swabs in any drugstore.

If you're shooting and have to take your eye away from the eyepiece, you must close the light trap. Otherwise, the film will be fogged with a bluish haze from light entering the eyepiece and bouncing off the viewing screen. To close, turn the light trap lever counter-clockwise. For unattended shooting—on remote heads or lock-offs—it's wise to cover the eyepiece with a piece of black Duvetyne.

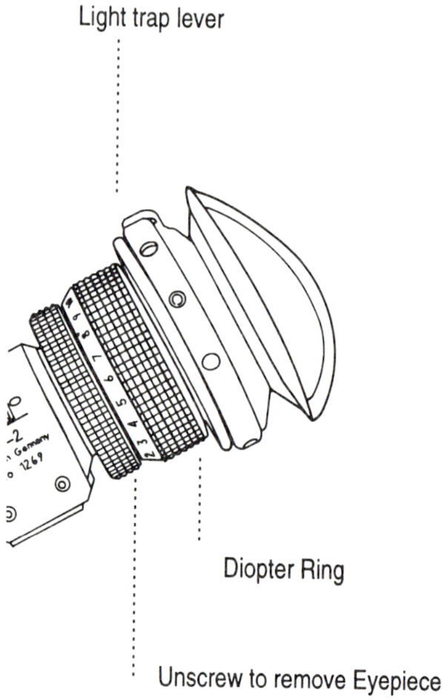

Rotate the larger of the two rubber rings (the one closer to the rubber eyecup) to adjust the diopter setting for your individual eyesight. Attach a thin strip of chart tape to mark different people's settings.

Punching a few holes in the rubber eyecup with a leather punch may help air circulation. Make the holes pinhole small, and cover them with the foam of the eye cushion. If direct light shines through, you could fog the film.

Finder Extender

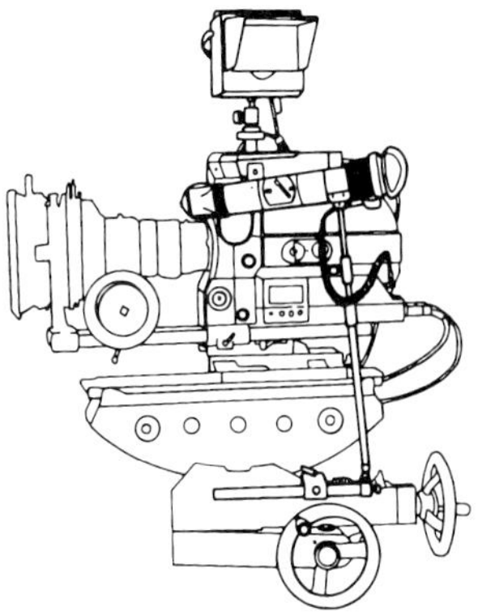

There are two finder extenders: FE-2 (7 ½") and FE-4 (10"). They make it much more comfortable when using a geared or fluid head. They have a 2 times magnifier (actually 17x, since normal viewing is 10x), accessible by flipping the lever forward, which is helpful for checking focus. The FE-4 has an ND6 contrast filter that flips into view.

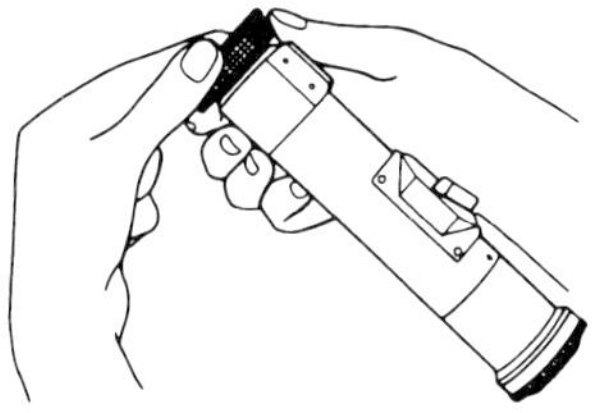

To install the finder extender, unscrew both end caps. The cap at the rear, next to the "FE" label, is removed by holding the rubber ring with one hand, and unscrewing the cap with the other hand.

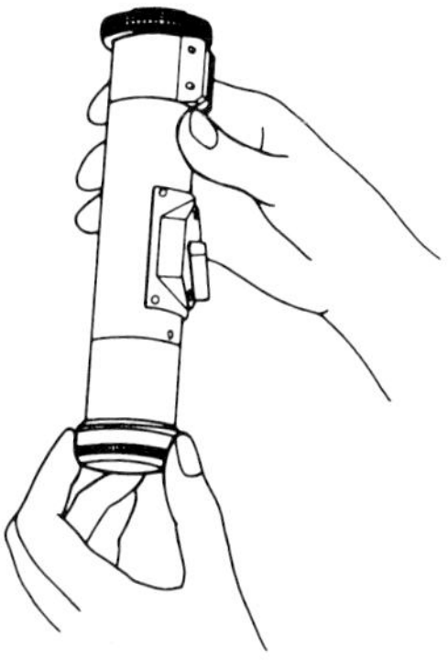

The other end simply twists off.

Next, swivel the camera's eyepiece so it aims straight up. This makes it easier to unscrew, with less danger of cross-threading or dropping, which are both common and expensive (over $4,000) mistakes. Unscrew the eyepiece from the camera.

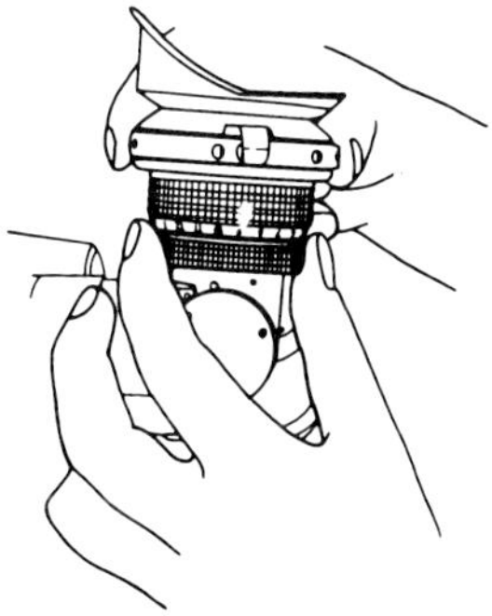

Hold the large rubber diopter ring with one hand—very securely—remember how much this little part costs. Unscrew the smaller ring with your other hand. Lift up on the eyepiece.

Attach the finder extender to the camera. The FE label faces up. The magnifier lever faces away from the camera. A guide pin inside the finder extender's mount faces forward, and engages in a slot. Insert, push down, jiggle it around to make sure it's really seated, and gently tighten the knurled ring. If not properly seated, it will cross-thread, so be careful.

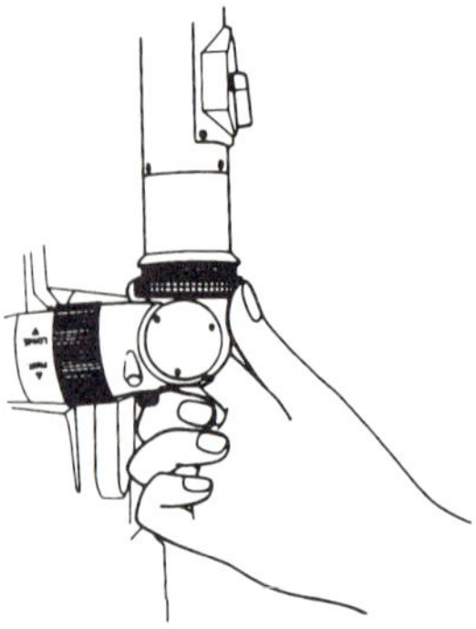

Attach the eyepiece. Engage the locating pin in the slot—there are two slots, and it doesn't matter which one you use. Jiggle, push down, gently tighten the lower, smaller rubber ring.

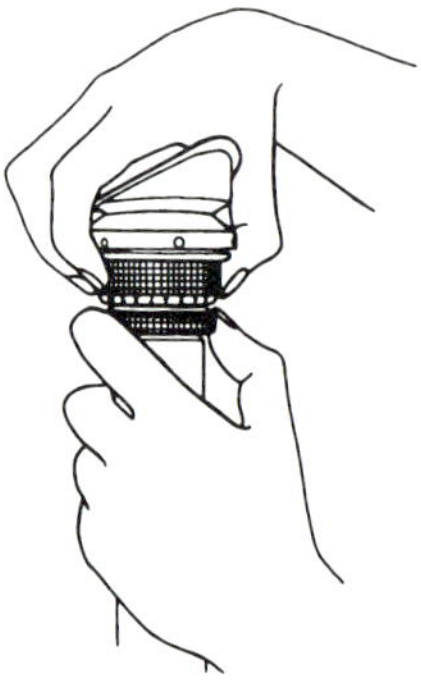

If you look through the finder now, the image will be upside down. To adjust it:

1. Loosen the viewfinder's friction adjustment. Turn the **FRICT—LOOSE** ring toward "**LOOSE**." Sometimes it is easier to hold the ring, while pulling up on the finder extender.

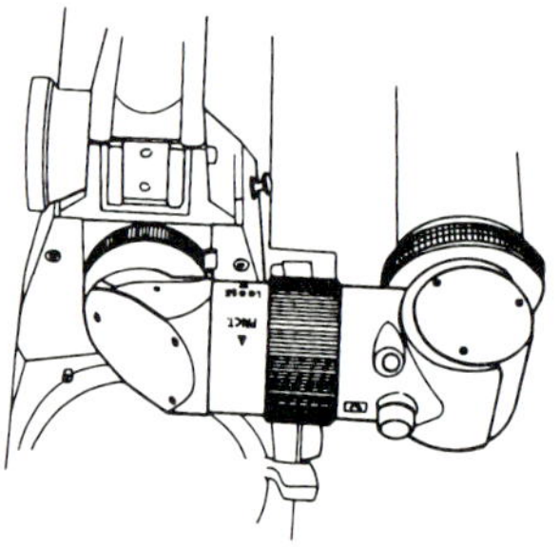

2. Push in on the silver release button, and keep holding it while you: Turn the black Prism Rotating Knob clockwise (direction of arrow). You can remove your finger from the silver release button. Notice that it is pushed in. Keep rotating until the silver button pops back up, and the knob stops turning.

3. Tighten the friction knob.

Finder Extender Leveler

A finder leveler will improve your operating ability and comfort when using a head.

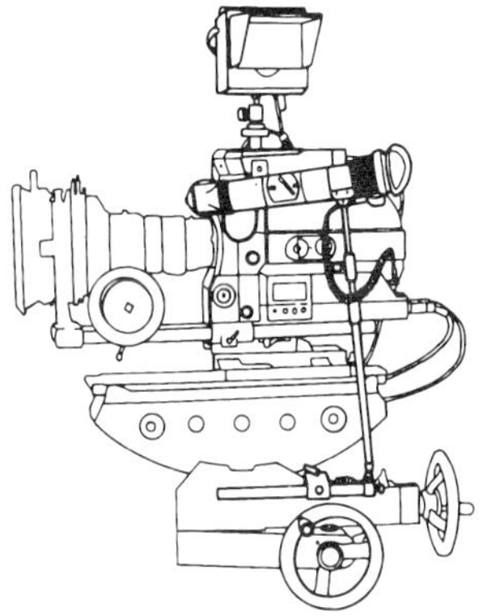

Full Studio Rig: 4" on-board mini-monitor, eyepiece heater, studio follow focus, mattebox, and eyepiece leveler.

Insert the round bottom rod into the receptacle of the head. This comes in two lengths.

Next, screw in the leveling rod. The two pieces should not be packed screwed together because the screw is delicate.

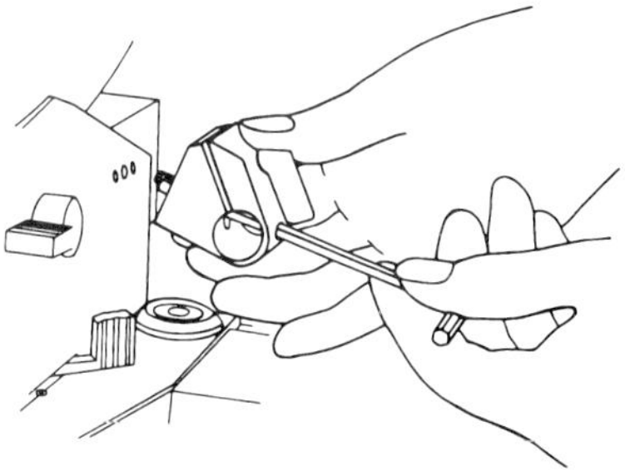

If the head doesn't have a finder extender receptacle, it is easy to install one.

Locating pins engage in the ARRIHEAD 2, and you tighten with an Hex key.

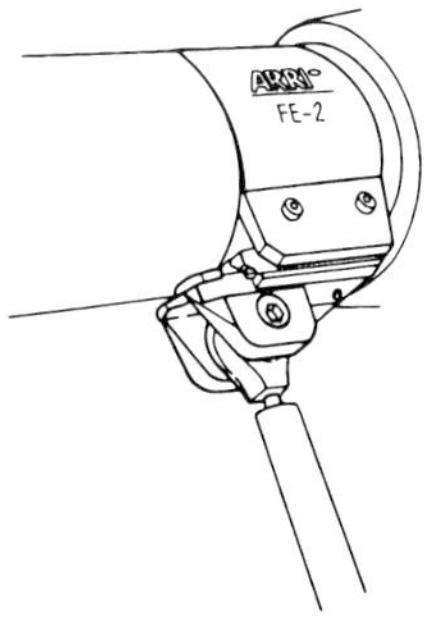

Insert the bottom rod, and turn the lever to tighten.

Attach the top of the leveling rod to the finder extender. It's a friction fit.

Before you use the finder extender with leveling rod, be sure to loosen the friction adjustment ring: ("FRICT-LOOSE"). See next page.

Failure to loosen will not only make it difficult to tilt, but will also damage the finder assembly.

Adjusting Viewfinder

To adjust the viewfinder's up-down friction, rotate the FRICT-LOOSE ring in the desired direction.

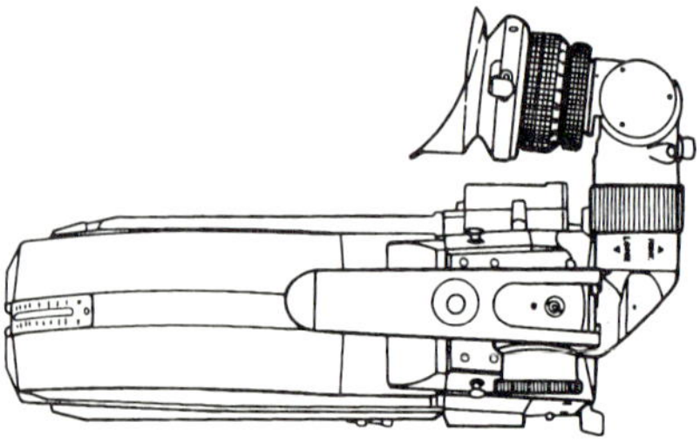

If the friction of the 25° swing-away (in-out) action of the finder needs adjustment, tighten or loosen 6 Hex screws equally on top and bottom with a 1.3mm Hex key (Tool A 16SR-17, Part# K 05.02825.0)

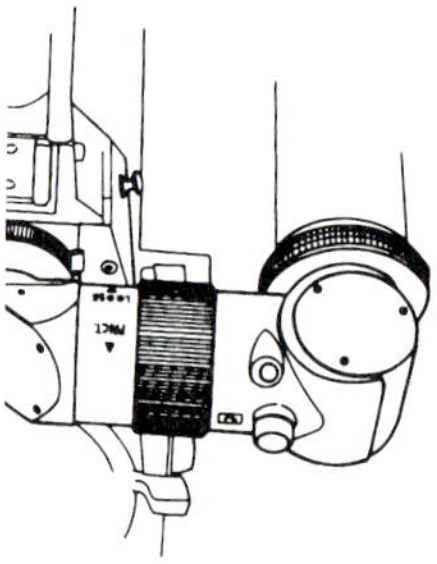

To increase or decrease the 190° left-right swing-over viewfinder tension, first loosen the bushing *(camera right, front top)* with the special twin-pronged driver tool A16SR-3 (part# K5.26129.0)

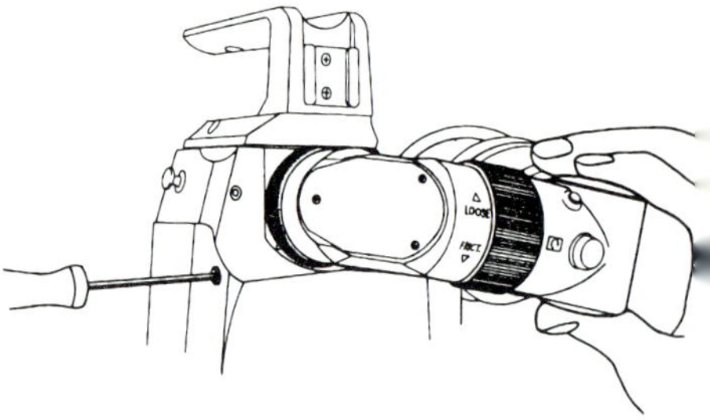

Turn the bushing about 1 turn counter-clockwise.

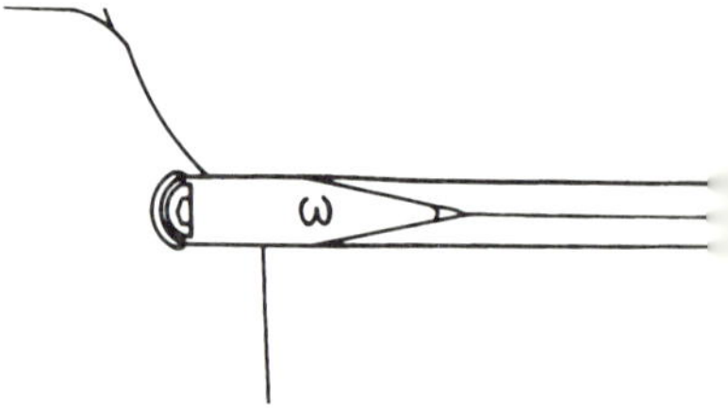

Insert a 2mm Hex key (ARRI tool A16SR-16, part # K 05.02431.0) into the socket.

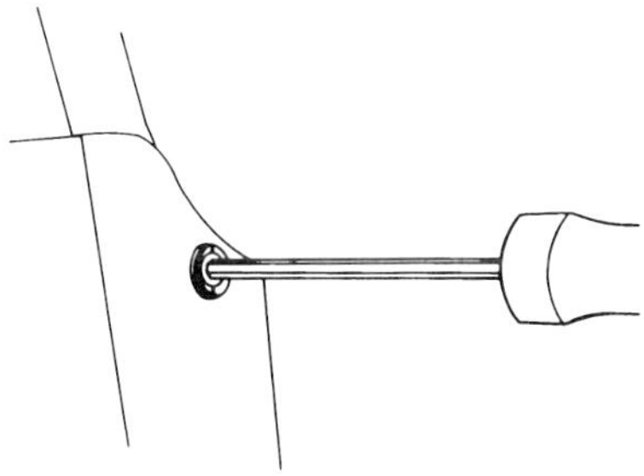

To decrease tension on the finder arm, turn counter-clockwise. To increase tension, turn clockwise.

Lock the bushing with the special tool when finished.

Here's the theory behind what we've just done.

The Hex screw is connected to a worm gear which rotates the knurled stainless steel collar nut holding the viewfinder to the camera body. The tighter the collar, the greater the pivot friction.

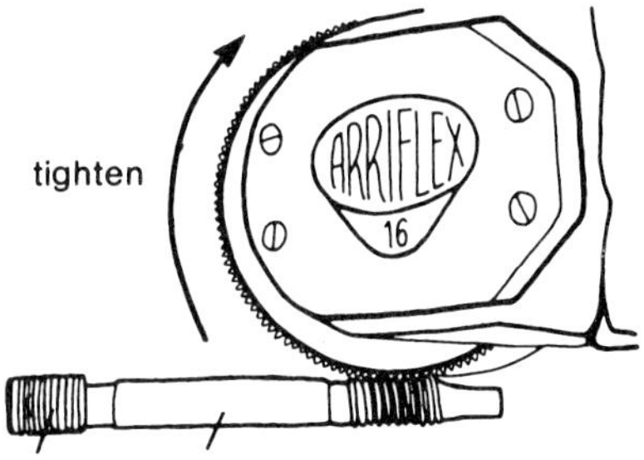

Tightening (turning the Hex screw clockwise) will seem easier than loosening (turning the Hex screw counter-clockwise), where you will encounter more resistance. This is because of the force of the worm gear pushing outward against the bushing lock ring. Just be sure that the bushing has indeed been backed off one turn.

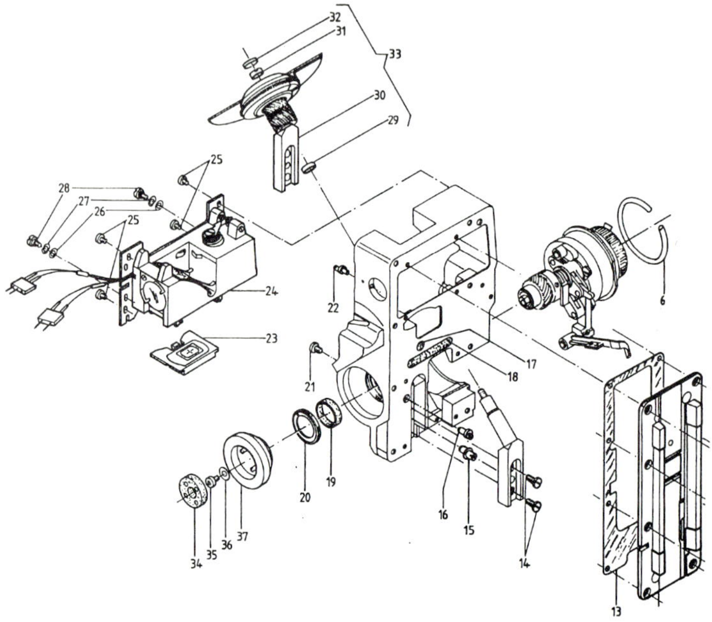

Exploded View of Gate and Mirror Shutter from Rear

Check the Rear

Remove Aperture Cover

Some 16 SR3 Camera Body Cases are configured to carry the camera without its magazine attached.

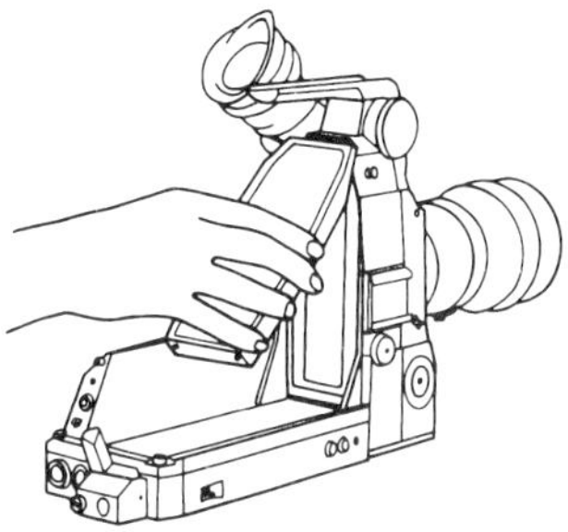

Note: it is safe to ship with the magazine attached.

If an aperture cover is used instead of a magazine, the cover pivots from the top and snaps in or out at the bottom.

Or, Remove Magazine

If an on-board battery is attached, swing it back.

It is held to the magazine with a magnet.

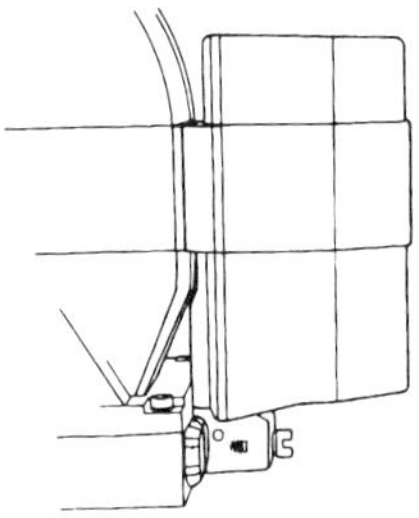

Grasp the magazine with one hand.

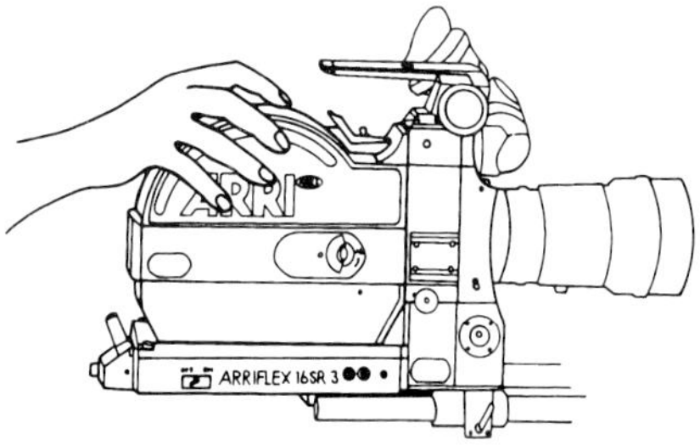

Hold the camera body or camera handle with your other hand if the camera is not securely mounted to a head.

1. With your index finger, flip the safety lock back to the "OPEN" position.

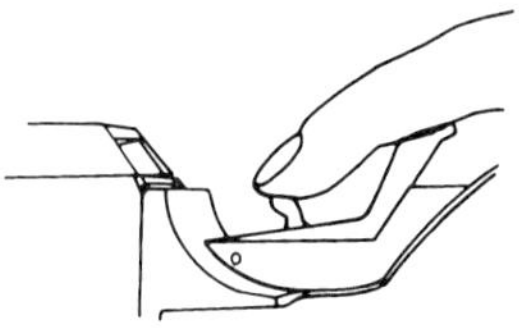

2. Depress the release lever.

3. Push it all the way down.

4. Lift up on the magazine.

5. Pivot the magazine from the top.

6. Raise the rear end of the mag until your index finger is almost touching the camera handle. At this point, the quick-change lock will disengage.

7. Pull the magazine straight back.

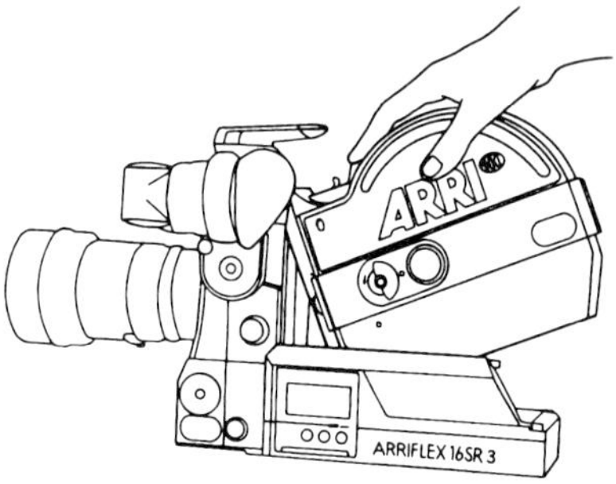

Video Assist Handle

Cameras fitted with video assist have longer handles. Some people prefer to swing the handle away when changing mags—but it's not essential.

Push the release button in, and swing the handle to the left.

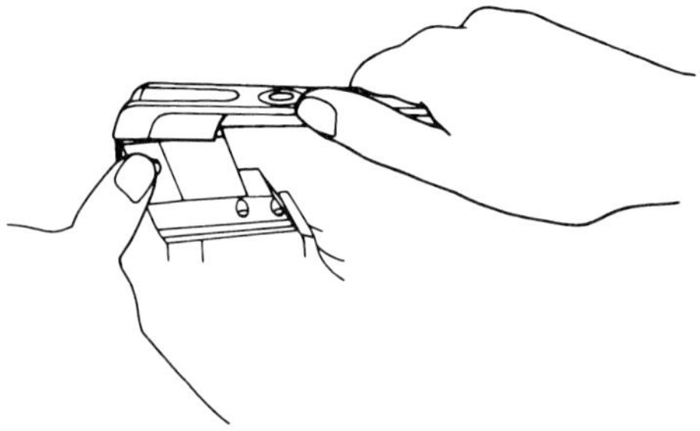

Check the Gate

Check the gate from the rear.

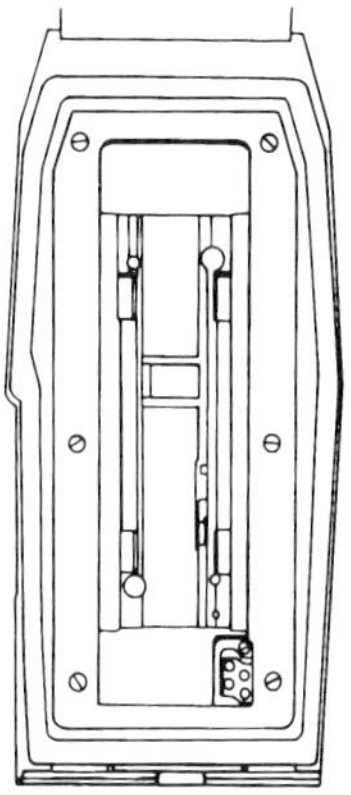

Do you see a silver bar on the left side of the aperture? If you do, the gate is set for **Normal 16**. See Super16 chapter beginning page 207.

Clean the gate, if it is dirty, with a plastic or wooden skewer—never a metal object. Do not use solvents. If there is a sticky emulsion build-up, clean it with a chamois or lint-free cloth.

In very humid conditions, you can reduce friction with a very minuscule amount of silicone applied with a pointed foam swab along the edges of the rails. Do the same to the edge of the magazine rails and guides. You should not be able to see the solvent—if you do, you have used too much. The problem with silicone is that it is virtually impossible to remove once put in the wrong place. Use caution.

Do not blow Dust-Off in from the back of the gate—you will blow most of the dirt into the lens cavity. Be careful not to damage the pull-down claw and registration pin.

Checking the Gate during Production

By the way, if you remove the magazine to check the gate after critical takes, you risk dislodging the errant piece of dust. The only proper way to check is **FROM THE FRONT**. Either remove the lens and use a Light/Magnifying Glass combination, or look down the barrel of the lens using a flashlight.

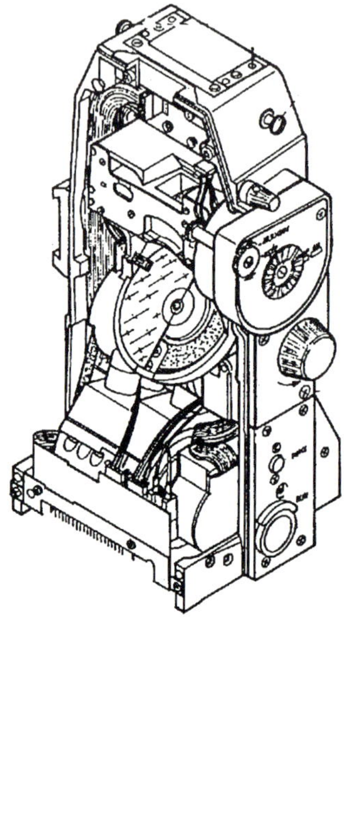

Exploded View of Motor and Mirror Shutter Front Assembly

Power

Plug In the Battery

Before plugging and unplugging batteries or accessories, make sure the main power switch *(camera right, rear)* is off – to prevent a rare case of shorting.

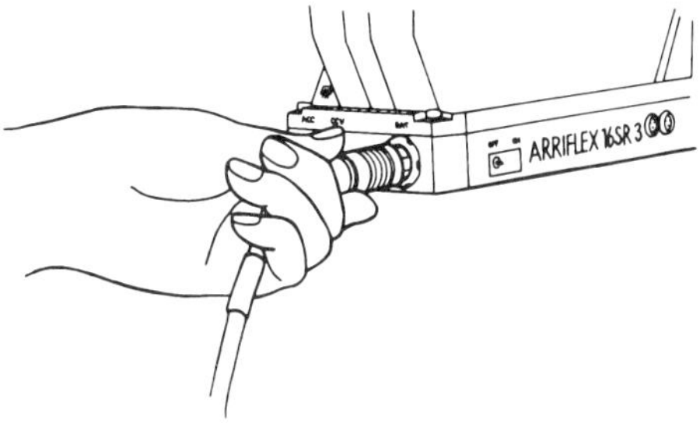

Like all the other members of the new generation of Arriflex cameras, the 16 SR3 runs off 24 volt batteries. Its predecessors, the SR1 and SR2 used 12 volt power supplies.

Plug the power cable into the back of the camera, where it says **BAT**. It is a two pin Fischer connector (camera side is male, cable is female). Pin 1 is ground, Pin 2 is +24v (10 amp max.)

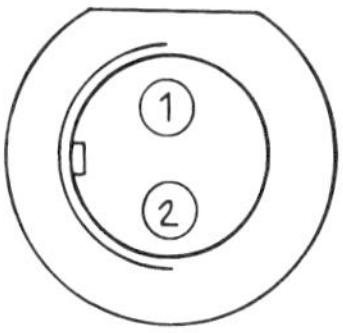

Plug the other end of the cable into your 24 volt battery. This is a 3-pin XLR connector.

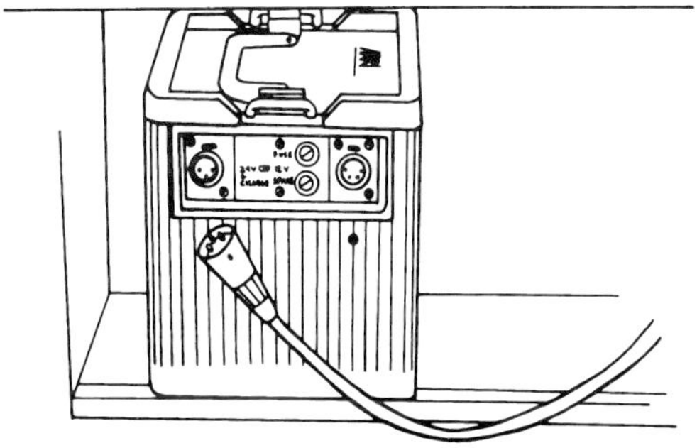

ARRI batteries are wired as follows:

pin 1 ground
pin 2 +24 v DC.

This differs from Panavision, where pin 1 is +24v, and pin 2 is ground.

Some rental houses use different configurations.
Otto Nemenz International and Clairmont Camera use 4-pin XLR connectors on the battery, with pin 1 as ground, and pin 3 as +24 v.

Clairmont Camera also uses Y cables, to put two 12 volt batteries or dual 12 volt batteries in series. These have the traditional 12 volt pinouts of 35-3 and 35 BL 12 volt cameras, where pin 1 is ground, and pin 4 is +12 v.

Block Batteries

There are many block batteries on the market. They have varying degrees of safety with unattended charging. I never felt comfortable leaving a battery alone overnight—in case of shorting or fire hazard. Make sure you charge it away from carpets or flammable surfaces.

ARRI Block batteries (NC 24/7 R) are switchable from 12 to 24 volts—7 Ah.

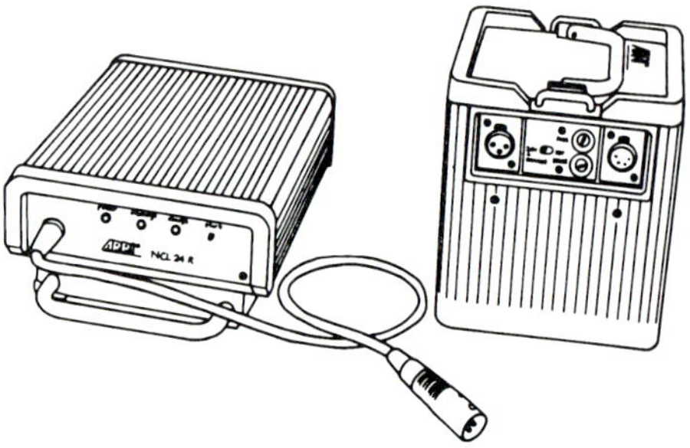

The charger (NCL 24R) for these batteries is interesting, because it has a built-in discharger to prevent memory effect.

1. First, check the voltage selector: 100-120-220-240.

2. To charge, plug the charger into the battery first.

3. Then plug the charger into the wall. A green LED power indicator lights up.

4. Push the **start** button.

5. The battery is discharged—indicated by a yellow LED—under a load of 1 amp until the voltage drops below 1 volt per cell. (A fully charged battery will take about 7 hours to fully discharge. You can bypass the discharge cycle by quickly flipping the battery output selector switch from 24 to 12 and back to 24 volts.

6. After discharging, the charger begins charging—a red LED goes on.

7. When the battery is fully charged (about 3 ½ hours), the red LEDs go out, and you may use the battery again. If you leave it plugged in, it stays on trickle charge.

8. When the helpful teamster unplugs your power cable, the battery will continue to be charged where it left off provided you have not unplugged it from the charger.

9. A flashing red light indicates over-temperature warning or someone unplugged the battery from the charger.

Battery Vest

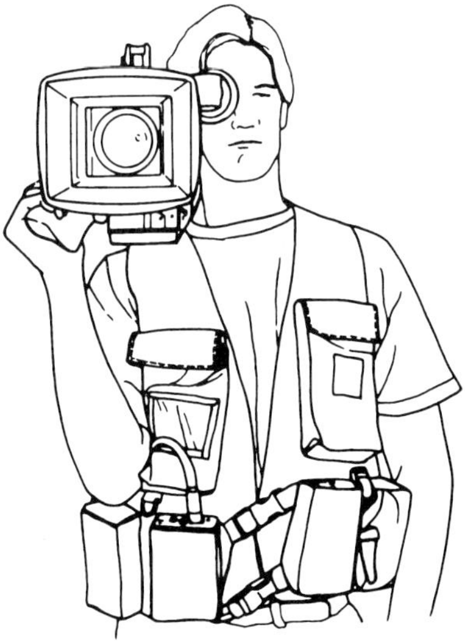

This innovative battery vest was designed by Norton Rodriguez of Miami. Unlike a traditional battery belt, the vest distributes its weight evenly across your waist and shoulders, and also adds enough shoulder protection to improve handheld comfort. It runs about 12 rolls of film. You can rest your shooting elbow on the cells for support.

It has pockets for your meters and other essentials.

NRG Research, Inc. distributes it. See Appendix.

On-Board Battery

The ARRI 16 SR3 uses an on-board battery, which frees you from cables and battery belts. Each on-board battery will run about five 400' magazines at room temperature, without video or numerous electronic accessories. We've shot as many as 8 rolls with new cells.

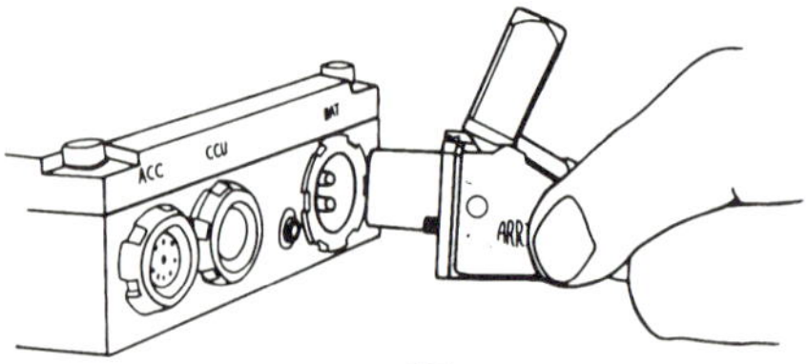

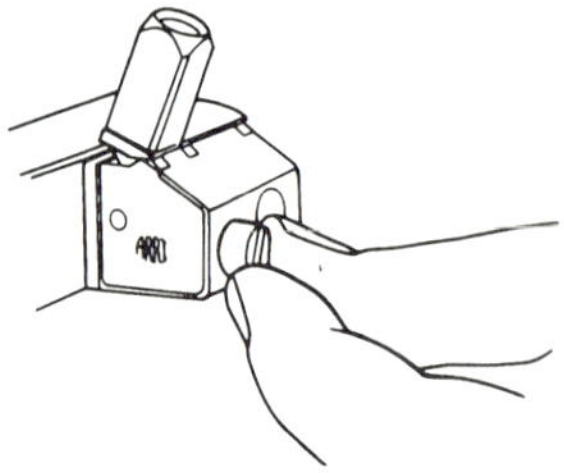

Attach the on-board battery adapter:

Push in and finger-tighten the slotted screw. It will loosen in time, with use, so check it occasionally.

Slide the battery onto the adapter's square metal shaft.

When you attach a magazine, the battery pivots against the mag, and is held in place with a magnet.

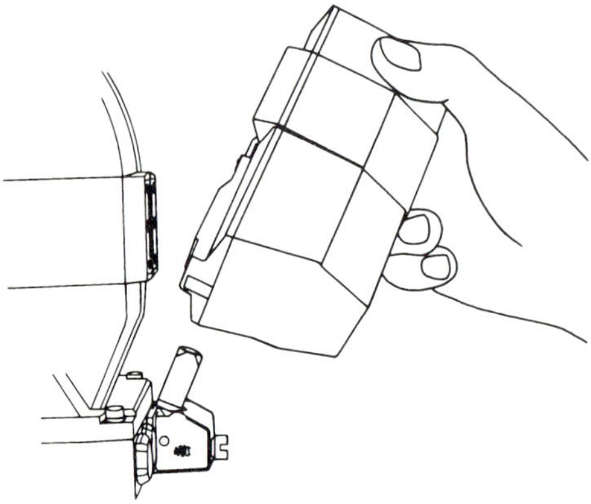

DO NOT SLAM the battery against the magazine. While this makes a satisfying sound, you might break the battery's plastic case.

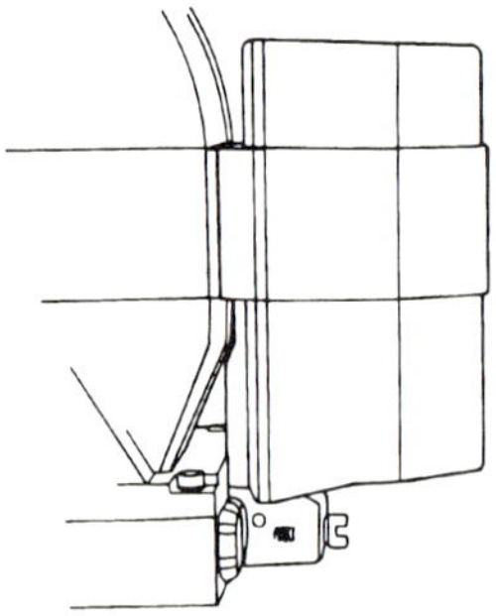

If you find you can't push the battery down, don't force it—you might have a 12 volt SR1 or SR2 battery by mistake. They have one pin inside the shaft; the SR3 has 3 pins inside.

Always slide the on-board battery straight up or down. NEVER wiggle the battery from side to side. You'll crack the socket.

Sometimes, it becomes difficult to slide the on-board battery on and off. Lubricate with an electrical contact cleaner such as Chemtronics Electronic Cleaner/Degreaser spray, CRC 2-26, or Chemtronics TF Pads. Ordinary lubricants will gum up the contacts, so do NOT use WD-40 or CRC 5-56 here.

It is best to run the camera until you see the low voltage warning: a flashing red LED in the eyepiece, and a "**bat**" in the main display. That discharges the battery enough to prevent "Nicad memory effect." You do not have to change batteries immediately upon seeing the warning—usually you can finish the roll.

Use ARRI's Double Charger (NCL 24/1.2) for on-board batteries. You can charge one or two at the same time.

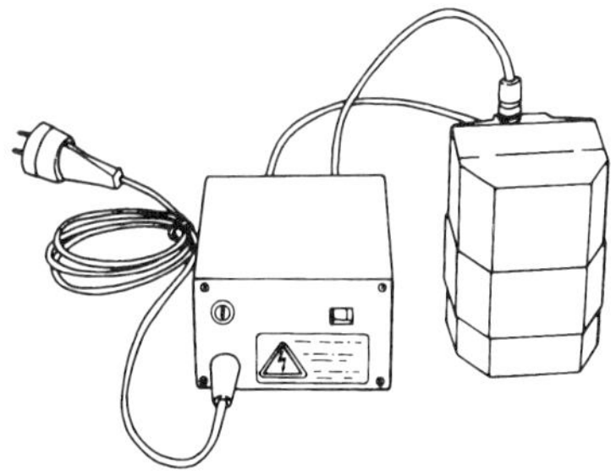

Check the red voltage switch on the front cover: 115 or 230 volts AC. Slide the switch to the correct setting. It runs on 50 or 60 Hz.

Plug in the batteries. Then plug the charger into the wall. Red LEDs will glow while the batteries charge. It takes about 7 hours for a full charge, at which time the charger goes into trickle mode, and the LED goes out.

When charging two batteries, connect them both at the same time. The charger has only one timer. If one battery is put on charge much later than another, it will not receive a full charge.

If someone unplugs the charger, or a helpful PA disconnects your extension cord, the charger will remember how far it went in the charging cycle as long as the battery is kept plugged in. When power resumes, the charger will continue where it left off.

Let's assume you've just finished charging two batteries, and want to charge two more. You must reset the charger's internal "clock," otherwise the new batteries will only be trickle charged. The red LED which indicates "charging" will not come on.

To reset the charger's internal 7 hour (approx) timer to charge more batteries, disconnect AC power and all batteries for at least 20 seconds.

There is a .25 amp fuse above the main power cord, on the chassis. Unscrew the fuse receptacle, and a plastic tray holding the fuse will slide out. Make sure you carry spares.

You can also charge on-board batteries with ARRI's block battery charger (NCL-24), using an adapter cable (KC 38, ARRI part K2.43196.0, Arriflex US part 331010.)

Power Notes

Like the Arriflex 535, 535B and 435, the Arriflex 16 SR3 uses 24 volt DC batteries. It will run with a DC power supply of 20 to 32 volts. If the voltage is out of that range (below 18v or above 34v), if there is a short in the battery or cable, or if polarity is reversed, the camera has an internal auto-reset current limiting circuit that prevents it from running. The camera will shut down, and takes less than a minute to reset. Make sure the main power switch is turned off, and you remove the offending battery.

If the polarity is reversed, the RUN LED will glow red. This could happen if you use Panavision batteries with ARRI cables. Both use 3 pin XLR connectors. If you have batteries from other manufacturers, make sure battery pin 1 is negative, and pin 2 is +24 volts DC. If not, you can make a reversing cable. Make sure you label it: "Panavision Battery to ARRI Camera Reversing Cable."

Table Of Battery Pin-Outs

3 pin XLR Battery pin #	16 SR3 ARRI Battery	Panavision Battery (needs adapter cable)
1	—	+ 24 v
2	+ 24 v	—
3	unused	unused

4 pin XLR Battery pin #	Clairmont / Nemenz 16 SR3 Battery
1	—
2	unused
3	+ 24 v
4	unused

4 pin XLR Battery pin #	16 SR1 and 2
1	—
2	unused
3	unused
4	+ 12 v

Camera's Power Receptacle

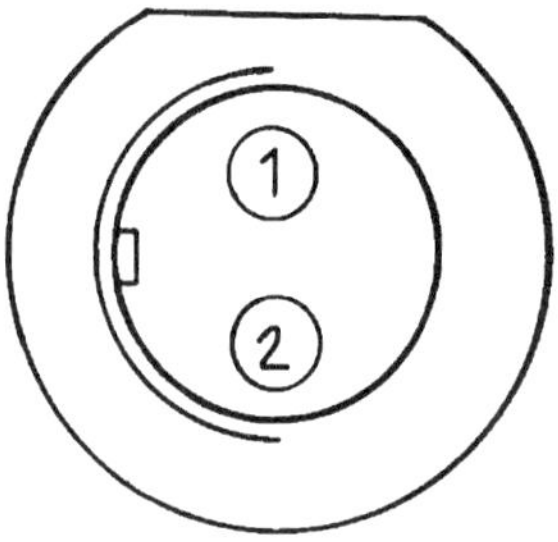

The two pin Fischer power socket on the camera is wired as follows:

Pin 1 is ground
Pin 2 is +24v. (max 10 amp)

Main Fuse

The camera is protected by a 10 amp Main Pico Fuse. A shorted handgrip or eyepiece heater cable could pop this fuse, as could overloading the accessory receptacles.

To check or change the main fuse, **remove your on-board battery or power supply. Turn the camera off.** Remove the magazine. Look at the camera's base.

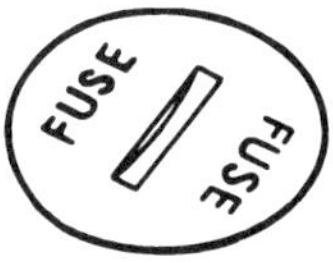

Use a coin to unscrew the fuse cover located at the right rear.

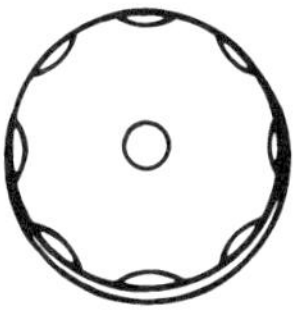

The 10 amp pico fuse can be removed with the ever-popular Hirschmann forceps. A spare fuse is located in the fuse cover. Unscrew the clear plastic cover to get it.

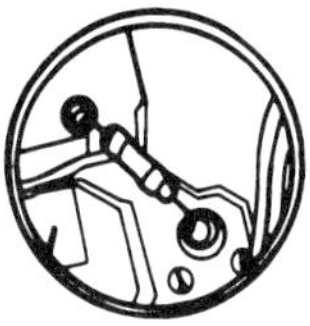

Replace the fuse and the cover. Make sure you buy more fuses, and find the cause of the fuse having blown.

Newer cameras (beginning version "E-3/4") are protected by self-resetting polyswitches located on the circuit board in the camera base. A 5 amp polyswitch protects the RS connectors. A 2.5 amp polyswitch protects the ACC, CCU and eyepiece heater receptacles .

Power Up the Camera

Turn the Main Camera Power Switch On. *(Camera Right Side, Rear.)*

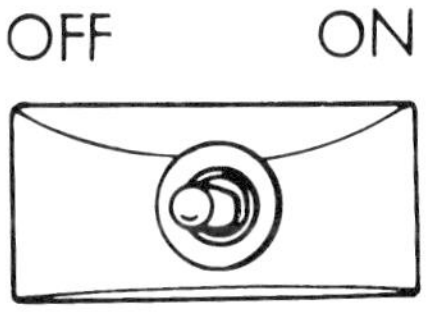

Check Status Light

The LED Status Light above the RUN switch will glow red for a second, and then go out. If it stays red or flashes, there is a power problem.

When the camera runs at speed, the LED glows red momentarily as the camera comes up to speed, at which time it will turn green.

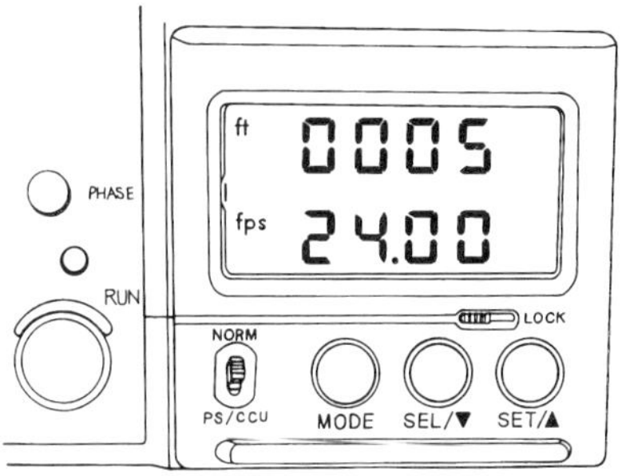

If the LED stays red, there is a problem. Turn the camera off, and unplug your power source.

Check Camera Speed

When the Power Switch is first turned on, the Main Liquid Crystal Display Panel will be backlit with reddish glow for about 30 seconds.

The backlight goes out to conserve battery power until you push one of the buttons below the display.

The bottom line of the display indicates the frame rate at which the camera will run. Press **RUN** once to start, and again to stop the camera.

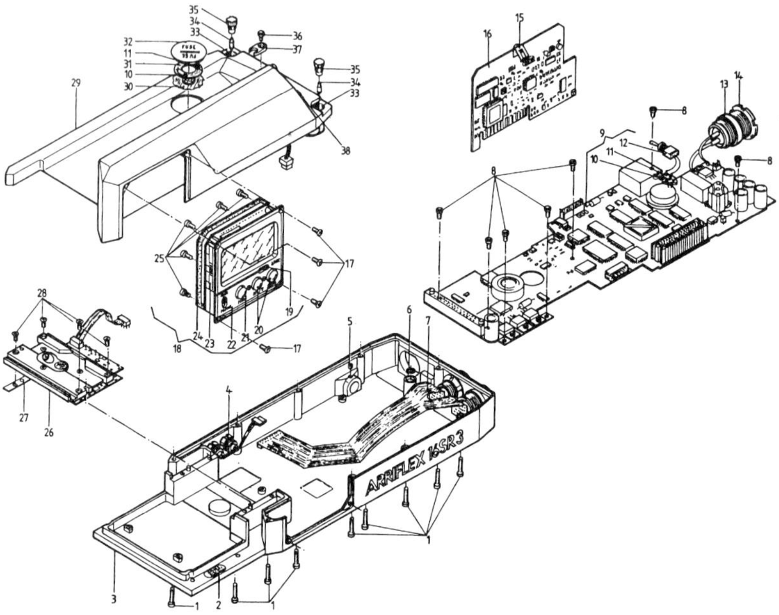

Exploded View of Base, Electronic Boards and Display

The Main LCD Display

and its 6 Modes (Pages)

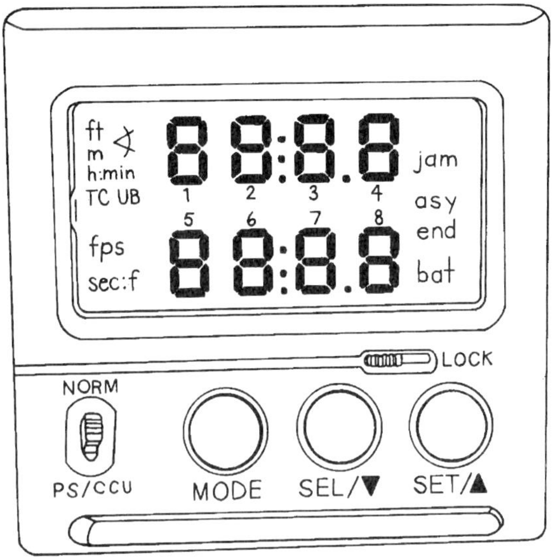

There are 6 MODES in the Camera's Main LCD Display. Think of each mode as a page on a computer screen.

Each time you push the MODE button, you advance one screen. After page 6, you circle back to page 1. You cannot skip pages.

Warning indicators

The LCD will display warnings, independent of Mode, for the following conditions:

TC	Timecode turned on
TC (flashing)	Timecode error
bat	Low battery, less than 20 volts
asy	Camera running off speed
end	Film has run out
fps (flashing)	ESU not picking up a valid signal

Home Page- Mode 1

Total exposed (or take) and default speed

When you first turn the camera on, you are at MODE 1—which could also be called Home Page 1. Home Page (or Home Plate, if you prefer a baseball analogy) is a good way to think of this screen, since that is where the camera retreats after 30 seconds of inactivity. Electronic engineers call this "standby."

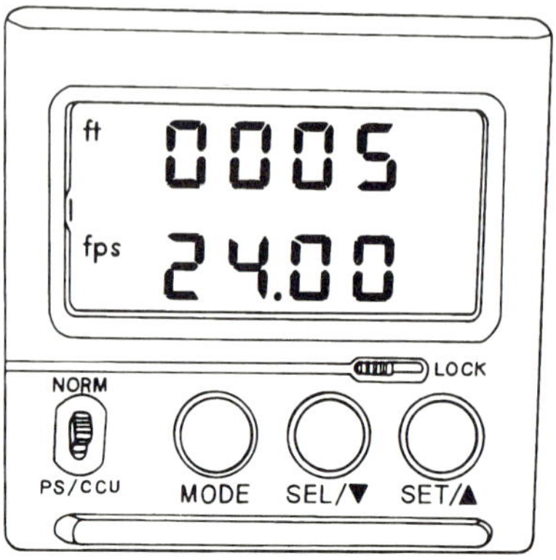

The top line is usually total footage exposed.

The top line can be programmed in meters or feet. Some people prefer the home page to display footage shot in the last take (instead of total shot on the current magazine)—in which case you will see a **t** (for take) in the top line. More on these things later.

Mode 1 - Reset Footage Counter

To reset the footage counter to zero, press **SET** for 3 seconds.

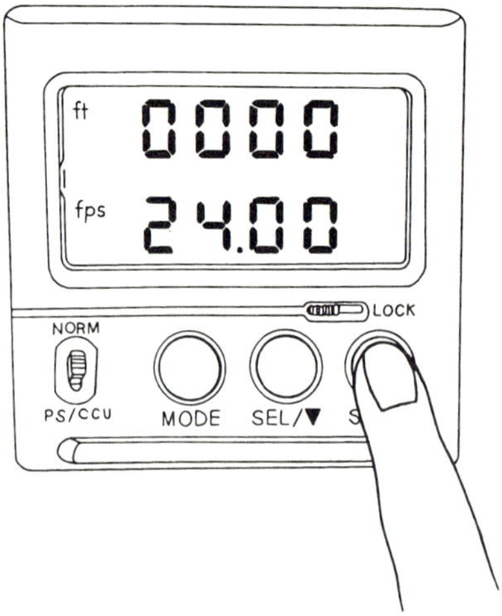

You should do this whenever you change magazines.

Mode 1 - Changing Default Camera Speed

Most jobs are shot at one main “default” speed. This should be set in Mode 1. It is usually 24 fps.

To change the camera’s default running speed, push **SEL** once.

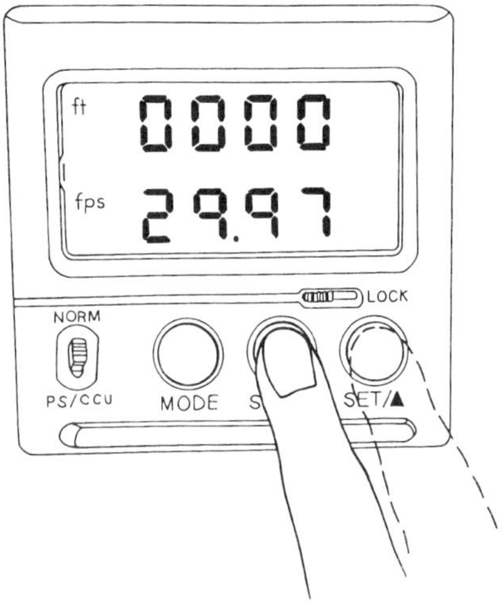

The speed will change to 25.00, and blink.

Push **SET** to accept 25 fps, or push **SEL** again to go to the next default speed, which is 29.97. Push again to go to 30.00. Push **SET** to accept 30, or push **SEL** again, and you revert back to 24.00.

(By the way, all the speeds entered from the keypad are crystal speeds.)

Mode 1 - NORM-PS/CCU

If you now slide the **NORM - PS/CCU** slide switch to **PS/CCU,** the bottom line of the display will no longer show a frame rate. Instead, it will read *PS* for Programmed Speed (but it will not show you what that speed is.) This is the camera’s second running speed quickly available to you at the flick of a switch. If press **RUN** on the camera now, it will run at the programmed speed, and now the programmed speed frame rate will display. You can switch back and forth between Normal and Programmed Speed while the camera is running.

To find out what the programmed speed is without having to run the camera, we go to the second page, MODE 2.

Mode 2

Programmed Speed

Push the black "MODE" button once: you'll see the pre-programmed "second" speed.

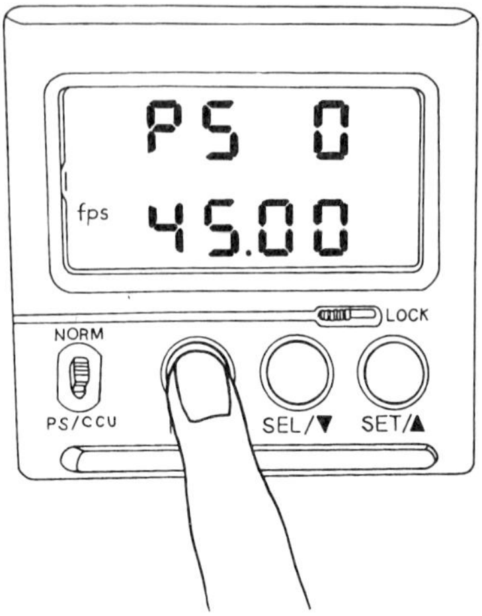

The top line says *PS*, followed by a digit. The digit is the third decimal place for speeds under 100fps, and the second decimal place for speeds over.

To change the programmed speed, press **SEL** once. The first digit blinks. Push **SET** for each higher value desired.

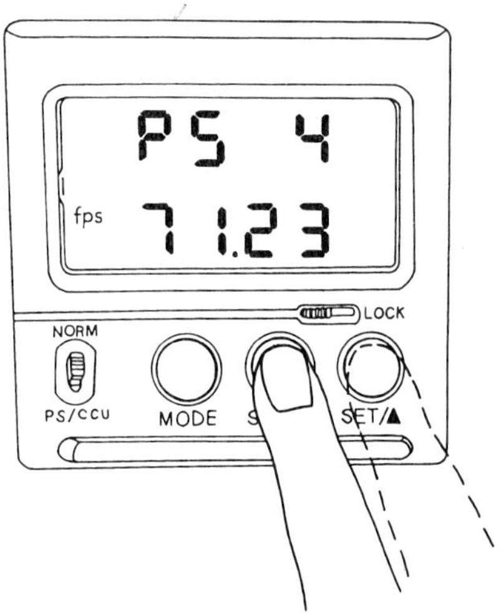

To go to the next digit, press **SEL** once. Set the value with **SET.** To skip digits (for example, to skip the decimal places,) push **SEL** without entering **SET.** The easiest way to store the number is to push **MODE**.

As mentioned, you can change from the default camera speed to the programmed "second" speed by flipping the slide switch, even while the camera is running.

Mode 2 - External Controls

If a remote control unit such as an RCU (which governs camera speed) is connected, the switch must be set to **PS/CCU**, and *PS* will be displayed on the top line, with the remotely set speed displayed on the bottom.

You do not have to run the camera while the display is in Mode 2—just use this mode while setting up and to check the preset speed.

You can fine-tune the camera's speed—when shooting computer monitors without an ESU, for example—by pushing **SEL▾** to decrease and **SET ▴** to increase the speed in 1/1000 fps increments while the camera is running.

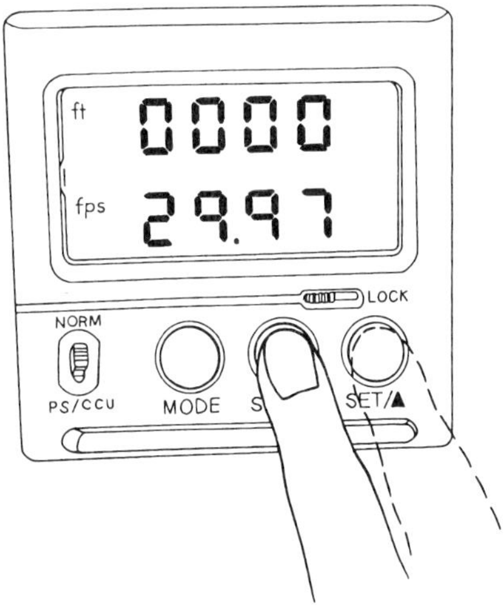

Exception: ESU

If you plug in an external sync unit (ESU), the top line displays *ESU*, and the bottom line will be the shooting speed. But you do not have to flip the switch to **PS/CCU** when using an ESU.

Mode 3

Take (or Total Exposed) and Voltage

Push the **MODE** button again.

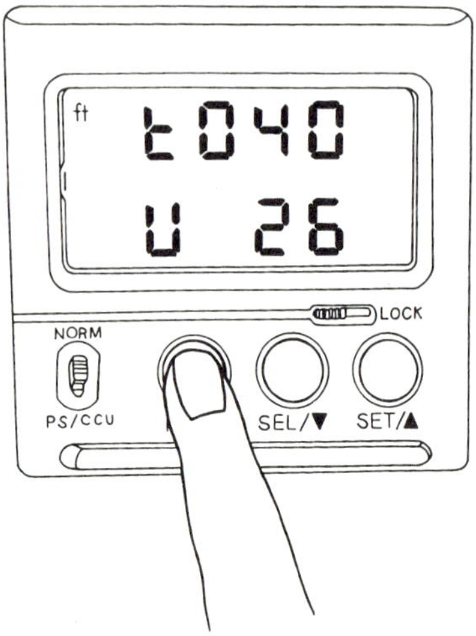

The top line is usually "footage shot in the last take," and is indicated by a small **t.**

If there is a *0* instead, this mode is showing "total exposed footage shot so far."

The bottom line is your battery voltage. Think of the "U" to the left of the number as a "V" for voltage—LCD displays have trouble spelling.

The quick way to tell you are in mode 3 is to look for the "U" in the bottom line.

To switch from feet to meters:

Push **SEL** once.
m or **ft** flashes.
Push **SET** to change and store it.

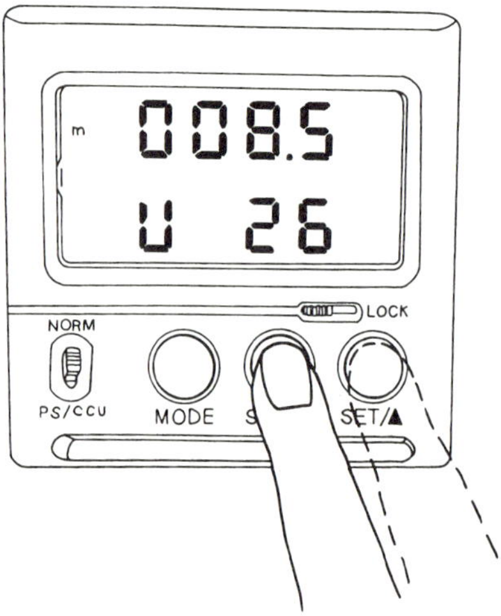

Meters will show a decimal point in the top line; feet will not.

Mode 3 - Switching take to total footage

To switch from "footage shot in the last take" to "total exposed on the roll so far" push **SEL** twice. Push **SET** to change and save the display setting.

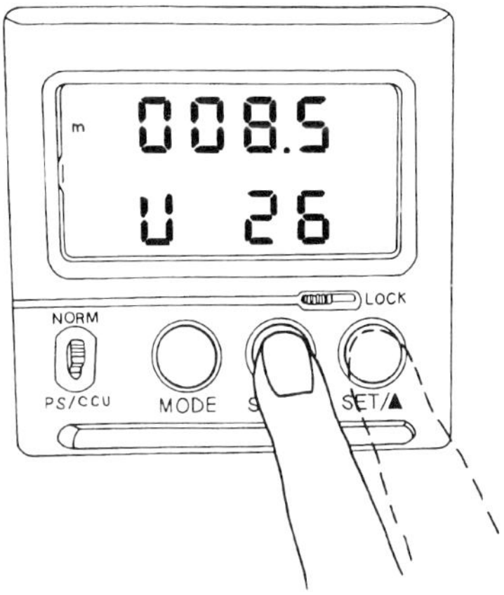

This action sends the "footage shot in the last take" display to the Home Page - Mode 1 readout. Note: if you do this, you must reset your total exposed counter from Mode 3 when you change mags.

Mode 4
Timecode

Push the **MODE** button again to go to the timecode display.

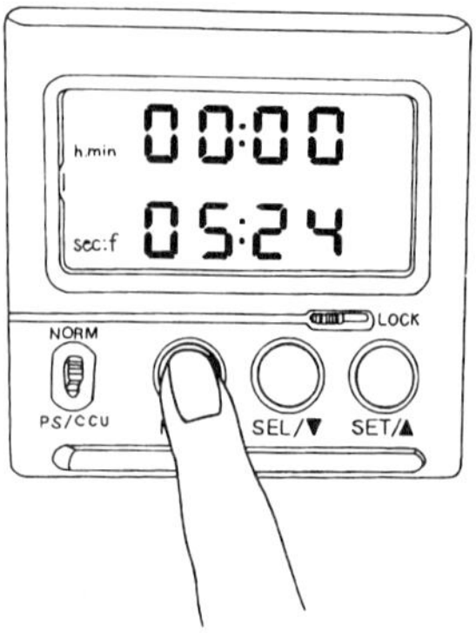

(Skip on to the next mode if you're not using timecode.)

To get timecode on film: "Jam-sync" the camera with another source. Connect the timecode output cable of a Nagra, DAT recorder, master clock, or video assist tape recorder to the 9 pin **ACC** socket of the 16 SR3.

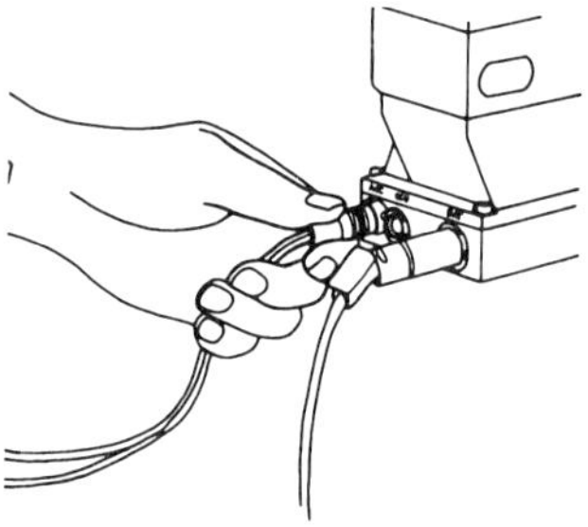

Before the job, check to see who has the cables—you, sound, or video.

The lower line of the camera's display will flash EC for "external code being fed." Anytime after it starts flashing CC for "correct code," you may unplug the jam-sync cable.

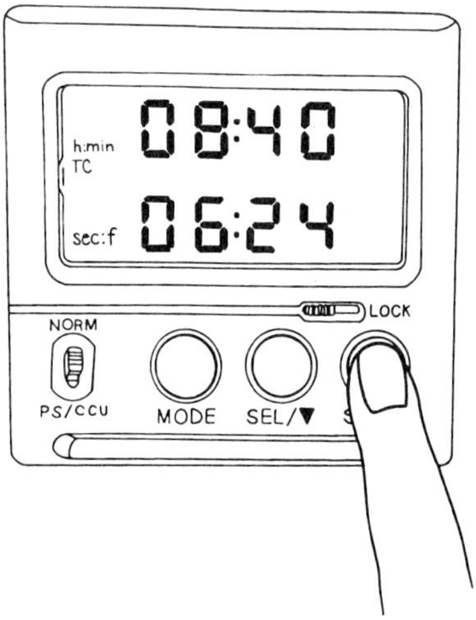

The letters **TC** appear in the display to indicate timecode is now being recorded on film. The last 2 digits are the timecode frame rate.

Push **SET** for 3 seconds to turn timecode recording off. Push **SET** again to re-enable it.

Make sure timecode sensitivity has been set on the magazine. See the section in this book on timecode.

Mode 5

User Bits

Push the **MODE** button again: User Bits are displayed. You cannot reset them here. They simply are numbers (0-9) and letters (A-F) the "user" can enter to identify date, camera number, and so on. The sound recordist can enter the user bits, or you can do it using an LCC or CCU.

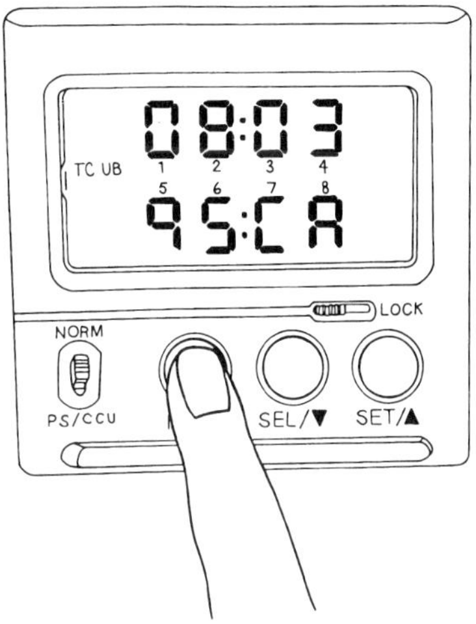

Error Messages

Mode 5 also shows timecode error messages if you have camera electronics version E-3/4 or later.

Push **SEL** . The bottom line of the display shows dashes. The top line displays error message numbers. (See timecode section for error message chart.)

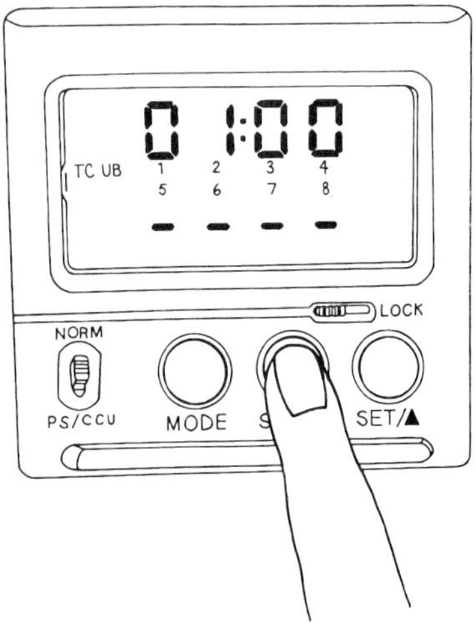

Error messages are usually caused by incorrect timecode.

The example to the right (*01:00*) shows that the camera must be re-jammed, since it has been more than 8 hours since it was last done.

Whenever there is an error, the *TC* display blinks on and off, and the camera usually beeps. To silence the beep, push **SET** briefly from Mode 1 (briefly, so you do not reset the footage counter). Then either turn timecode off (push **SET** for 3 seconds in Mode 4), or re-jam timecode.

Mode 6

Beep Settings

Push the **MODE** button again:

The top line displays start/stop beep status.

Push **SEL** to get the two dashes after *LS* (loudspeaker) to blink.

Push **SET** to cycle through the settings: up is on, down is off. The left dash is the start beep, the right dash is the stop beep.

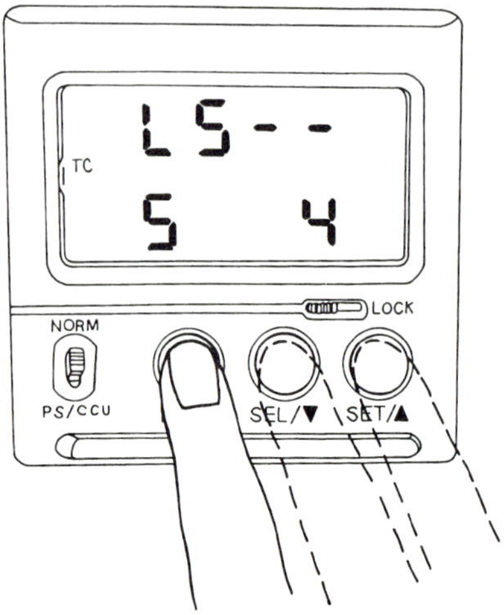

Mode 6 - Timecode Sensitivity Display

A number after the S in the bottom line of Mode 6 shows the timecode sensitivity setting when a timecode-equipped magazine is attached. The timecode sensitivity must be set on the magazine. It controls the intensity of the LED which exposes a barcode on the film. (See the sensitivity chart in the timecode section).

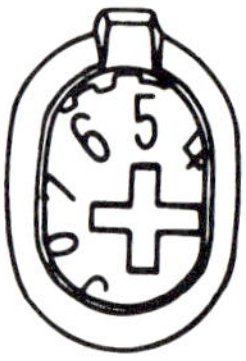

Back to Home Page - Mode 1

Push **Mode** again — we're back where we started: footage shot and fps.

If you are in modes 2 - 6 without setting data, the camera returns to the Home Page after about 30 seconds.

It's sort of like a digital watch.

Check Shutter Angle

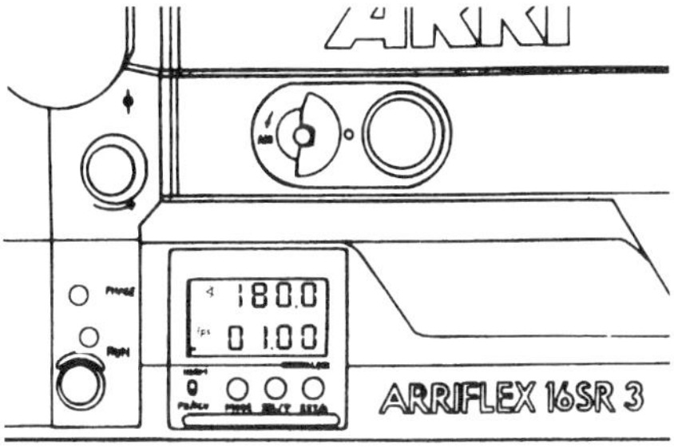

The mirror shutter of the Arriflex 16 SR3 is manually adjustable: 180°, 172.8°, 144°, 135°, 90°, 45°.

To check the shutter angle without having to remove the lens, push the **PHASE** button for at least 3 seconds. An angle symbol ∢ displays on the LCD panel.

The main power switch must be on. You can run this test from any display mode.

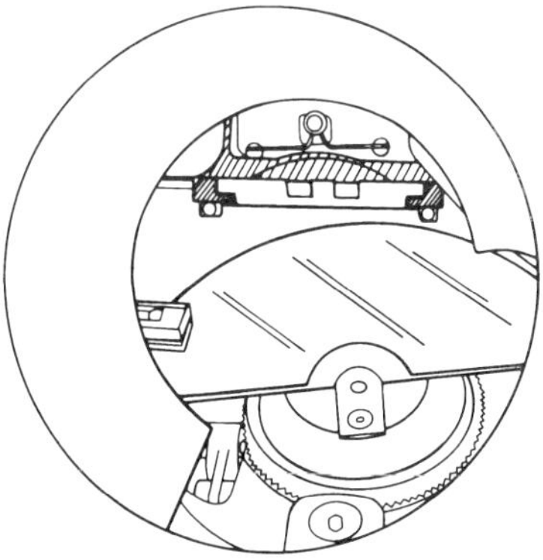

The shutter angle will display after two seconds. The camera runs at 1 frame per second, as the shutter angle is measured by an LED and photo receptor.

Replace Aperture Cover

Never leave the camera open for more than a few minutes without the aperture cover or magazine in place. Dust will surely fly in. Sometimes insects will get inside. If you see a King Kong like object crawling over your image, it is probably an insect inspecting your fibre optic viewing screen.

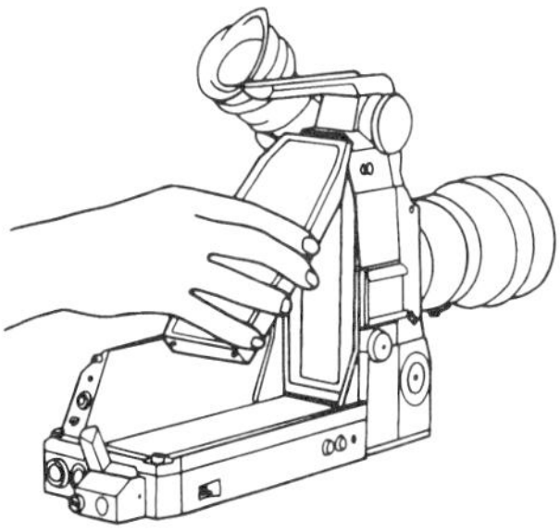

Attaching the Magazine

To continue with the checkout, you might want to use a magazine that isn't loaded, or at least contains film you do not mind wasting.

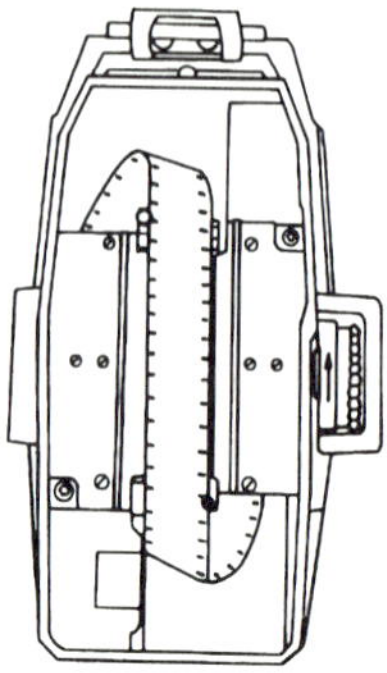

If the magazine is loaded, make sure the film loop is centered, and held in place by the four side guide hooks. (We'll discuss loading later.)

1. Grab the mag with one hand. Hold the camera with the other hand if it is not mounted on a head.

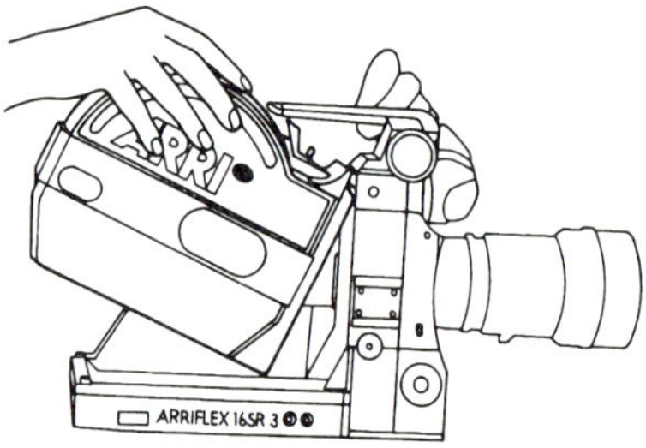

2. Angle the magazine about 30° above the base.

The release lever need not be pressed when you attach the magazine.

3. Slide the guide pins of the magazine into the slot of the camera. The flap, which goes up as the mag goes in, will snap down when properly inserted. If you don't hear a click, wiggle gently, and pivot the mag up and down until you hear the click.

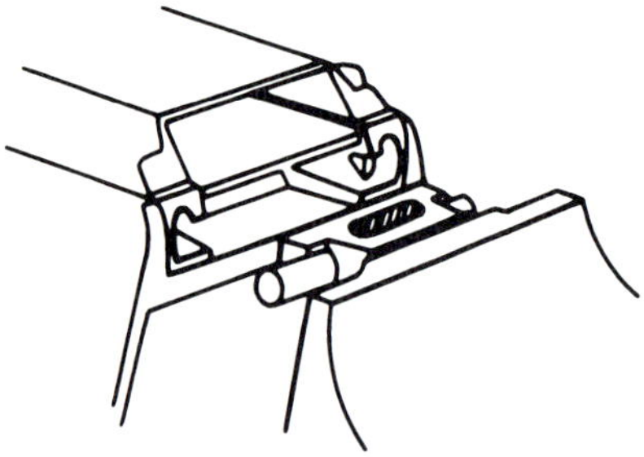

There is a red bar on the top of the magazine. It is a warning indicator, which will be visible if the magazine is not engaged properly.

4. Next, pivot the mag down gently until it locks in place.

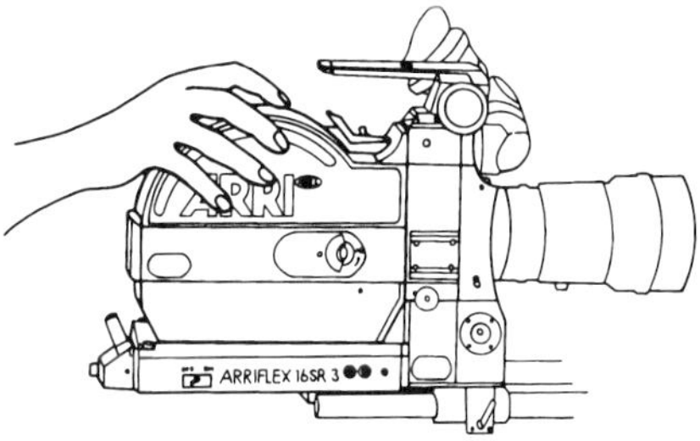

DO NOT SLAM TH E MAGAZINE.

You will burr the magazine gears.

5. Slide the mag SAFETY LOCK to the **LOCK** position.

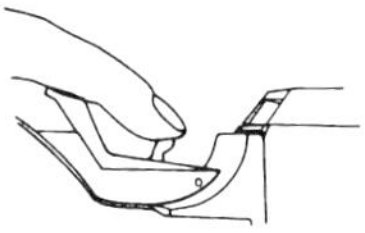

6. Press the **PHASE** button. (This was the TEST button on SR1 and SR2). It runs the camera slowly, at 1 frame per second, to gently engage the pull-down claw into a sprocket hole.

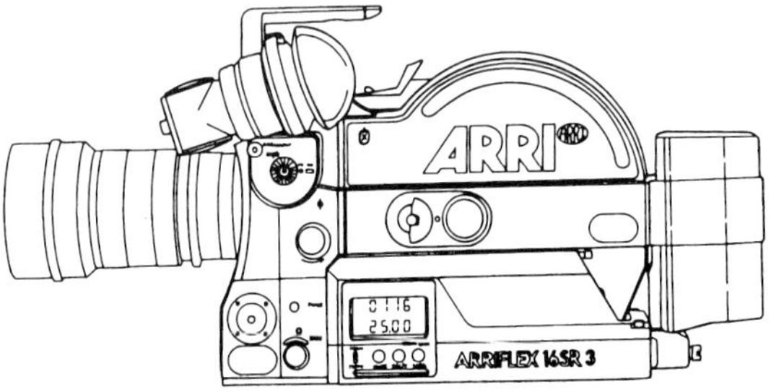

Or inch the camera manually: turn the inching knob counter-clockwise.

With film loaded, you will sometimes hear the pulldown claw click into a film perf with a definitive and satisfying click. Keep the **PHASE** button on until you hear that click. Sometimes it takes a few cycles to engage.

Although the camera will run without first pressing the PHASE button, or inching manually, you could damage a perf.

Remember- if you slam the magazine onto the body, you could punch an extra, unwanted perf in the film. So, gently attach the mag to camera.

Important: Highspeed vs. Regular Mags

1. DO NOT USE REGULAR MAGAZINES ON HIGHSPEED CAMERAS

2. DO NOT USE HIGHSPEED MAGAZINES ON REGULAR CAMERAS

3. 16 SR3 Magazines and Cameras are the same color gray, whether high speed or regular.

4. Highspeed magazines are labeled "HS" in yellow.

5. Regular speed magazines are not labeled.

6. You should not interchange HS with Regular mags.

7. You may, however use 16SR1 and SR2 magazines on SR3 cameras—and SR3 mags on the SR1 and SR2—but again, keep regular with regular, and highspeed with highspeed.

8. If your magazines are black, they are for 16 SR1 and 16 SR2 Regular speed cameras (up to 75 fps).

9. If the magazines are gray and black, and marked HIGHSPEED, they are for 16 SR1 and 16 SR2 Highspeed Cameras (up to 150 fps.)

10. If you try to use regular mags on a Highspeed camera, your film might be out of focus. This is because regular magazines have a spring-loaded pressure plate. At high speed, the film can cause the pressure plate to breathe, and focus is lost.

11. Using 16HSR Highspeed magazines on regular 16 SR cameras can also cause unsharpness because the Highspeed magazine uses a different kind of pressure plate, and the back focus is set differently on the regular camera.

Check for Scratches

When checking out a camera, run a scratch test on each of the mags before the job.

You can use loaded magazines or test film.

Run about four feet of film. Then remove the magazine, and open the take-up side door.

Or, run the camera with the take-up side magazine door open. This was easier to do on the SR1 and SR2, because you could just open the door. The SR3's camera left electronics base prevents the magazine from being opened while it is on the camera. You can open the mag take-up side first, then attach the mag to the camera. Be careful to hang onto the loose door.

Inspect the film with a magnifying glass. There should be no visible scratches or abrasions.

The area along the edge of the film by the sprockets may show marks.

This is normal.

If you do find scratches, check all obvious sources: gate, pressure pad, loop size, etc.

Proper loop size is especially critical when using the HS camera in Super16 format. Also, loops that are too large can scratch against the un-channeled areas of the magazine throat.

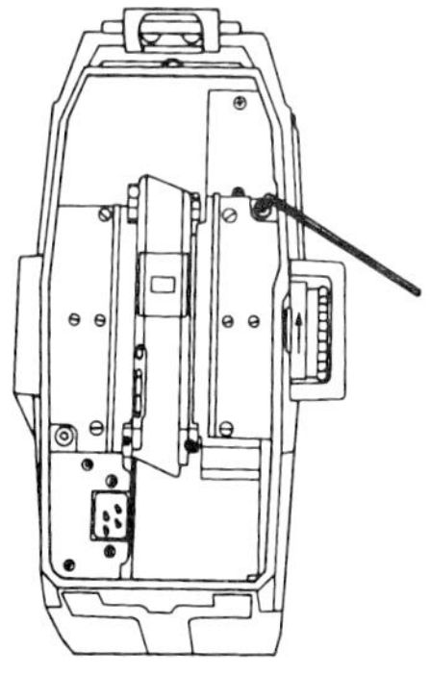

If you see scratches and can't determine the cause, you should remove the magazine sprocket cover now.

Removing Mag Sprocket Cover

DO NOT REMOVE COVER WITH UNEXPOSED FILM LOADED IN MAGAZINE!

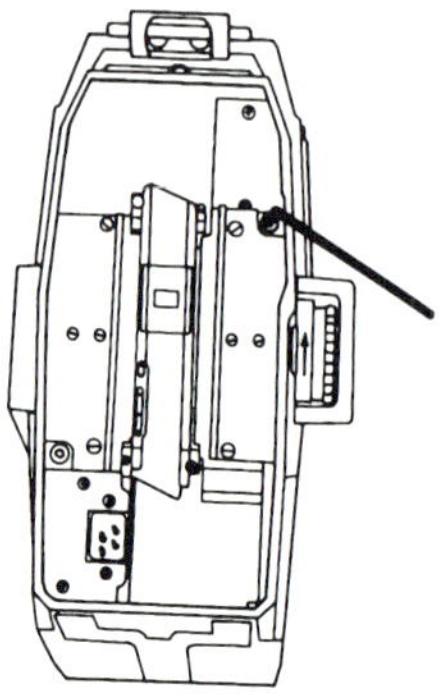

1. Put the magazine on a flat surface, facing you.

2. Use a 2mm Hex Key or Hex driver to remove the 2 screws at 1 o'clock and 7 o'clock. They are very tight. Turn counter-clockwise.

Note: on SR 1 and 2 magazines, these were flat-headed screws—which had to be removed with an ARRI flat-bladed screwdriver .

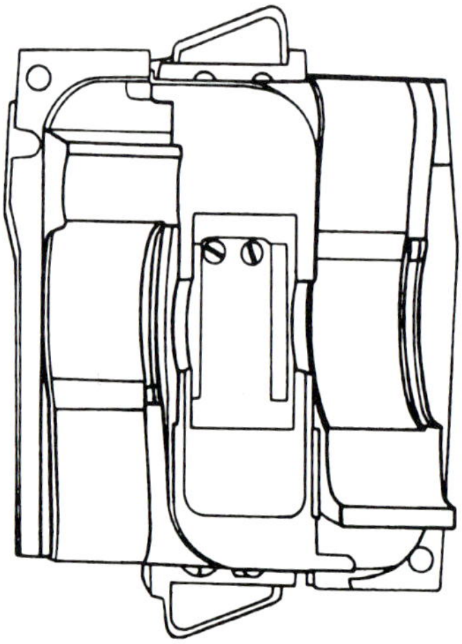

3. The entire assembly will lift away to reveal the film channels. Don't scratch any of the surfaces on either side. This is where the film travels.

4. As you look at the inside of the sprocket cover, note that the left side of the channels have only one thin ridge on the outside. This is to keep single perf film from being touched in the Super16 picture area. 16SR1 and 2 mags used for Super16 must be modified the same way.

5. Emulsion or chips may be found in these channels. Pull the chips away with double-sided tape, camera tape or something sticky.

6. Do not scrape anything with a METAL OBJECT.

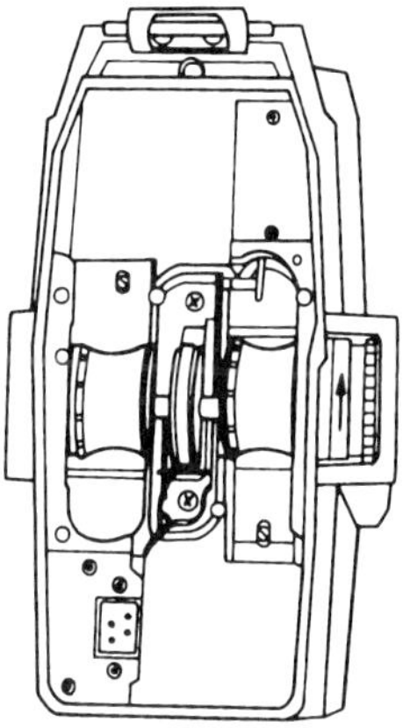

Use wooden or plastic skewers—or Kimwipes moistened with alcohol—to remove any emulsion build-up.

7. After chips are gone, blow with air.

8. Replace the cover—it will only go on one way. (The cutouts for pulldown claw and registration pin face down). Wiggle the cover around to be sure it is seated properly.

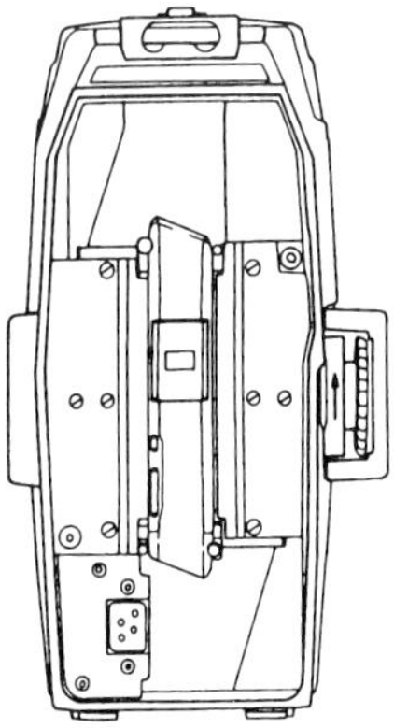

9. Insert the 2 hex screws. Tighten one. Then the other. Last turn of screws will be tight- but don't force.

10. Screw tightness does not affect image sharpness, and has no effect on pressure pad or fixed gap film channel.

Check Timing of Movement

The 16 SR3 employs one motor to drive both the pull-down claw/registration pin assembly and the mirror shutter. The mirror shutter is connected to the motor by a timing belt. Although very rare, it is theoretically possible for the belt to jump out of position after a severe film jam, or if improperly serviced.

The consequence of this would be a "smeared" image; because the film would be moving while the shutter was still open.

To check timing, use a roll of film loaded in a magazine. With a marker, draw an "X" on a frame of film in the center of the throat. Draw squiggly lines above and below the "X."

While viewing from the front of the camera, position the "X" in the gate area. Now, slowly advance the inching knob forward and back. You should not see the "X" move while the gate is in view.

Rods, Lens, Follow Focus, Mattebox

Loosen both levers at the front of the baseplate receptacles (turn counter-clockwise).

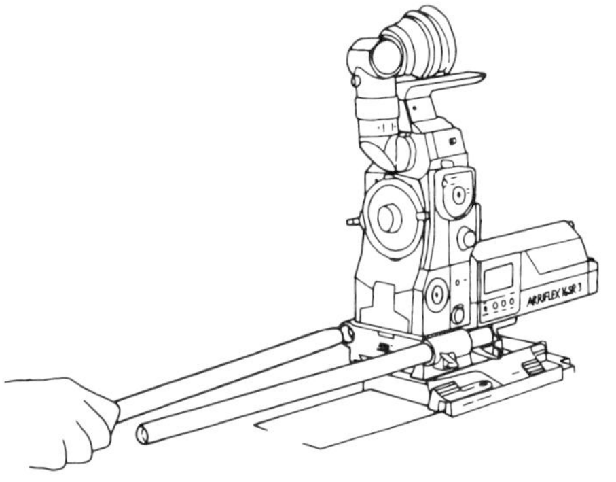

Slide the rods in, and tighten.

There are two sizes of rods in use: the new 19mm diameter and the older 15mm diameter.

Make sure all your accessories match the size rods in use.

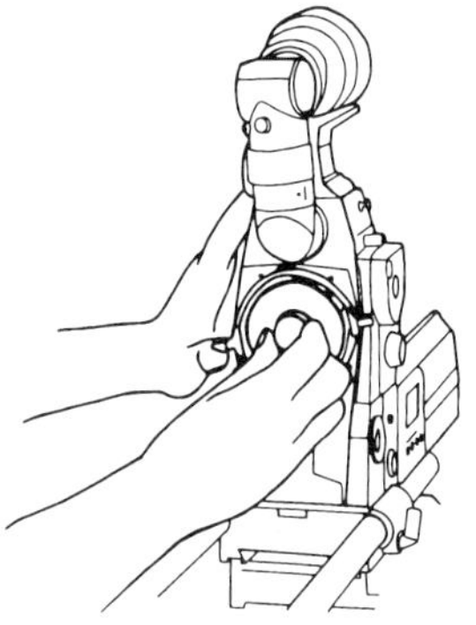

Remove the PL cap by turning the PL lock ring counter-clockwise. Pull the cap straight out.

Keep the cap in your pocket or pouch, because it is a good idea to replace the cap whenever a lens is removed.

Keep the cap clean—do not get lint all over it. Wrap it in a cloth.

Also, be sure the PL mount itself is clean and dry. Wipe off any grease—because it attracts dirt and grit which can affect your flange focal depth. Do not lubricate the with the gooey ARRI grease familiar to older cameras.

Install the lens, tighten the PL lock ring clockwise.

Remember:
(CLOCK=LOCK).

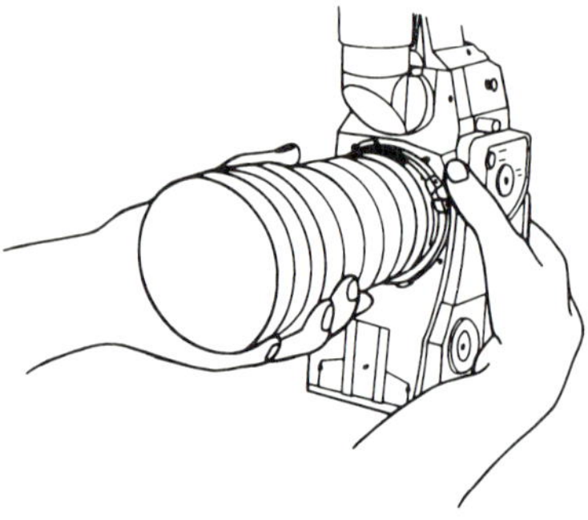

If you are using a long or heavy lens, attach the lens support and tighten.

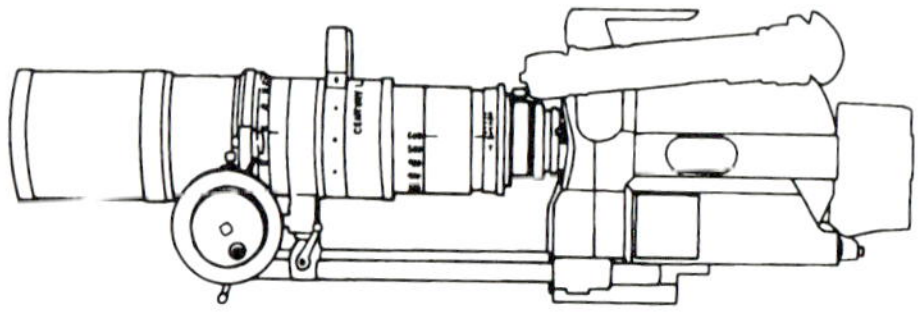

Follow Focus

Make sure the black locking lever is loose (counter-clockwise).

Decide whether you want the follow focus gear to come from above or below the lens. Your preference. Position the drive arm accordingly.

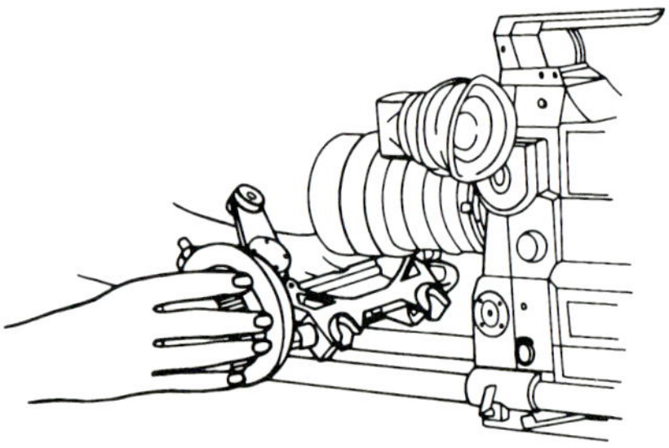

Choose the correct lens drive gear for the lens you are using: they differ in width and diameter to fit various lenses.

Attach the follow focus to the rods. It is often helpful to angle the follow focus forward so you don't bang into the lens.

Slide the follow focus along the rods while engaging the lens drive gear into the geared focus ring of the lens. Tighten the black locking lever and the adjustable arm lock. Tighten the lens drive gear's knurled screw.

The follow focus has a quick release design, so you can take it off at any time, without having to remove the mattebox or lens supports. The new style FF-2 has two speeds.

Mattebox

Prepare the mattebox with an appropriate lens donut for the lens diameter in use. You'll find them listed in ARRI catalogs as "reflex prevention rings." They mean "reflection," since donuts are critical when using filters in the mattebox. Without the donut, you'll have light reflecting a mirror image of the lens front from the rear surface of the filter.

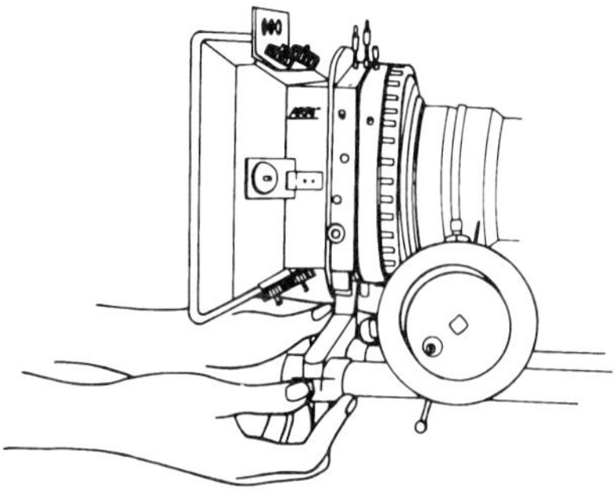

Loosen both levers on the mattebox support, and slide the mattebox onto the rods. Lock the levers.

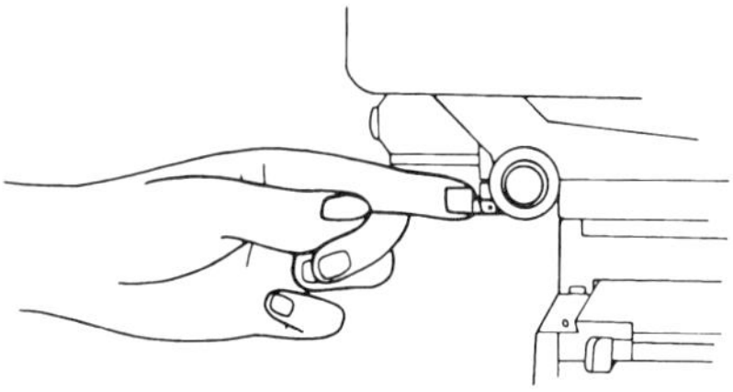

Lightweight support

A lightweight support is useful in documentary mode to attach a mattebox, lightweight follow focus or zoom motor.

Unscrew the locking ring (counter-clockwise). Slide the square shiny plate into the square receptacle on the front of the camera. The locking ring should be above the rods—if not, you are mounting the support upside down. Tighten.

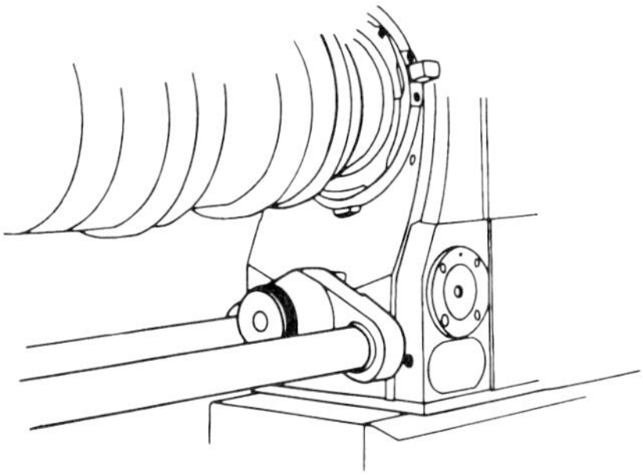

The lightweight support has a 15mm diameter. Rod to rod distance is shorter than the standard baseplate, so different accessories are used.

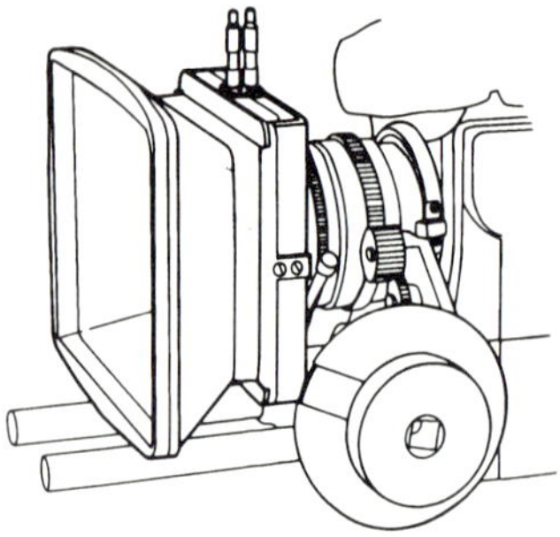

The lightweight follow focus and lightweight mattebox slide onto the rods from the front, and are tightened with knurled screws.

Preston Cinema makes a good lightweight bracket for Microforce motors. A small insert sleeve converts the 19mm diameter to 15mm, so you can use the bracket on all rods.

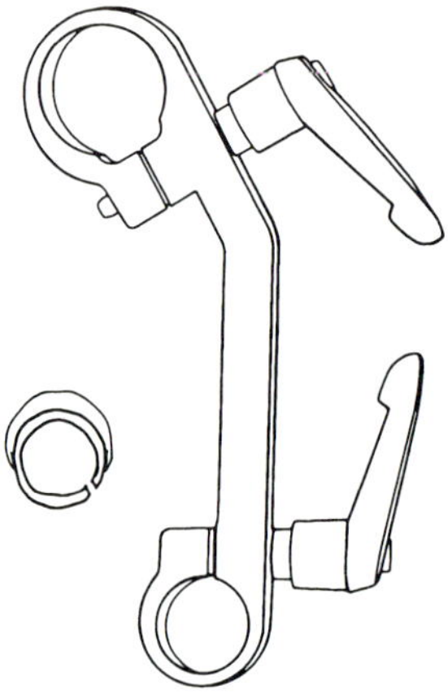

Mattebox Choices

Some of the popular Mattebox styles are:

6.6" x 6.6"	MB-14	in 15 and 19mm rod size
5" x 6"	MB-15	in 15 and 19mm rod size
4" x 5.650"	MB-18	in 15 and 19mm rod size
4" x 4"	MB-16	in 15 and 19mm rod size
4" x 4"	MB-17	for lightweight support
4" x 4"	LMB-3	clip-on mattebox

PL Lens Mount

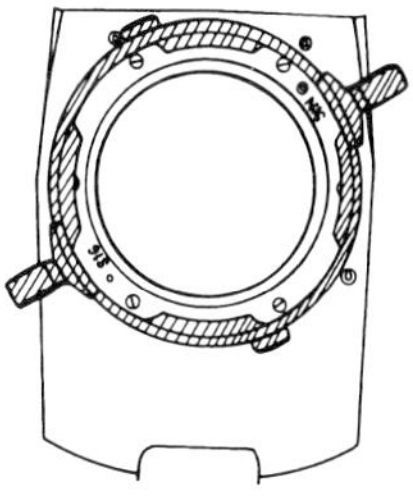

The PL Lens Mount on the 16 SR3 is the same size as on Arriflex 535, 535B, 435, 35 BL4, and most 35 BL3 and 35-3 cameras. (Some of the earlier models were bayonet mount)
The diameter of the PL mount is 54mm.

With the PL Lens Mount, you can usually orient the lens so the witness marks face one of four directions: top, bottom, left or right. The favorite position is facing camera left.

Most lenses are marked with footage and metric distance scales on opposite sides—so you have a choice.

Mounting PL Lenses

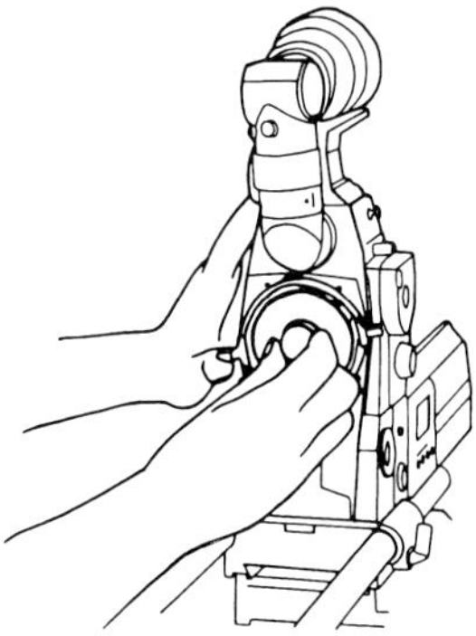

Remove the black plastic PL cavity dust cap by rotating the PL lock-ring lever counter-clockwise.

Look at the lens locating pin at 1 o'clock. The format for which the mount is set (Regular—N16 or Super16—S16) is engraved in red on the ring.

See the Super16 section for instructions on how to change it, page 211.

When handling lenses, always hold them by a nonrotating part—not the focus, zoom or aperture barrels.

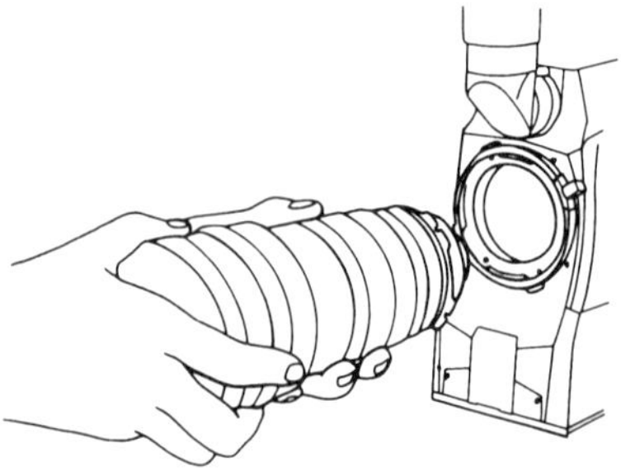

Note where you want the witness marks.

Line up the PL mount index pin located at 1 o'clock with one of the four slots on the lens mount.

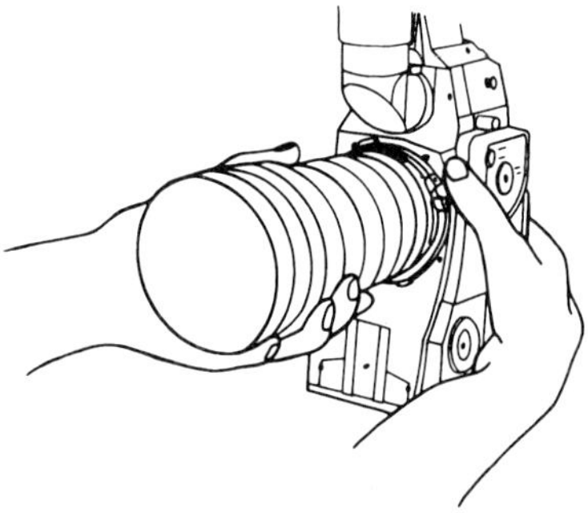

Insert the lens into the mount.

Rotate the PL lock-ring clockwise. Remember: CLOCK=LOCK.

Tighten. To get the feel of how tight, try opening again. If you lock the ring too tightly, it will be difficult to open.

The World's Worst Assistant uses a hammer to unlock his lenses, which damages the mount.

Mounting Bayonet Lenses

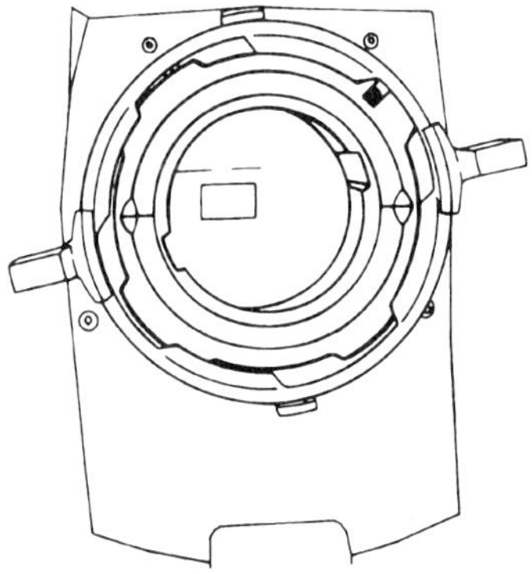

16 SR1 and 2 cameras and lenses had a bayonet (twist-the-lens) mount. If you have one of these lenses, you can mount them with a Bayonet-to-PL Adapter.

Insert the Bayonet Adapter into the PL mount, and tighten the lock-ring.

To attach a bayonet lens: Engage the two bayonet tabs of the lens into the two channels of the mount. Push in all the way. Rotate clockwise until you hear a click. Rotate gently.

Removing Bayonet Lenses

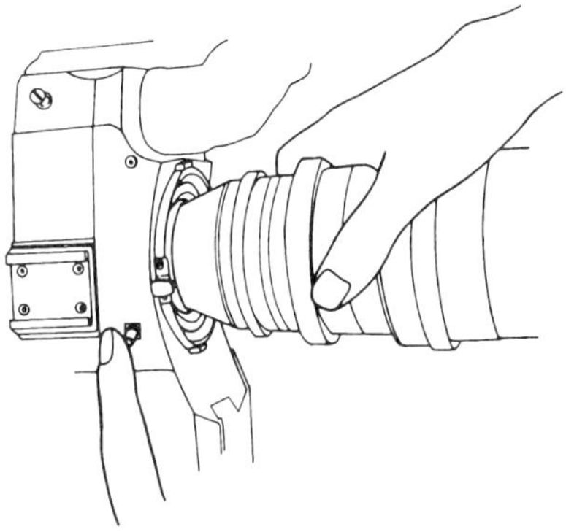

Press the Bayonet Adapter Release Button on the camera right side. Rotate the lens counter-clockwise. Pull out. Remember, you don't have to push the lens release button to put lenses back in.

PL cavity dust caps won't fit—you need a bayonet cavity cap.

If you have ARRI Standard lenses—pre-bayonet, probably inherited from an Arriflex S—they will still fit in the bayonet adapter, but they might spin on axis because there is no locating pin.

Some lenses will damage the mirror shutter if they spin on axis. The 5.9mm Angenieux has metal rear element protectors, which can hit the mirror. When in doubt, check with an Arriflex service technician. Most have special gauges to check lens rear element to mirror clearance.

To remove the Bayonet Adapter, rotate the PL lock-ring counter-clockwise, and pull the adapter out. Now you can use the PL cavity cap.

Simple Lens Tests

You arrive at the rental house the day before a shoot to pick up the equipment. The camera and lenses are packed in their cases. You are assured that all is well, and that camera and lenses are all
coexisting in that blissful state known as proper collimation.

But since you already know that the camera assistant will be blamed for any conceivable mishap in the course of conspiring events, you will certainly want to check things out yourself.

Rental houses appreciate your concern. Since they are often busy, cannot spend lots of time going over the camera with you, and cannot lend you their expensive test instruments, various conventional procedures have evolved:

Check Viewing Screen Depth

First, we want to check our viewing screen depth, using a lens we know is properly collimated. Some rental houses keep such lenses specifically for testing purposes. These lenses do not go out on location.

Set up your camera on a tripod. Insert the test lens or a Zeiss prime lens—50mm is a good one. Position the camera 6' from a lens chart or flat wall. Many rental houses have pedestals and suspended lens targets, to make things easier. If not, tape a lens chart on the wall. Use the charts in this book.

Measure out 6 feet from camera to target with a steel tape measure. Stanley Powerlocks seem popular.

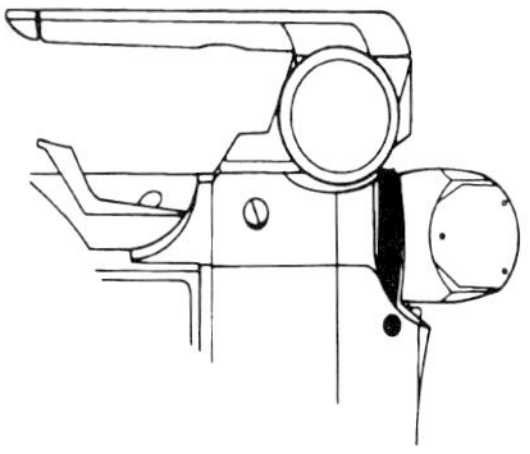

This is a good time to see if your cloth tape measure has shrunk from years of abuse. Hook the end of your cloth tape measure over the tape hook on either side of the camera. Both hooks are even with the film plane.

Adjust the eyepiece to suit your eye. Rotate the large diopter ring (rubber covered with numbers) until the crosshairs and image both appear sharpest.

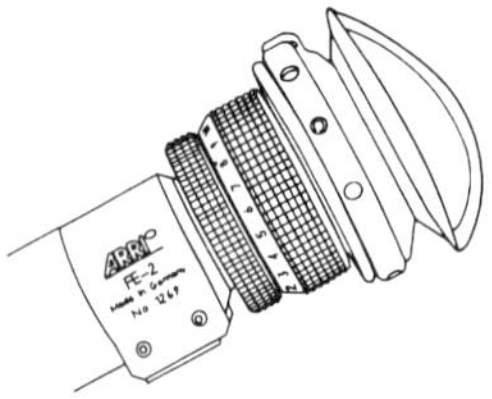

Note—on the SR3, unlike previous models, you don't have to lock the diopter ring with a secondary FIX-LOOSE ring.

Focus on the target. The lens focus scale should read exactly 6'. If not, then either the lens or the viewing screen is out of alignment, and you can confirm which of the two possibilities exists by checking with another lens. If the second lens is also out, then the chances are good that the viewing screen needs adjustment. Read the viewing screen section of this book first—then bring the lens to your friendly service technician.

Check your lenses

Next, check the lenses you will use on the job. Zoom lenses should be checked in both wide and telephoto positions.

Most lens charts aren't big enough, so you can tape up five targets photocopied from the back of this book to fill the center and all four corners of the frame.

At 6' from the wall, with an 11-110 lens at 11mm, the area to cover on the wall will be about 56" wide x 42" high.

Since this is a qualitative test (is the lens good or bad) rather than quantitative (how many lines does it resolve), charts with Siemen's stars work best. They snap in or out of focus very clearly.

Position two lights level with the camera, one on either side, at 45° angles to the chart to prevent glare.

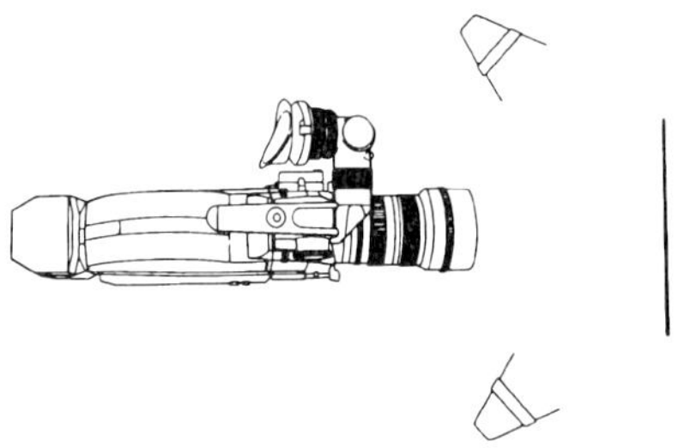

Open the lens to its widest aperture. Zoom in to full telephoto. Focus on the center of the chart. The lens scale should read 6'.

Now zoom out. The crosshairs in the eyepiece should remain centered. This is called "tracking."

The image should remain sharp throughout the entire zoom range.

If time allows, a film test could be shot at this time. Check all your lenses.

Check Infinity

Check the infinity settings of all your lenses. Take the camera outside, or to an open window. Open the lens to its widest aperture. Set the lens on infinity. Zoom out to the widest angle position.

Sight on a distant object. Telephone poles, wires, buildings —anything with a hard edge. Zoom in to full telephoto. Focus the lens. The objects should be sharp, and the lens barrel should read "infinity" (∞).

Some lenses focus just a touch past infinity, which is acceptable, and even preferred by some. Just alert the cinematographer, who may assume that infinity is where the lens stops rotating. Mark the infinity setting. (More on this in the next section.) If the lens goes way past infinity, or doesn't reach infinity at all, send it back.

Setting Up the Lens

Many zoom lenses for 16mm do not have exact focus points inscribed on the lens barrel. Instead, only the number appears, which is not exact enough for critical follow focus.

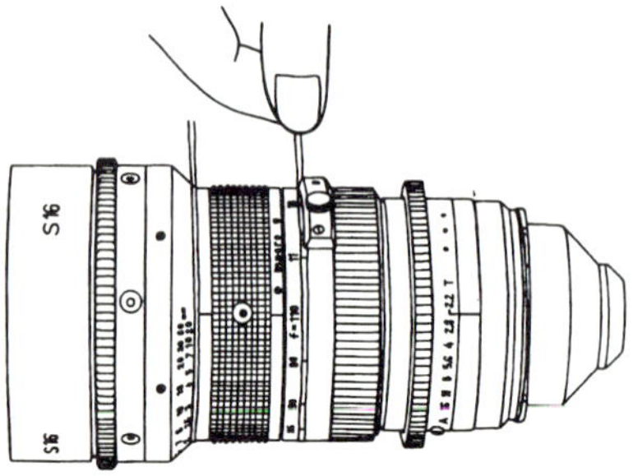

For critical follow focus when measuring distances by tape measure, set up the lens in advance with exact focus index marks. Attach strips of camera tape or drafting tape to the lens.

This is easy at rental houses with moveable targets. Just send the target to each distance indicated on the lens barrel, zoom in all the way, focus, and draw an index mark with a Pilot Ultra Fine Point Permanent SCA-UF marker.

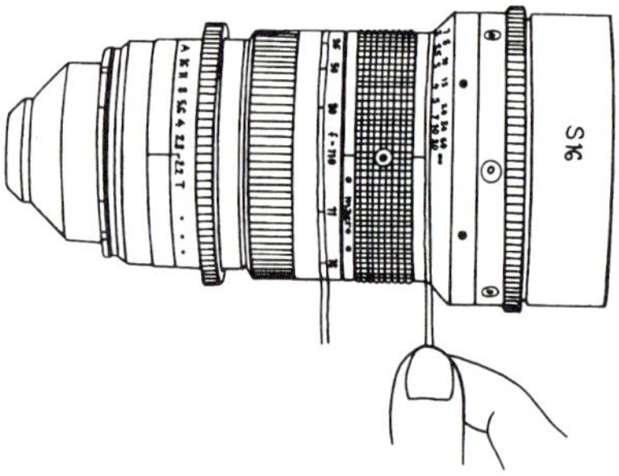

Or, set up and move a tripod.

Sometimes you will be pulling focus from the other side of camera. Zeiss 10-100 and 11-110 lenses have indexes printed on both sides. Some lenses do not. Copy the lens scales onto chart tape, and attach to the camera right side.

Letraset "Letraline" works very well: matte finish, easy to write on, 3/16" wide, very thin, comes in a multitude of colors for aesthetic touches, in handy plastic dispensers.

It's a good idea to put chart tape on all lenses for temporary focus, zoom and aperture marks using a pencil or erasable marker.

Removing old chart tapes is not easy. The gunk residue can be removed with dry camera tape.

ARRIGLOW

ARRIGLOW is used to illuminate the frame lines in low light conditions. It's an adjustable red light source that shines on the viewing screen.
You can have ARRIGLOW or you can have Light Meter, but you can't have both.

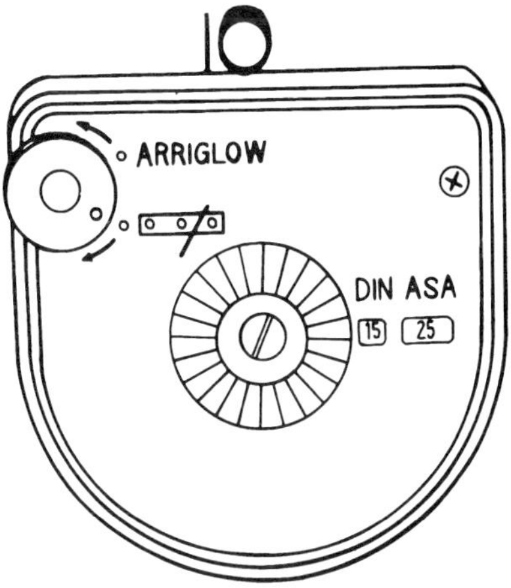

To choose frame line illumination, turn the ARRIGLOW/Meter Selector Switch fully clockwise to the ARRIGLOW position. There is no intermediate, middle position. The markings on the dial are not intuitive. Looking at the arrows, one would assume you turn in the direction of the arrow to activate that feature. Not so. Turn to the dot. If it's your camera, I suggest you paint out the arrows.

To adjust the intensity of ARRIGLOW—turn the knob above the word ARRIGLOW clockwise to make it brighter. Don't go fully clockwise—it gets too bright, and the whole finder is washed in a reddish haze. Turn counter-clockwise to make it dimmer.

Check ARRIGLOW Timing

The frame line illumination turns off as the film is exposed, and on while the mirror is in the viewing position.

If, through some technical fault, the ARRIGLOW is on while film is exposed, you will have a red haze on your film. If this is not an effect you desire, the "timing" of ARRIGLOW to mirror shutter should be checked.

Turn the ARRIGLOW on. Rotate the brightness to full. Look through the front while pressing the PHASE button. You will see the ARRIGLOW turn off while the mirror shutter is clear of the aperture. The fiber screen will glow red again when the mirror covers the gate.

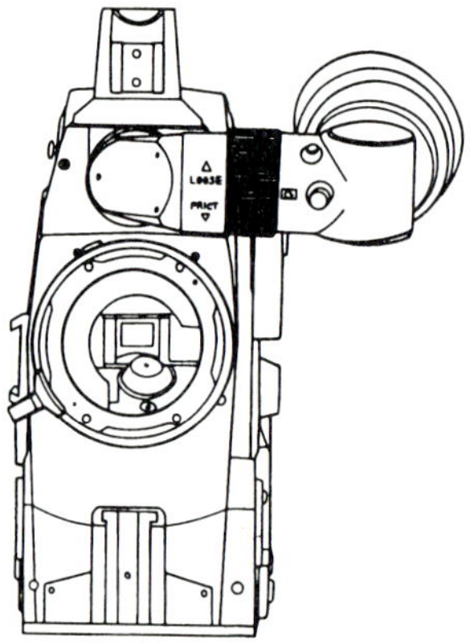

Manually turning the inching knob will not work, unfortunately.

If there is any doubt, shoot a test with the ARRIGLOW intensity cranked up to the max.

Light Meter

Light Meter Theory

The light meter in the camera reads 1/4 of total picture area, center-weighted—meaning that exposure is more sensitive in the crosshair area.

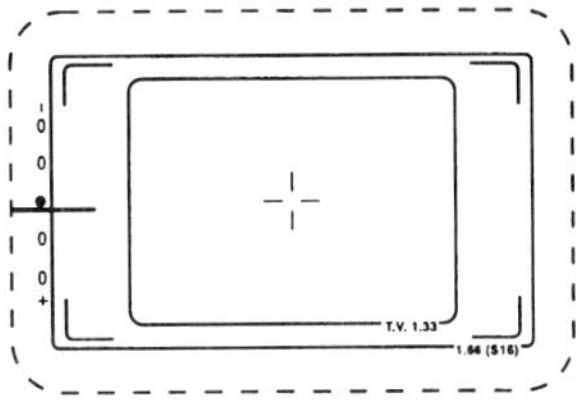

The center dot on the left is for normal exposure. The other dots represent one stop each, over and under normal exposure.

Above the center dot, you have two stops underexposed (-). Scene is too dark. You've stopped the lens down too much. You need to open up to a wider aperture. Remember: Minus (-) makes darker.

Below the center dot, you have two stops overexposed (+). Scene is too bright. Lens is open too much. You need to stop down. Remember: Plus (+) makes brighter.

But don't consider the match-needle as law. It's very accurate, but keep in mind it calculates for average scenes. For example, let's assume you are filming an actor on a set with a dark background. The actor is lit. The background, if you measured with a spot meter, might be 5 stops below key. You're exposing for the actor. However, because the camera reads the center quarter of the picture area, it assumes you want an average between the dark background and the bright actor. The resulting shot, if you went by the meter, would give you a greyish background, a washed out actor, and a washed-up cinematographer.

But, you can still put the meter to great use. Before shooting, you can zoom in to fill the frame with the actor. Now you will have the correct reading. Use the camera as a spot meter, then zoom out to your correct frame.

Perhaps the most useful function of the match-needle is to check for changing lighting situations. If you were shooting a live performance, and lighting cues on stage changed constantly, you could correct while shooting. If your pre-established exposure gave a reading in the viewfinder that was two dots (stops) above center (underexposed), and the lights on the actor brightened as she walked downstage, you could adjust your aperture to keep the match-needle two dots above center.

Or you might be shooting under quickly changing available light conditions. The sun goes behind a thick cloud. The match-needle will alert you immediately.

Or the camera is on the end of a 30 foot jib arm, mounted to a remote head. You're shooting an impossible angle straight down into a cauldron of molten steel. You could climb up and take a spot reading. Or you could look at the match-needle on the Powerpod's video display.

When shooting with HMI lights, don't rely on the meter when the camera is running. The phase difference between the lights and the spinning shutter could throw you off by as much as a stop. Measure with the camera stopped.

Setting the Meter

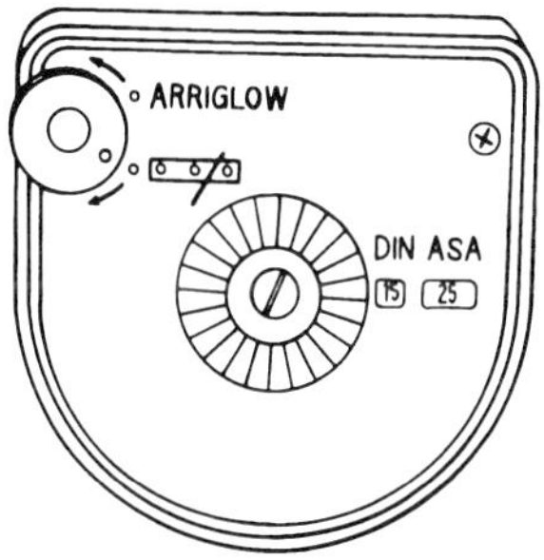

Check the dial of the Film Speed Selector. What film is being used? How will the film be rated?

You should then set the ASA / DIN dial on the camera to the unfiltered rating listed for the film. Push in and rotate the knurled ring until the correct rating displays in the window. DIN and ASA settings will turn simultaneously. DIN is the European equivalent of ASA.

Film manufacturers used to rate film speed in units called "ASA." Recently, they changed the nomenclature to "EI" for Exposure Index. For our purposes, they are the same thing— except you'll see "EI" on the film can and "ASA" on the camera.
By the way, you will see ASA on Minolta meters, and ISO on the new Spectras!

You'll find the film speed labeled as "EI" (Exposure Index) on Kodak cans, and occasionally as "ISO" on other brands.

Example: you are shooting with EXR 200T 7293. The film can label reads:

o	Filter No. 85	EI 125/22°
✳ 3200 K		EI 200/24°

On the camera, set the film speed selector to ASA 200. Even when you put filters on the lens, you will leave that dial at ASA 200. You will NOT have to redial it to ASA 125.

The reason is simple. The 16 SR internal light meter gets its reading from the center ¼ of the fiber optic viewing screen. Light passes through the lens, bounces off the mirror shutter and collects as a focused image on the viewing screen. If you put an 85 filter on the lens to balance for daylight, that filter absorbs light—2/3 stop. You will naturally be cutting down the intensity of light hitting the fiber optic screen (and being evaluated by the meter) by 2/3rds of a stop.

The 2/3rds of a stop is represented by the El rating difference between 200 and 125 on the film label.

So, you ask, why don't you change the SR exposure computer dial to 125, just as you re-program your incident light meter from 200 ASA to 125 ASA?

Your incident light meter evaluates light hitting the white photosphere. You change ASA settings to account for the light loss of the 85 filter on the camera lens. But you didn't put an 85 filter over your photosphere. If you did, you would not have had to change settings—you could have kept it at 200 ASA the same way you left the 16 SR meter at 200.

Therefore, no matter what filter you put on the front of the lens, the 16SR exposure computer will account for it; you do not have to change settings.

Note that some cameramen rate EXR 7293 at El 250. In that case, you set the dial to 250. In effect, you are just under-exposing by 1/3 stop, which will slightly desaturate colors, increase grain, render whiter whites and greyer blacks.

Likewise, if the film is to be pushed, you would set the dial to the pushed film rating. Example: you are rating the film at El 400—effectively pushing 1 stop— set the dial to 400. However, don't be so hasty in your instructions to the lab. With '93, you can sometimes achieve better results by having the lab print the dailies up by that one stop, without pushing. It depends on the contrast and composition of the scene.

Meter compensates for FPS

On the 16 SR3, the exposure meter compensates automatically for the frame rate (frames-per-second) which has been set.

We'll get into this later, but these speed changes can be made on the camera's keypad or a variety of external sources: RCU, RSU, CCU, LCC.

Shutter Speeds

You don't really need to remember this, since the SR3 does the math automatically. But to calculate shutter speed for a 180° shutter, the formula is:

$$\text{Shutter Speed} = \frac{1}{\text{fps} \times 2}$$

To calculate exposure time for any shutter angle, the formula is:

$$\text{Shutter Speed} = \frac{\text{shutter opening}}{360 \times \text{fps}}$$

Meter doesn't compensate for shutter angle

However, shooting with any shutter angle other than 180° does not automatically compensate. You can make manual adjustments. Each click of the ASA wheel is 1/3 stop.

Shutter Angle	Exposure Change	Clicks (Open)	ASA Setting
		turn dial counter-clockwise	example
180°	normal		200
172.8°	very close to normal		200
144°	- 1/3 stop	1 click	160
135°	- 1/3 stop	1 click	160
90°	- 1 stop	3 clicks	100
45°	- 2 stops	6 clicks	50

If you change the ASA of the meter, you invite mistakes later unless you add a piece of camera tape to the mattebox or camera as a reminder of what you've done.

There's a better way. Leave the ASA setting alone. Less chance for error. Look at the chart above (or any good cinematography calculator) to see how much light you lose with the new shutter angle. Compensate by opening up on the iris. Observe how much distance the match-needle moves. Keep that relationship on every new lighting setup involving this shutter angle.

Video Assist

2 Carrying Handles

There are two handles for the 16 SR3:

regular

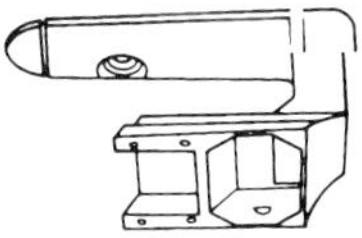

video

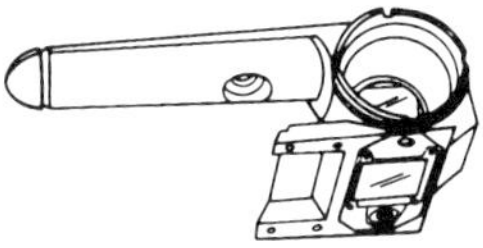

Let's assume your camera is fitted with a regular handle.

To enable video assist, you must first install the video handle, which houses the beamsplitter and video camera mount.

Swapping Handles

1. Remove the regular handle by unscrewing 4 black 2mm hex screws.

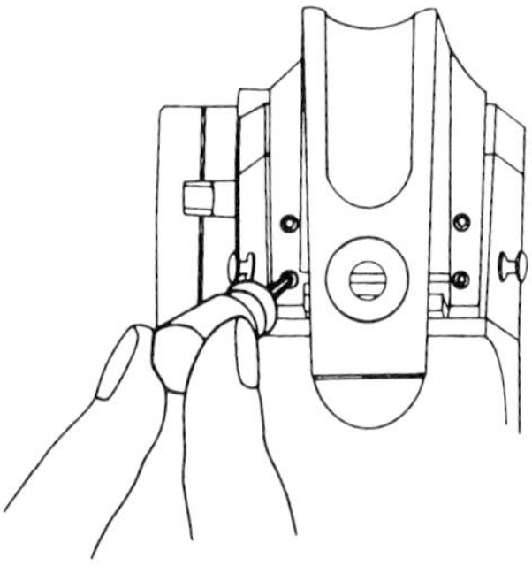

2. Lift the handle straight up.

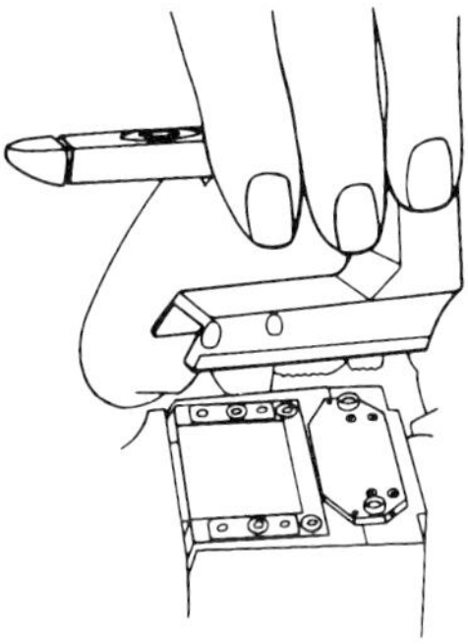

3. Unscrew the 4 black hex screws with a 1.5mm hex driver. Do not remove the two guide screws with green paint.

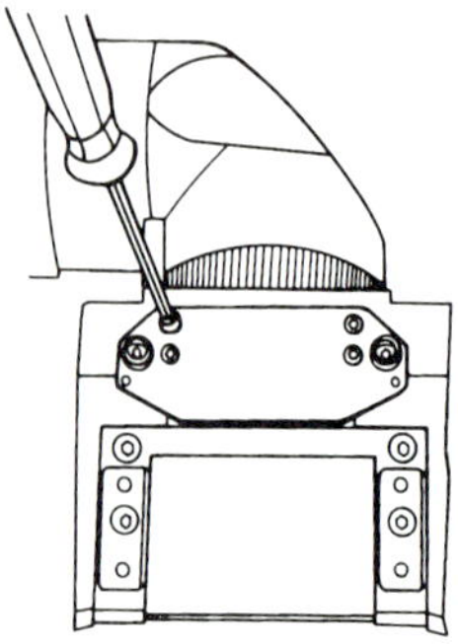

If the 4 hex screws hold down a solid piece of black metal (as opposed to a glass prism), you are removing a 100% beamsplitter—so named because it sends 100% of the light to your viewfinder.

4. Using two fingernails, lift up on the beamsplitter assembly.

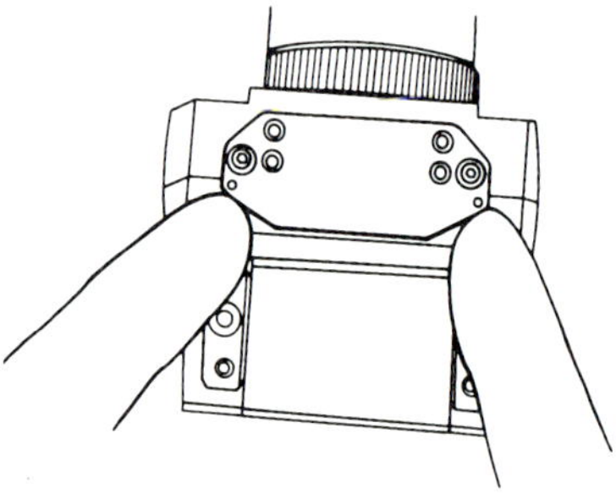

5. There are 3 beamsplitters for the 16 SR3: 100% as mentioned, 80-20 B+W (80% to the viewfinder, 20% to the video camera) and 50-50 COLOR (50% to the finder and 50% to video).

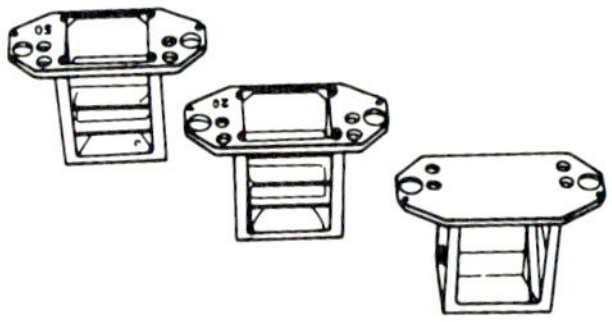

The 80-20 B+W beamsplitter gives you the brightest viewfinder image while shooting with video. Although it is recommended for black and white video assist cameras, we had good results with color video cameras in most situations except low light conditions.

6. Replace the beamsplitter. Tighten the 4 black 1.5mm hex screws.

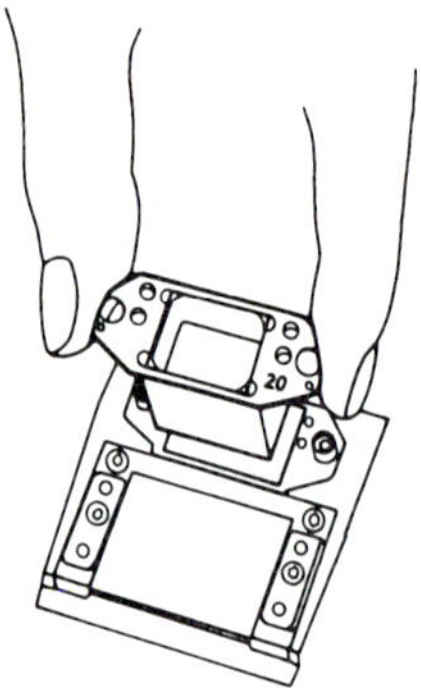

7. Install the video handle

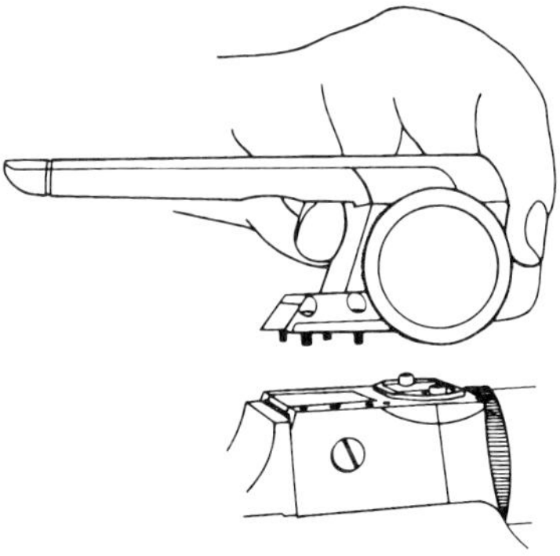

8. Tighten the 4 black 2mm hex screws of the carrying handle.

Periodically make sure these screws are tight—since they hold the entire camera's weight.

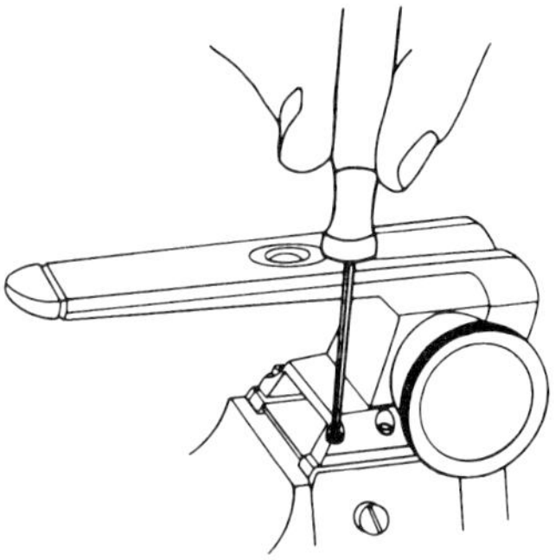

9. To attach the video assist camera, unscrew the video handle dust cap.

Attach the video assist camera by lining up its locating pin, and turning the lock ring clockwise.

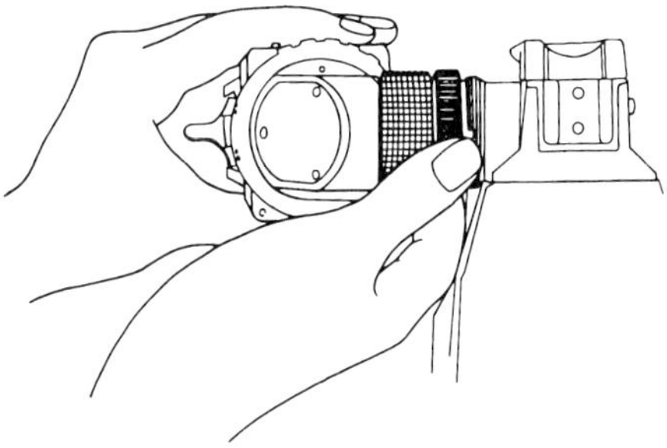

If you look underneath, you will see the adjustment rings for video camera focus and iris.

The iris should be adjusted in addition to electronic aperture settings on the video camera.

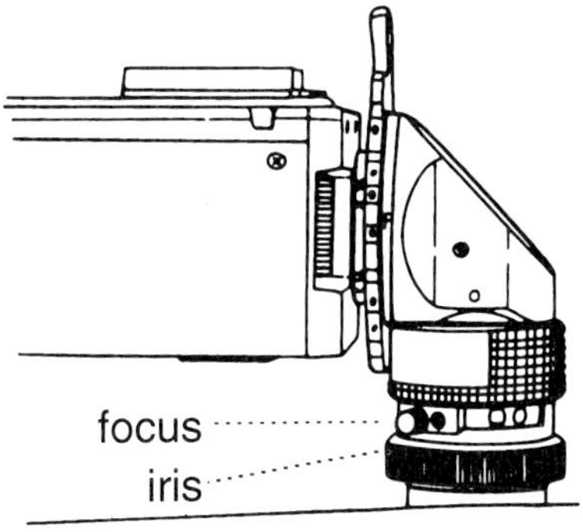

Adjusting the Video Image

Sic Transit Video

When the SR3 is shipped with the video tap attached, the video image sometimes gets bumped out of alignment. It is best to ship the video tap nestled in its own compartment of a case. The video assist camera should remain attached to its video elbow, because it is difficult to reassemble the two parts after they have been separated.

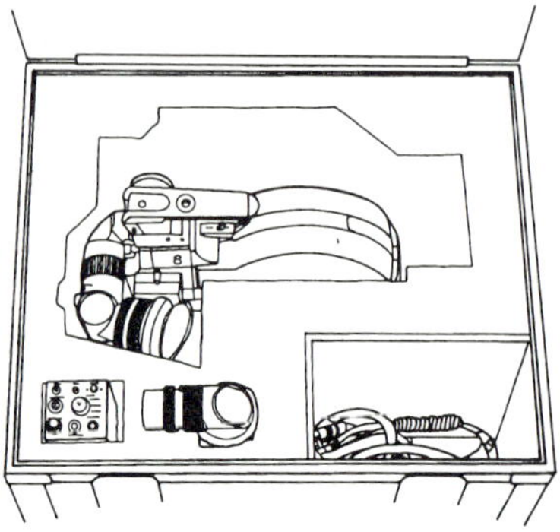

To adjust the video image, the video camera is physically twisted or slid up-down , left-right or on axis relative to the ARRI video elbow, while watching the resulting image on a monitor.

Because of the optics involved, moving the video camera up-down shifts the image left-right on the monitor, and moving the camera left-right shifts the image up-down.

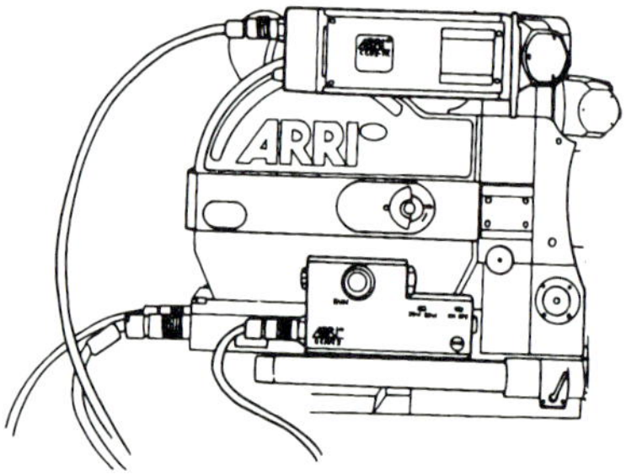

You should start with the simple procedure (adjusting 3 hex screws) that follows.

If that is not enough, you graduate to the advanced procedure. Tweaking while watching a regular video monitor is an Olympic event in hand-eye coordination.

For mere mortals, the quick fix when performing the advanced video adjustment procedure is to turn the monitor 90° onto its left side. That way, left is left and you regain your bearings.

Minor Adjustments of Video Tap

1. Plug into a video monitor. Slightly loosen the knurled black collar, which locks the video camera to the video optical elbow. You will rarely see the two tabs on the collar—they are inconvenient and best removed. (They are needed on 35mm cameras.)

2. If the video image is not level to the horizon, twist the video camera slightly clockwise or counter-clockwise.

3. If the image is *slightly* off-center, adjust up-down and left-right with the X and Y hex screws using a 1.3mm driver.

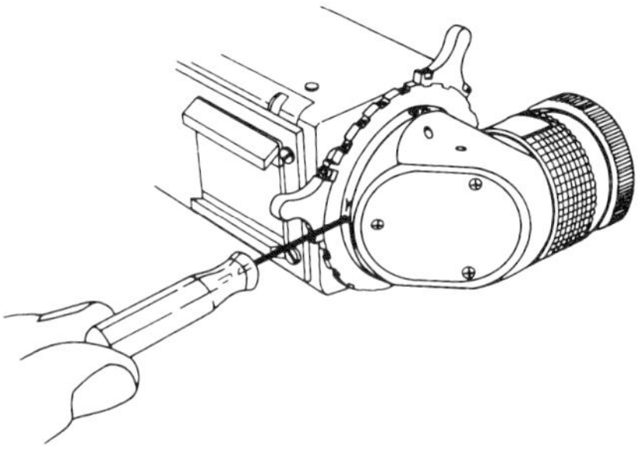

4. If you feel too much tension or are restricted in one direction, back off the 1.3mm hex set screw on the bottom of the elbow by a couple of turns. It is labeled "F." This set screw adjusts a spring which pushes the assembly against the other two hex adjustment screws.

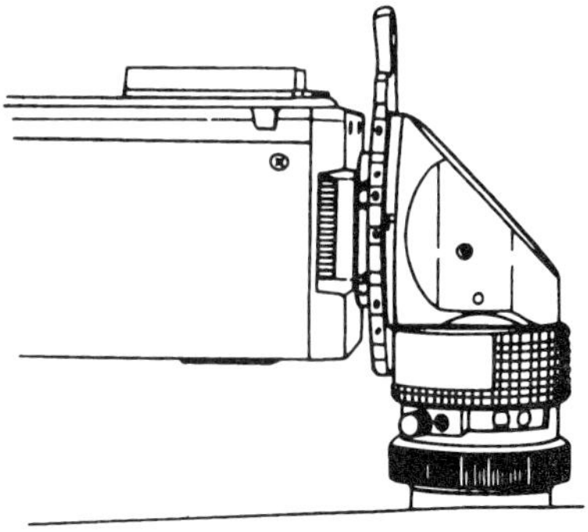

5. Adjust the X and Y screws again.

6. Tighten the F screw.

7. Tighten the collar.

Major Adjustment

If the image is severely out of position, proceed with these next steps.

8. Loosen the knurled ring.

9. Back off the X and Y screws a few turns (1.3mm hex)

10. Loosen (counter-clockwise a few turns) the 1.3mm hex set screw (labeled "F") on the under side of the elbow.

11. Gently slide the video camera back and forth. Now you see why it helps to turn the monitor on its side: left-right is actually up and down.

7. When you have roughly centered the image, gently tighten the knurled collar—but not all the way.

9. Fine tune your adjustments of the X and Y screws.

10. Tighten set screw F on the bottom.

11. Now tighten the knurled collar.

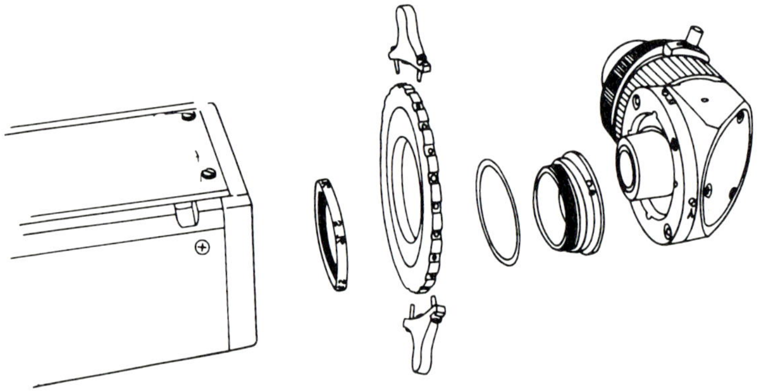

Super16 Adapter

Notice the ring closest to the video camera above. This is the red spacer necessary when shooting Super16. It positions the video camera further away from the video elbow—effectively allowing the larger image area to cover the CCD surface.

ARRI CCD2 + AFP2

(CCD Camera + Anti Flicker Processor)

Mounting and Cabling

Unless modified, you must use both units together. The AFP2 not only reduces flicker, it is also a voltage regulator—stepping down the camera's 24 volts to the 12 volts required by the CCD2.

Mount the Anti-Flicker Processor on the dovetail below the color video tap. You will need 2 cables:

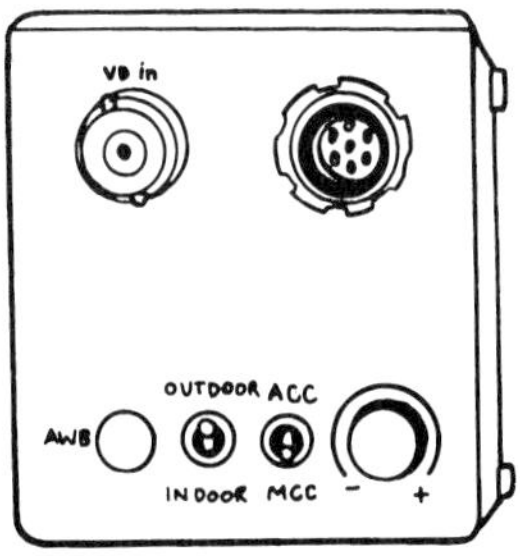

KC 34 (7 pin male to 7 pin female) connects between the video camera and the AFP **VIDEO CAMERA** receptacle.

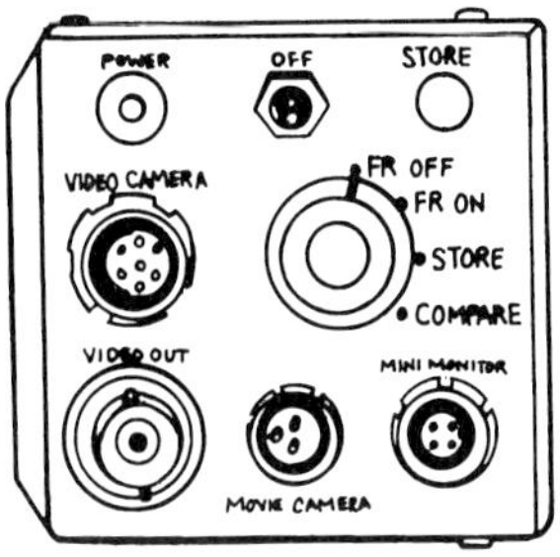

KC 37 (3 pin male to 3 pin female) connects between the **MOVIE CAMERA** receptacle on the AFP and any 3 pin RS socket on the 16 SR3.

Connect your BNC video cable to **VIDEO OUT** on the AFP.

A common mistake is to plug the video cable into the top BNC connector: **VD in** on the CCD is for input of a video signal (genlock).

Power On

Turn the power switch on.
The **POWER** LED glows.

AGC/MGC Gain Control

Auto Gain Control/Manual Gain Control lets you choose between automatic or manual video exposure. We prefer Manual in most cases, and adjust video level with the manual electronic gain knob(+ -). Make sure the mechanical iris is also adjusted on the video elbow.

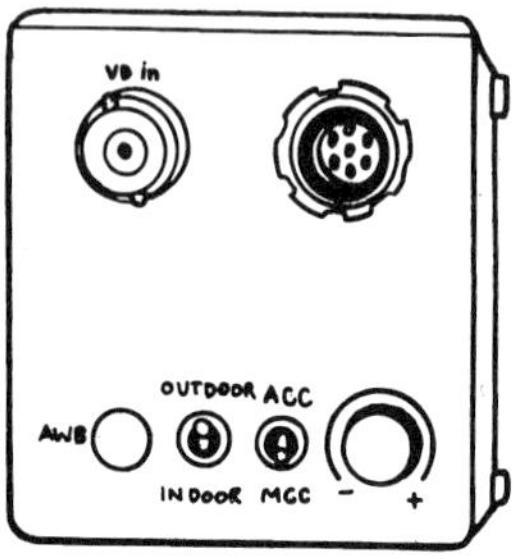

Color

For automatic control of video color, set the **Outdoor/Manual/Indoor** switch to either **Outdoor** (5600°K) or **Indoor** (3200°K).

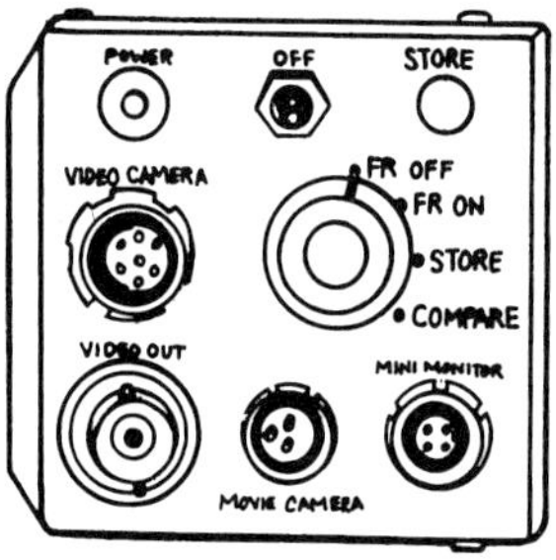

Set the **Outdoor/Manual /Indoor** switch to the middle position for manual control of color.

Push the **AWB** (Auto White Balance) button for a couple of seconds while filling the frame with an illuminated white card.

Some shops have modified the CCD2 camera so it can be cabled directly to the 12 volt output of the DC to DC converter, and the Genlock **VD in** is modified to supply video out. Of course, you will not have flicker reduction with this modification.

Flicker Reduction

When shooting, set the 4 position knob to:

FR OFF	flicker reduction off
FR ON	flicker reduction enabled

With flicker reduction enabled, a small white dash-like cursor blinks in the lower right corner of the video monitor when the 16 SR3 is rolling.

The bottom of the AFP has a rotary switch. It should be set to “A” or “5” for best flicker reduction.

Frame Store

To store an image in memory while shooting, press the **STORE** button with the flicker reduction knob set to **FR OFF**.

STORE	To view the stored image
COMPARE	Compares the stored image with the live one.

Mini Monitor

You can plug a mini-monitor into the 4 pin receptacle, using one cable for video and 12 volt output. Sony and Sharp 4” LCD monitors are useful for knowing exactly how the camera operator is framing for critical focus. These monitors can easily be modified slightly to accept the single power-video cable.

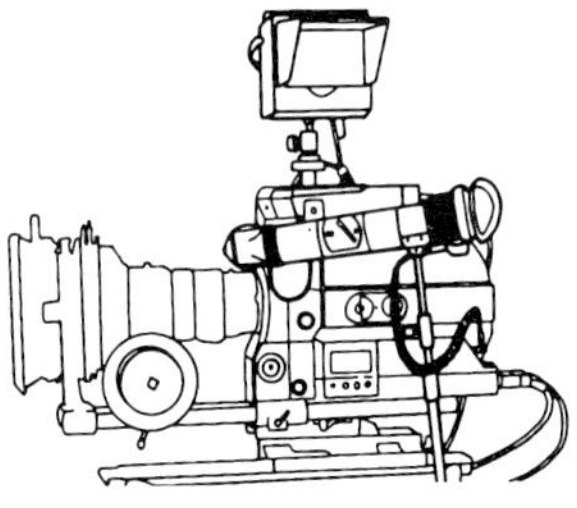

Some popular monitors are Sony FDL-x40, XVM-40, Sony FDL 330S, and Sony FDM-027 watchman. LCD screens are difficult to see outdoors. Try to find an active matrix color display.

CEI Color IV

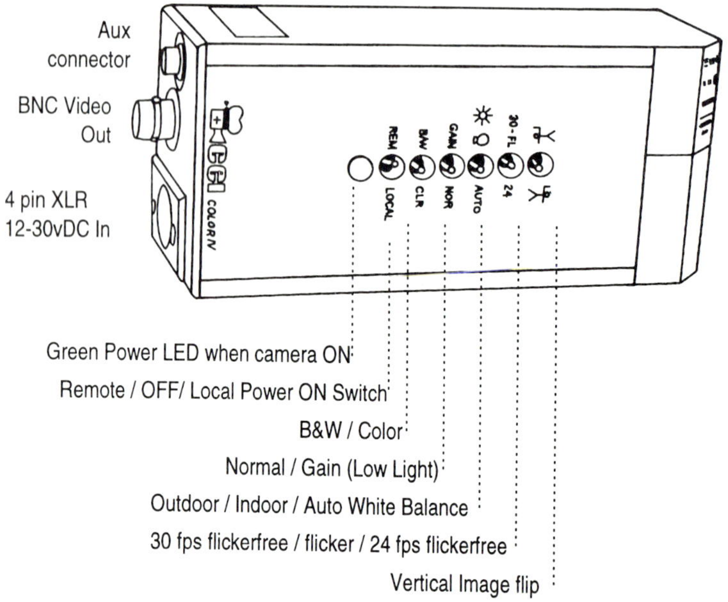

The CEI Color IV mounts to the ARRI video optics elbow with the black knurled lock ring. However, a 5mm blue spacer ring (provided with the CEI camera) must be used. When shooting in Super16, you will use both the blue CEI spacer and the red 2.75mm ARRI spacer rings.

The CEI Color IV plugs into the 12 or 24 volt DC power receptacle on the SR3 (or directly into a battery).A number of different cables are available.

Most of the time, all the small switches can be set to the right (bottom) position for normal operation.

The 3 position Rem/Local is the Main On/Off switch.

There is no manual gain—this video camera is automatic. The "Gain" position of the Gain/Norm switch is used to boost the video signal in low light.

CEI makes an auxiliary support that mounts under the dovetail accessory bracket on the camera.

Adjusting the Mirror Shutter

Picture the mirror shutter as a circle. Put a shaft in the center. Draw a line across the diameter, and cut the circle in half. Throw away one half. You have just manufactured a 180° mirror shutter. The mirror covers the aperture while the film is advanced, and bounces the image into the viewing screen. When the open section of our circle reveals the aperture, the film is held stationary, and exposed.

The 16 SR3 carries this theory a little further with its adjustable mirror shutter. The 180° portion of the mirror remains the same. However, a metal shutter has been attached to the center shaft. It is attached to a gear. You can adjust the "open" portion of the circle from 180° all the way down to 45°. The shutter angles are 180°, 172.8°, 144°, 135°, 90° and 45°.

Closing the mirror shutter is useful for a number of tasks. Shooting at high speed with a narrow shutter angle "freezes" objects such as water droplets. Above and below water scenes can also be "sharpened" with the smaller shutter angles. You can also shoot with non-electronic ballasted HMI lights at various speed/shutter angle safe combinations.

Some useful shutter angles—by no means a complete list:

Shutter angle	frame rate fps	HMI frequency
180	24	60
172.8	24	50
172.8	48	50
144	48	60
144	40	50
135	45	60

If you are shooting at 24 fps, a 180° shutter angle gives you a shutter speed of 1/48th second. Shooting at the same 24 fps speed with a 45° shutter angle will provide a shutter speed of 1/192 second.

$$\textbf{Exposure Time} = \frac{1}{\text{fps}} \times \frac{\text{shutter angle}}{360}$$

Adjustment Procedure

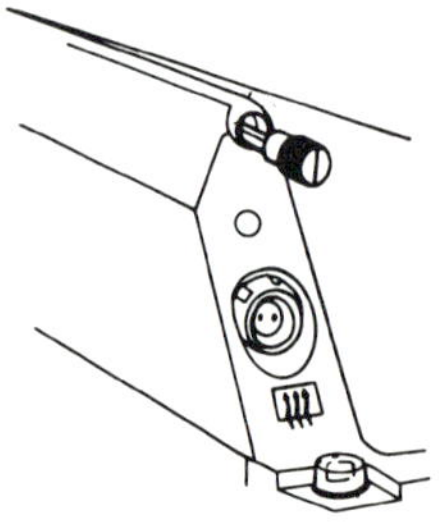

Use the special 2mm Hex tool that is stored in its own compartment at the left rear corner of the camera—just above the heated eyecup power receptacle.

The tool has a rubber collar to prevent damage to the mirror shutter. If you've lost the special tool, you can improvise by wrapping electrical tape around the lower shaft of a 2mm hex driver, starting 3mm from the end.

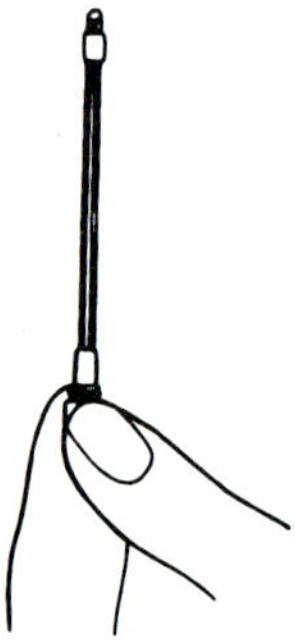

The rubber collar prevents the mirror shutter's edge from being chipped when it hits the tool's shaft—as we shall now see.

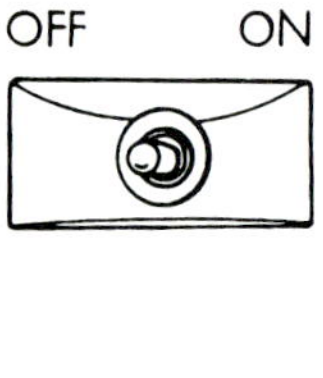

Important. Turn the camera off. Imagine your embarrassment if the camera starts while you're fiddling around and you shatter the $4,000 mirror shutter.

Remove anything in the PL mount. Rotate the manual inching knob with your right hand, so the mirror is on top and you can see the black shutter adjustment hex socket at 6 o'clock—just below the silver geared ring.

Gently insert the special 2mm hex tool, and push in.

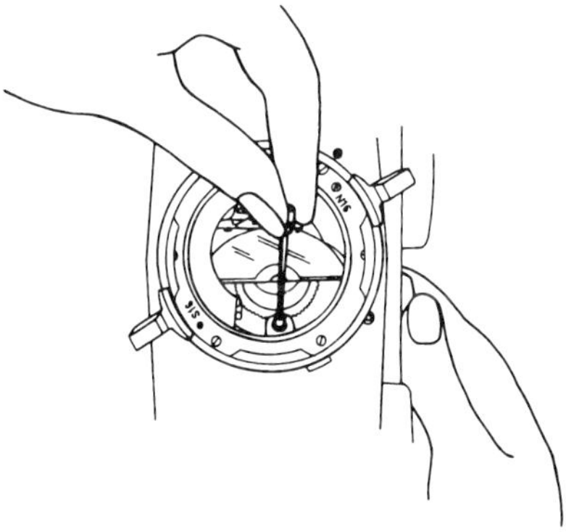

This engages a small gear against the silver geared ring, which rotates the metal shutter out from behind the mirror.

As you push in on the special hex tool, push in on the manual inching knob as well to hold the mirror shutter in place.

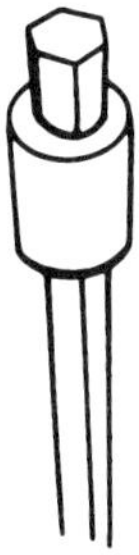

Turn the hex driver counter-clockwise to close down the shutter (smaller opening—smaller number). Remember: Counter=close shutter.

It sometimes helps to gently turn the manual inching knob the opposite direction. So, if you are closing the shutter by turning the hex driver counter-clockwise, apply a little clockwise force on the inching knob.

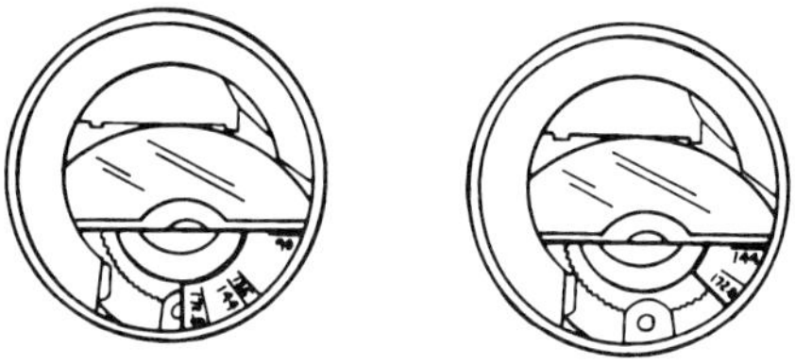

Turn the hex driver clockwise to open the shutter to a wider setting—higher number. This is where the rubber cover on the shaft is essential. You do not have to hold the manual inching knob. The mirror shutter will rest against the tool's shaft.

As you turn the special tool, you will feel the shutter presets click in slightly. You will also see the settings' index marks. If you do not see any shutter angle indexes, it is set to 180°.

It is possible to run the camera with the shutter in an intermediate position. This is not advisable, because it almost certainly will change while the camera is running.

Check your shutter angle by powering the camera up, and pushing the PHASE button for a few seconds. The shutter angle will appear in the top line of the main camera display.

Also remember: if you close down the shutter, you have to compensate your exposure. Open up the lens aperture one stop for 90° and two full stops for 45°.

Magazines

The main difference between 16 SR3 magazines and previous ones is the timecode sensitivity dial where the manual footage counter was, and a timecode lens, which should be periodically opened with your fingernail, and cleaned with lens cleaner.

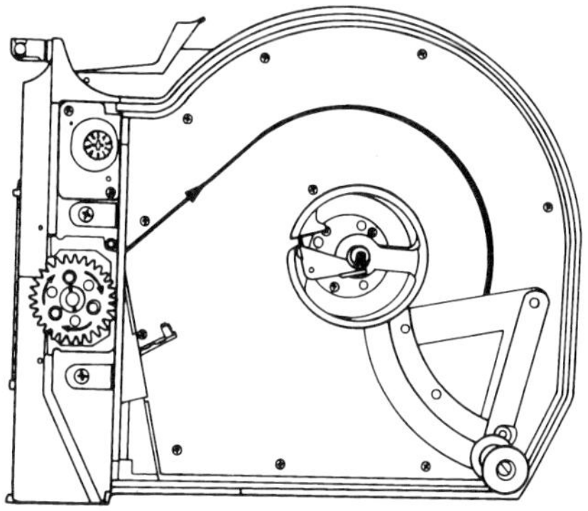

Do not slam magazine onto the camera.

The main drive gear of the magazine is made of plastic. It engages against the main drive gear of the camera. Many people slam the magazine into place on the camera. If the two opposing gears are not perfectly lined up, the teeth can become chipped or dented when slammed together. That is why it is a good idea to **gently** lower the magazine into position. Replacement gears can be purchased that are honey colored, and have a consistency reminiscent of Gummi Bears. They are less prone to chipping.

Loading Magazines

Arriflex 16 SR magazines are among the fastest and easiest to load of any camera. It takes about three minutes in and out of the changing bag. While the procedures are extremely simple, I have gone into great detail on the subject of loading to save you time on the job, make things simple and routine, and to insure foolproof and silent running.

In my considered opinion, there is only one changing bag to be used for 16mm shooting: the Harrison Changing Tent.

It has miniature tent poles to keep the fabric from touching your hands and film. As a result, you are less likely to get hairs in the gate—which most often result from lint or dirt.

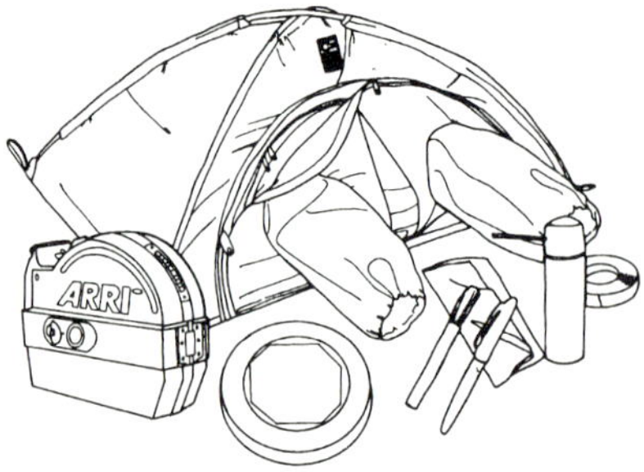

Pick a comfortable place to work. On location, if you don't have the luxury of a darkroom in a camera truck, use a table, the tailgate of a 4x4 vehicle, or the back of a van.

Be sure your work space is clean. Wipe it free of dirt and dust, or unfold a Space Blanket under the changing bag.

Shake out the changing bag first. Turn it inside out. Brush off lint.

Check for arm hairs that may have stuck to the fabric. This obsession with a clean bag will save much aggravation later on.

The cause of most gate hairs (dirt or dust in the camera aperture) is a dirty changing bag.

The 16mm frame is very small, and gate hairs are very large in comparison.

Cleanliness now will save reshooting later. Most 16mm shows are being shot on negative, any dirt or dust on the film will look like snow, and is horrible to look at. So, mag and bag must be scrupulously clean.

When you are loading and unloading film in the changing bag, play it safe—out of direct sunlight. How do you check if the bag has pin-holes? Put it over your head and check for light leaks.

What do you do if you forgot the bag? Use the bathroom. They usually don't have windows. Seal the door with black tape.

Opening, Closing, & Care of Magazines

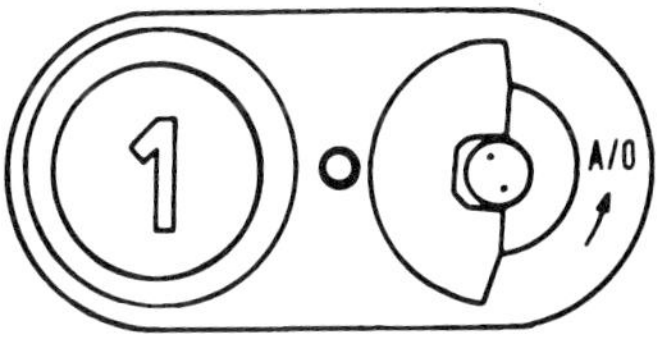

1. To open the magazine door on either side of the camera, push the red safety button all the way in.

2. Grasp the knob. Rotate in the direction of the arrow to the "**A/O**" (Auf/Open) position (counter-clockwise). Do not force. If there is any resistance, you are not pushing the red button in far enough.

3. The camera right door (FEED) swings open by pulling on right side.

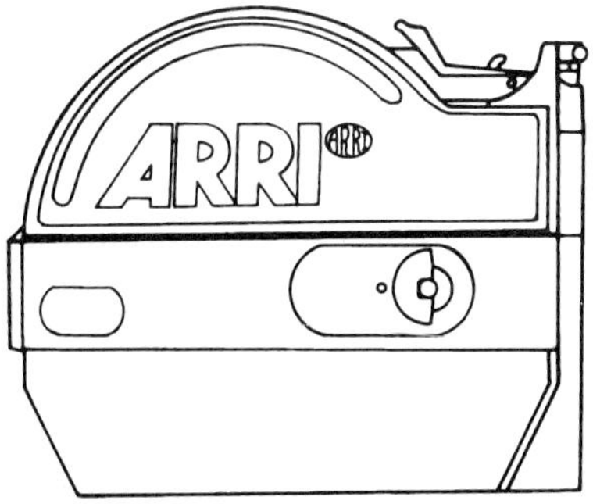

4. The left door (TAKE-UP) opens by pulling up on the left side.

5. ***DO NOT HOLD THE MAGAZINE BY ITS HINGED COVER***. You could bend the hinges.

6. ***DO NOT SLAM THE MAG COVER SHUT***.

7. ***DO NOT CLOSE MAG COVER WITH KNOB IN THE LOCKED POSITION***. You could bend or break the spring metal locking tabs.

Cleaning Empty Mags

Do your cleaning away from the changing bag so the dirt doesn't settle there. If you are using a darkroom, make sure your clean changing surface doesn't become dirty.

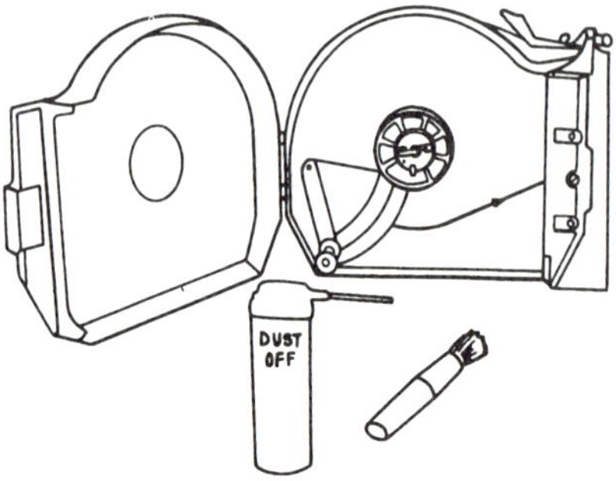

1. The insides of your magazines should be even cleaner than the inside of your changing bag.

2. You will find that dust and slivers of film settle on the somewhat sticky insides of the mag after every roll. So, clean thoroughly every time.

3. Use a Nylon Brush to get rid of gritty dust.

4. Follow with blasts of Dust-Off.

5. Swing away the footage counter guide roller. Don't lift up on it—you could break the track.

6. If there's a core in the feed side, take it off now to save time in the bag. DO NOT WIGGLE THE CORE FROM SIDE TO SIDE - you could bend the feed spindle. PULL STRAIGHT UP AND OUT.

7. Some core holders are stiff. If so, release the spindle retainer, pull off the core and core holder, separate the two outside the mag, and put the core holder back on. Remember to re-attach the spindle retainer.

Spindle Retainers

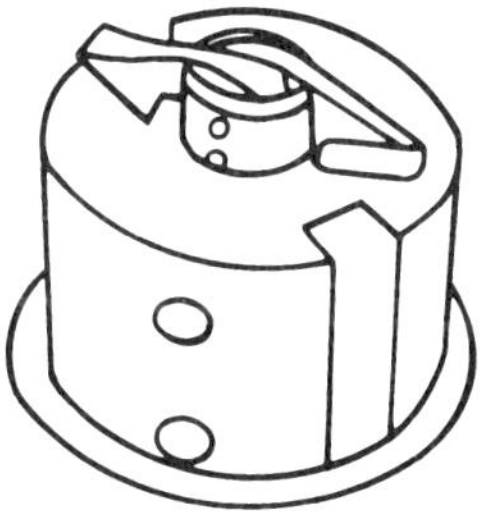

The spindle retainer is made of two bars that move in a scissor-like manner.

To remove the core holder, slide your fingernail under one of the bars. Pull up on one bar, then the other. Lift the core holder up. To replace, push the core holder back down on the shaft, and push the two bars down.

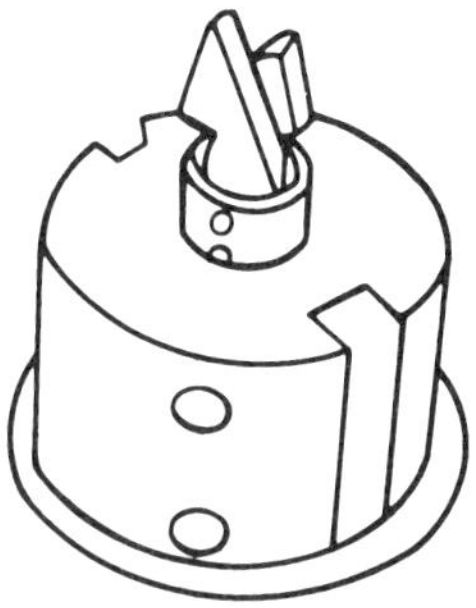

MAKE SURE THE SPINDLE RETAINER BAR IS TIGHTLY LOCKED.

When loading film into the feed side, don't push down on the film itself—it will "cone" and make noise. Push down on the core.

The spindle itself is attached to the mag with 3 small press-fit rivets. Wiggling the core back and forth to remove it will ultimately loosen it. Pull cores straight off.

When you have to remove film from the feed side, it's best to unlock the retaining bars, and pull both the core and core holder off the spindle—squeezing the circumference of the film. Then separate the core from the core holder out of the mag.

Remove core holders when using daylight spools.

The ARRI 16SR accepts up to 400' on cores, up to 200' on daylight spools. NASA uses 400' loads on specially modified daylight spools, which have been ground down.

Preparing Film For Loading

It's a good idea to leave cans of unexposed film inside their cardboard containers until ready to use. The cardboard helps absorb shocks and humidity, insulates, and above all, is absolute proof that the roll is indeed UNEXPOSED.

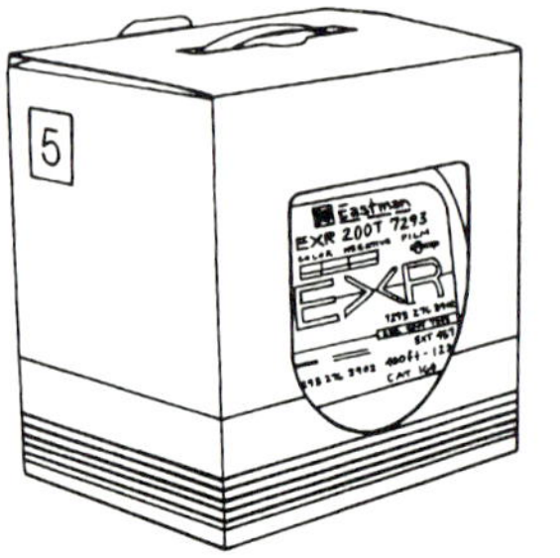

Save the cardboard for storing exposed cans of film, and again, to absorb shocks.

Unwind the tape from the manufacturer's can onto a smooth surface - desk top or equipment case, car window or wall - NOT on a carpet, clothing or priceless painting. Just make sure the tape will come up easily, without pulling up other things. You will need this identification tape again.

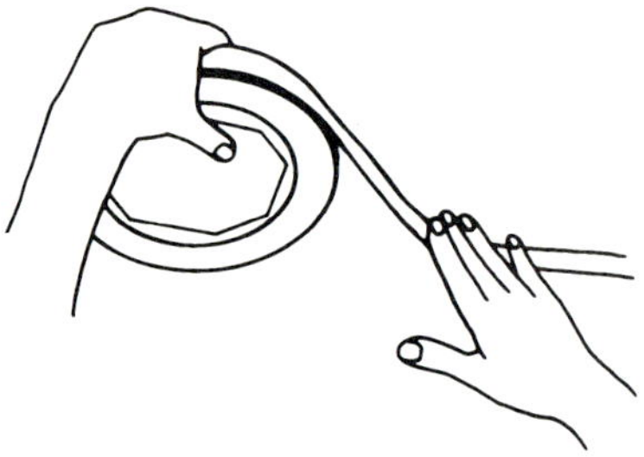

In the rest of this chapter, we will go over some of the different ways of loading 16 SR3 magazines:
Empty Magazine.
Magazine with Exposed Film Inside
Magazine with a Short-End to be Discarded
Magazine with a Short-End to Keep

There are many different ways to load magazines: these are just a few ideas. As Jonathan Ercole says, the main thing is to be consistent. In the Camera Prep film, notice that he and Anne Gwynn both keep unexposed film on the left side, and exposed film on the right when loading.

Loading An Empty Mag

1. If you're in the darkroom, place in front of you an UNEXPOSED FILM CAN (STILL CLOSED!), and a MAGAZINE (closed, feed size up).

2. If you're using a changing bag, put those same two items inside: the UNEXPOSED FILM CAN (Still Closed) and the Magazine.

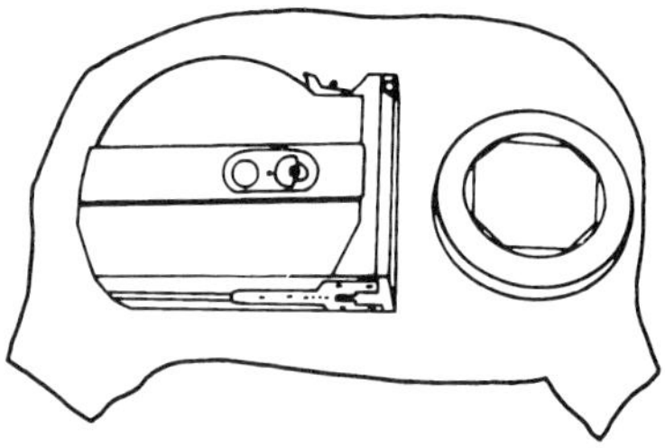

3. Zip up both zippers of the bag. Stick your hands into the sleeves of the bag, in over your elbows.

4. ***DOUBLE CHECK: ZIPPERS SHUT?***

5. If you're in the darkroom, close and lock the door. Turn out the light.

6. Open FEED door of mag. Push in the Safety Button. Turn lock knob counterclockwise. Open film can. Without turning film over, remove it from black bag with your right hand. Stick your thumb through core hole.

7. With fingernail of left hand, peel tape off end of film roll— top to bottom (counter-clockwise). The way Kodak packs the film, the whole piece of tape should come off (until they change their system.) Actually, it's a label, with film ID printed on it.

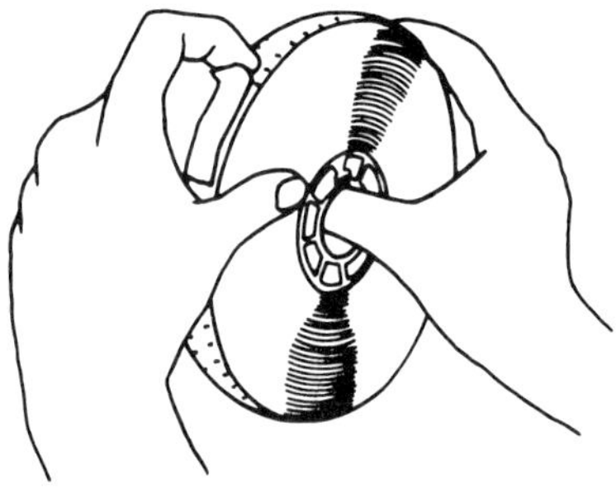

8. ***IT IS CRITICAL TO GET ALL THE TAPE OFF THE END OF THE ROLL— FAILURE TO DO THIS WILL CAUSE MAG JAMS.*** Check: run your finger over the end.

9. Put the tape on the OUTSIDE of the now empty can. You will look at it later when you open the bag to check that it's all in one piece. You can also double check the type of film you are loading, because the label or tape often identifies the type of film. If the tape is ripped, you MUST account for every piece, like a surgeon counting sponges.

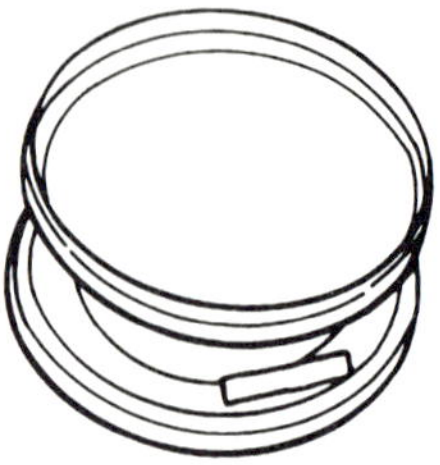

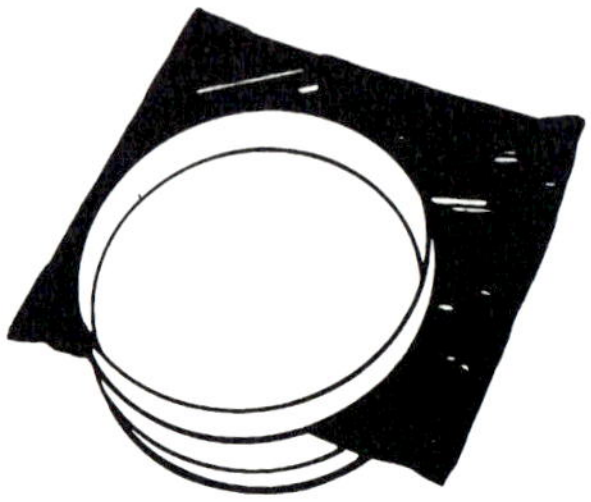

10. By the way, when taking the lid off the film can, put it under the can with open end facing down. This way, lid can't nestle into can and is easier to separate later on.

11. You have the roll of unexposed film in your right hand. We'll assume it's a 400' roll on core.

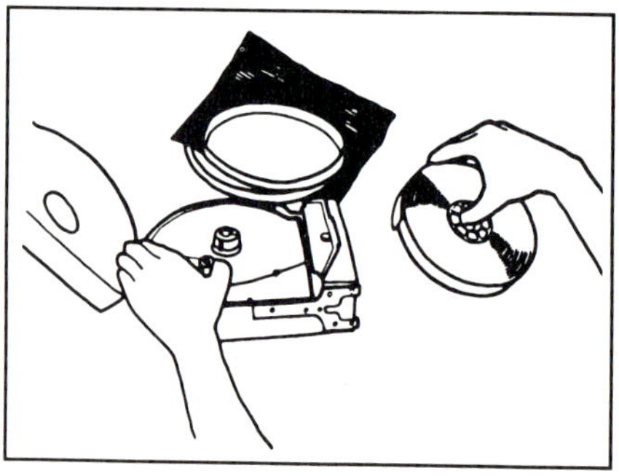

12. With your left hand, slide the guide roller arm (footage counter arm) all the way to the left until it clicks. DON'T LIFT UP ON IT (as you would with an ARRI S—it may break).

13. Hold the film roll over the center of the magazine. Locate the core holder with your thumb, which is sticking through the center of the core.

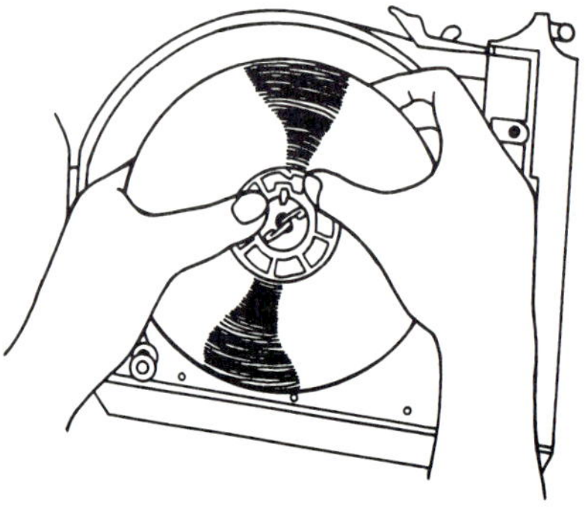

14. With your left hand, push the core down on the core holder as far as it will go. DO NOT PUSH DOWN HARD ON THE FILM ITSELF—JUST PUSH DOWN ON THE CORE. Otherwise, the film will cone and make noise.

15. Next, push the head of the film into the magazine feed slot. Some people feed the film into the slot before putting the roll of film onto the core holder. It's harder and takes longer that way.

16. Hold the magazine drive gear with right index finger.

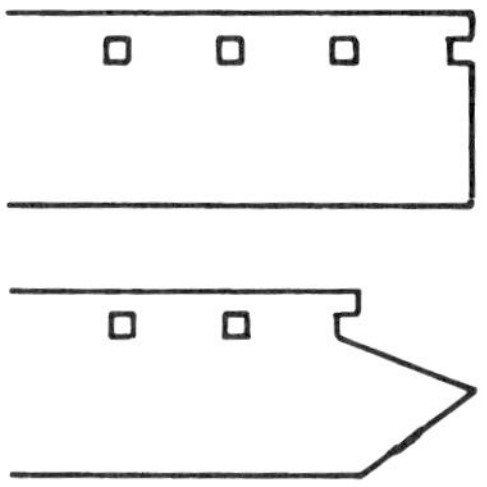

17. If the film has been cut straight across the sprocket holes, it will enter the slot easily. Sometimes, the film has an arrow notched at the head of the roll. So, you'll have to wiggle the end around a bit to get it in.

18. The easiest way to get the film in the slot: locate the end of the film and rotate the roll so the end faces the feed slot. Use your left index finger and thumb to guide it into the slot. Start near the bottom of the mag, and push the film end up along the edge until it pops into the slot.

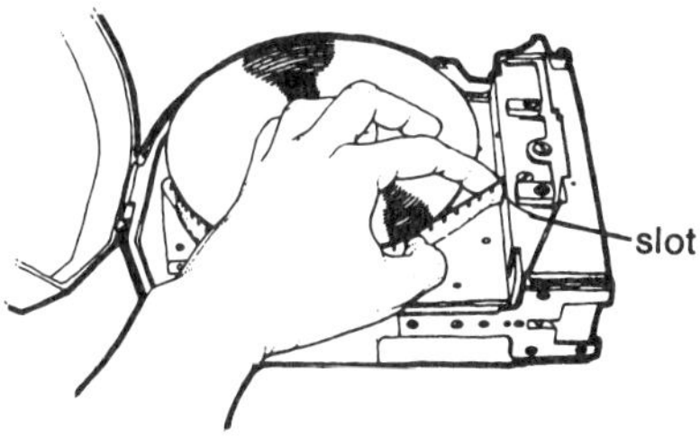

19. As the film pops into the slot, push gently until you feel the resistance of the internal sprocket gear.

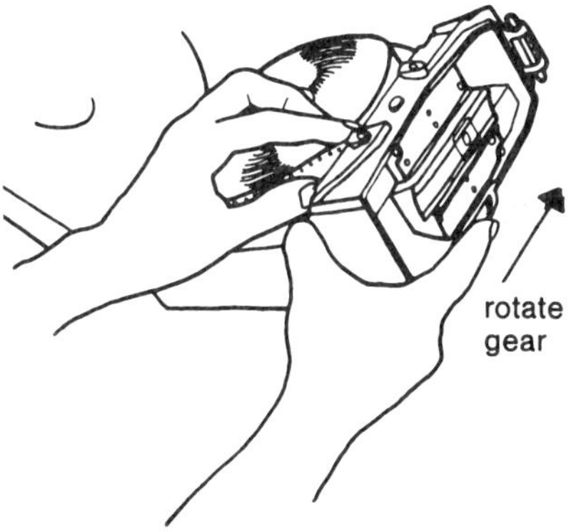

20. Very gently advance the mag drive gear with your right index finger, in the direction of the arrow (which you can't see, because you're in the dark). With the feed side up, turn the gear counter-clockwise (up—towards the top of the mag). Use just a slight amount until you feel pressure on the film.

21. Then, pull back gently on the film with your left fingers until you feel a sprocket hole snap in place internally over a sprocket gear tooth.

22. ***NEVER FORCE THE FILM.*** If you do, you'll tear the sprocket holes and deposit emulsion inside the tracks.

23. If you're having trouble, maybe the film is curling inward. Try bending it out slightly to give it a straighter path to follow.

24. Turn the mag drive gear a few more turns to advance the film all the way into the magazine throat.

Here's What Is Going On Inside:

The film finds its own path.

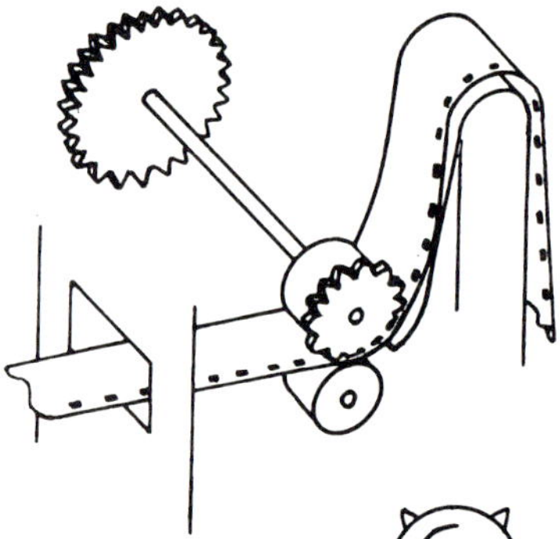

A. If the film has been cut straight across the sprocket holes, the end of the film pushes against the sprocket roller gear as you push it in. The sprocket gear engages naturally in the next sprocket hole.

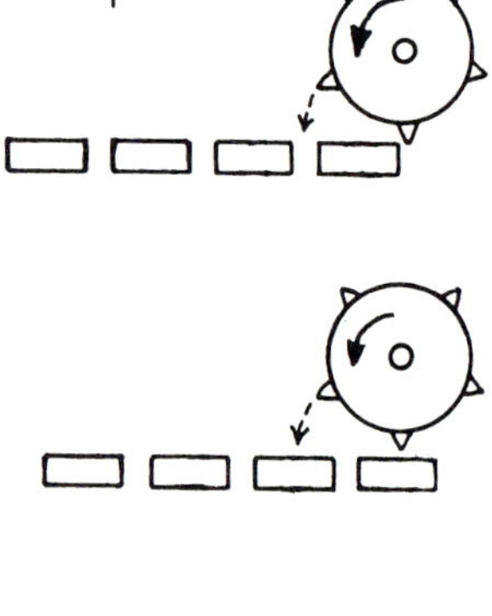

B. But, film doesn't usually come that way. The head of the film roll is either notched or cut midway between the sprockets. In this case, the end of the film pushes the sprocket roller, and the next sprocket gear does not engage in a sprocket hole, but rather the film itself. So, you then have to pull the film back a little bit until the sprocket hole pops in place.

25. Be sure spindle lock retainer is tight over core holder, as described earlier.

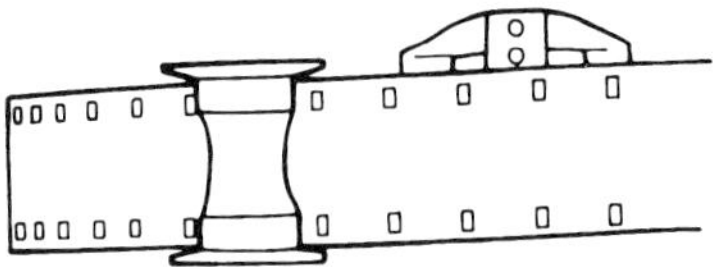

26. Now, disengage footage counter guide-roller by sliding it gently toward the roll of film.

27. With your finger, make sure both lips of the footage counter roller ride evenly over top and bottom edges of film.

28. If the rollers are not riding evenly, pull up or push down on the whole roll of film - very gently, by grabbing around the circumference and moving it until the roller pops into position. DO NOT MOVE ROLLER—MOVE FILM.

29. ***DOUBLE CHECK: IS FOOTAGE COUNTER GUIDE-ROLLER IN PLACE?*** This is the most common mistake made when loading.

30. Take out slack in the film by advancing the magazine main drive gear, or winding the feed roll back clockwise.

31. Check that magazine lock knob is all the way open (counter-clockwise).

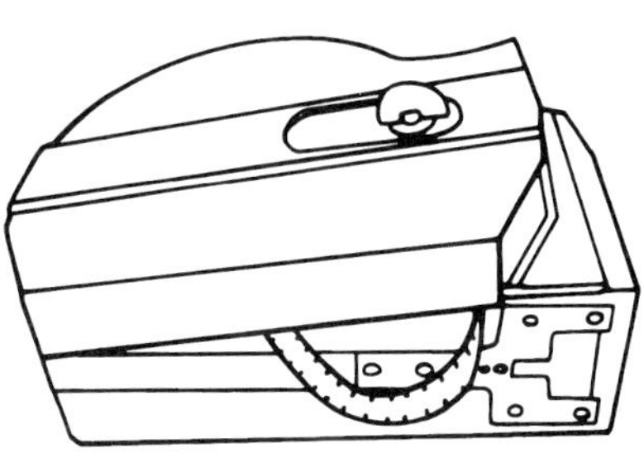

32. Gently shut magazine feed door. Be careful not to catch any slack film that may be hanging out.

33. DON'T slam the door shut—it's delicate.

34. DON'T close with the mag lock knob in the locked position - you might bend the brittle metal tabs, or break them off.

35. Once closed, run your fingers around the edges of the mag to be sure you haven't caught the changing bag or black film stock bag inside.

36. Lock the mag. Turn lock knob clockwise until it clicks.

37. ***DOUBLE CHECK***—try to pull the mag open by pulling the cover on all corners. Mag is now shut.

38. ***Think again: mag shut, locked, no film left in bag.***

39. Open changing bag, remove mag. Or, if you're using a darkroom, turn on the light.

40. If the head of the film roll is notched, or otherwise less than perfect, cut across the sprocket holes with the scissors of your Swiss Army knife.

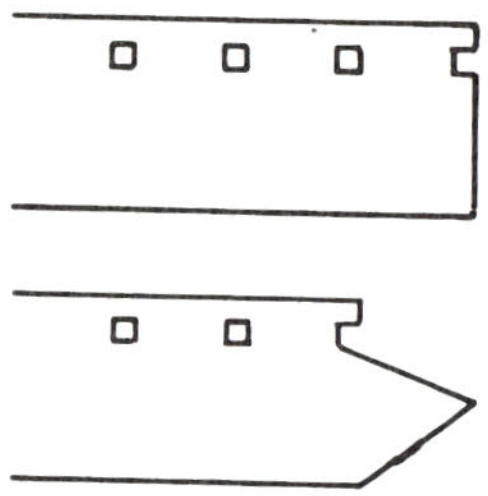

41. It's a particularly good idea when you're rushed, because it may save you time in the long run, not having to jiggle film in and out.

42. When cutting off the notch, make sure you dispose of this small piece of film in a place where it will not interfere with any equipment. Small chips always wind up in the places where they do the most harm.

43. Stand the mag up on its hinges, throat up, drive gear away from you.

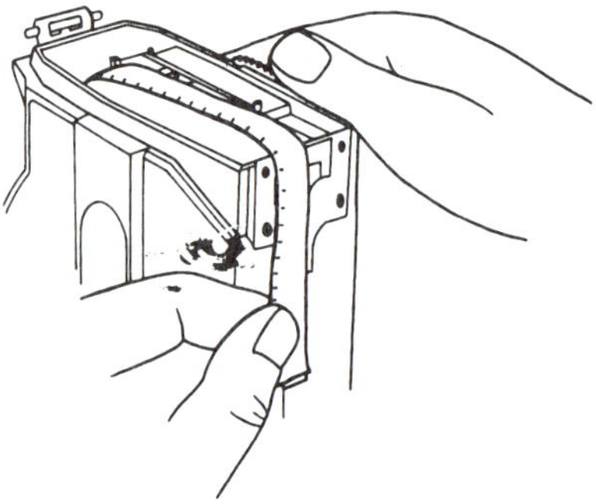

44. Pull the film out of the throat with your right hand, while using your left index finger on the drive gear as a brake.

45. Continue pulling across the throat and along bottom of mag to the white index line. The film comes out on a slight diagonal. Don't try to straighten it out along the shiny film channel guide rail.

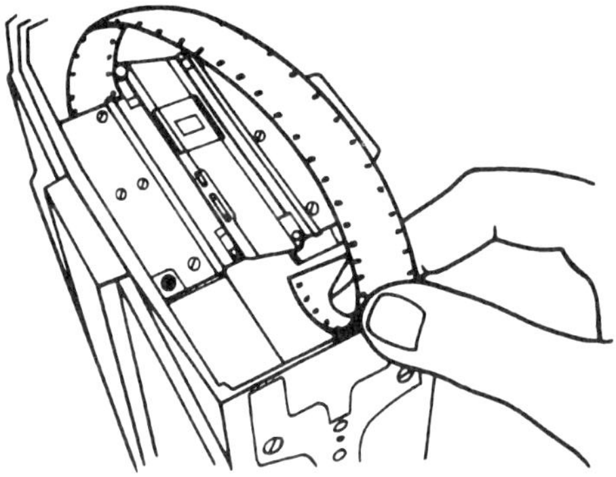

46. If you didn't cut the film head across the sprocket holes, measure the film to the first set of sprocket holes over the index line.

47. Now, hold on tight to the drive gear with your left index finger to keep the loop size from slipping.

48. With your right index finger and thumb, press the film end down onto the smooth guide rails and into the slot.

49. The drive gear will rotate as the film enters - same principle as when loading the feed side. When the film sprockets engage, rotate the drive gear in the direction of the arrow about five revolutions.

50. As before, don't force the film in. If you have trouble, be patient. Delicately feel with the film, hold drive gear, gently pull the film back until a sprocket hole is engaged.

51. If the loop has become too large, you can turn the mag drive gear in reverse (opposite direction of arrow). Just remember that the feed spindle will not take-up the slack, and the film will just accumulate loosely in the feed chamber.

52. Open the TAKE-UP side of the magazine. Clean it out with Dust-Off and a brush.

53. Lay the mag down, take-up side up. Pull back guide roller.

Collapsible Cores

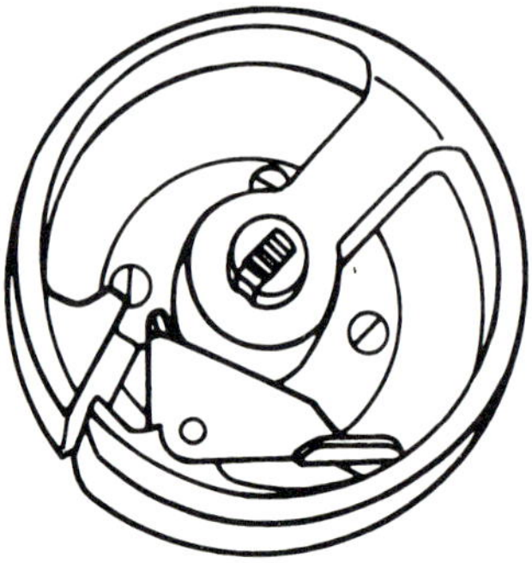

54. Most Arriflex 16 SR3 Cameras come from the factory with collapsible cores on the take-up side. I am still convinced you will have less chance of negative and lab dirt if you use regular plastic cores—but more about that later.

55. The only advantage of the collapsible core is that it's a little faster to load, and you don't need an extra supply of cores when dealing with short-ends.

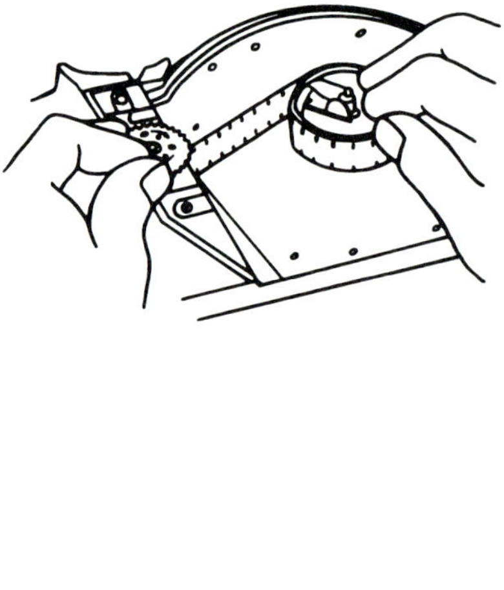

56. Make sure the collapsible core's lever is disengaged (pull it away from the center spindle).

57. Pull the film from the take-up channel, and insert about ¾" of the end into the collapsible core's slot. Don't fold the end. If you insert too large a piece of film into the slot, it will most likely make noise by rubbing on the mag's cover.

58. Lock the collapsible core's lever to bite down on the end of the film, and expand the core's circumference.

59. Rotate the core and the mag drive gear in opposite directions to take up slack.

Plastic Cores

60. If you're using a plastic core—pull about 2 feet of film through. You can pull on the film directly, without turning the mag drive gear.

61. Fold the film end over once.

62. Make the fold even, and smooth it out with your fingernails.

63. If you are in a hurry, and the end is notched, fold over twice.

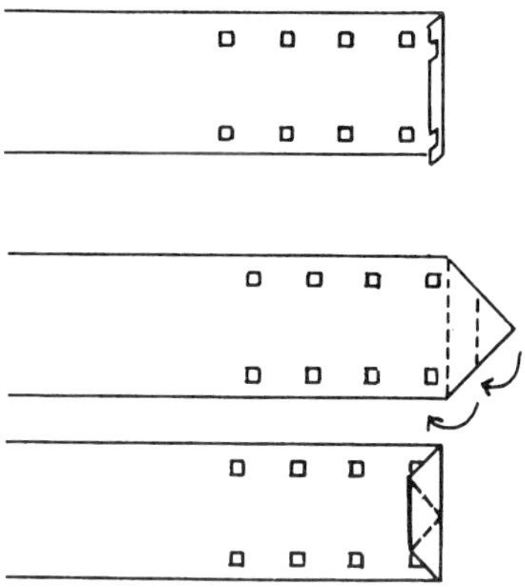

Double perf film: not for Super16!

64. Insert folded end of film into slot of core, as shown.

65. Smooth the fold with your fingernail. Any bump will make noise as the guide roller passes over it when the camera is running.

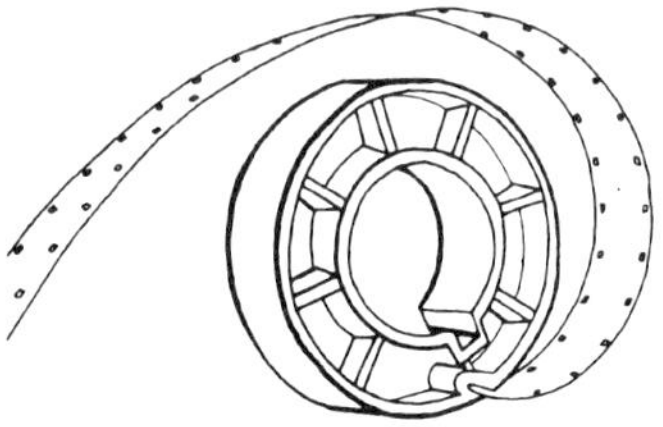

66. Be sure film and folded ends do not protrude out of the core slot.

67. Wind about five turns around core to be certain film is secure. Index finger and thumb of left hand should guide film evenly on core, while right hand rotates core.

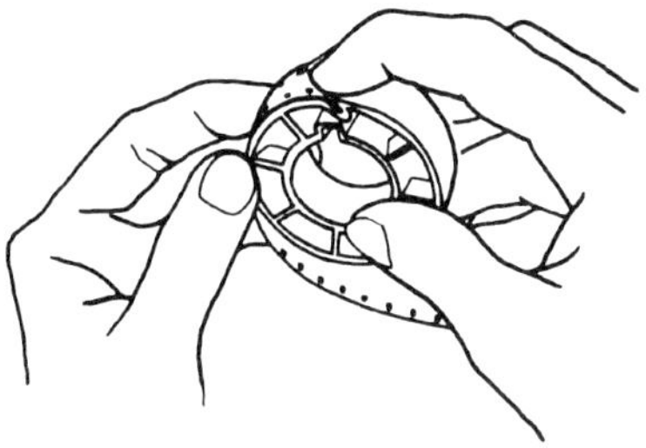

68. Take-up will then be even, smooth and quiet.

69. This is done with core out of the magazine. More on cores later.

70. Slide the core onto core holder. Push down on the core all the way.

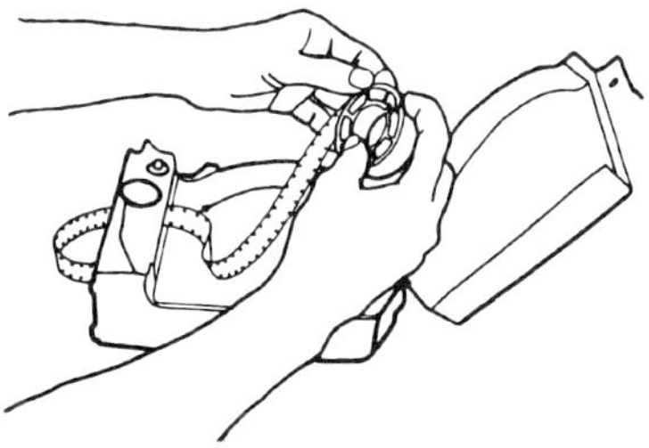

71. The next steps are the same, whether you are using a collapsible or regular core.

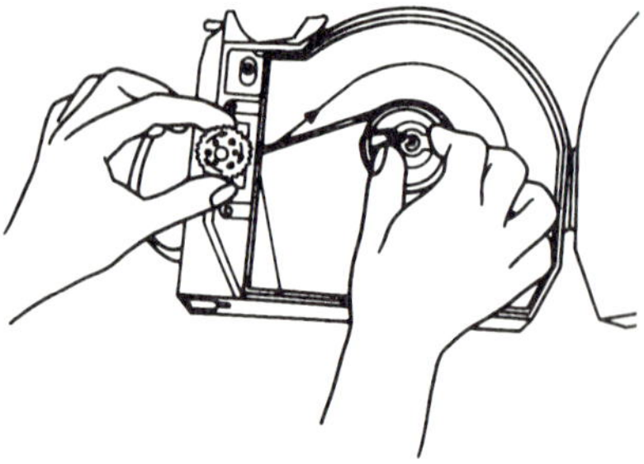

72. Engage theguide arm roller by sliding it into place. Hold drive gear with left hand, and core with right. Gently turn the two away from each other to take out any slack. Don't force. Now, rotate drive gear with roller in place to be sure that take-up is even. Close the mag cover, and lock. Test by trying to open it by the cover.

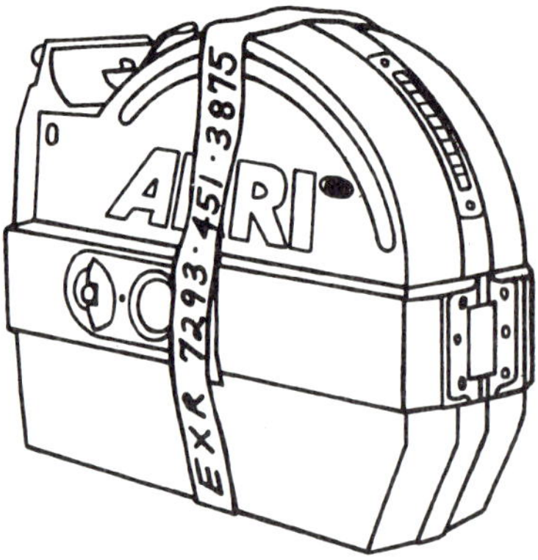

73. Check the footage counter. If you don't see the white pointer, you forgot to engage the feed guide roller arm. Back into the bag or darkroom.

74. Again—make sure mag cover is closed. Wind film identification tape around the mag to prevent accidental opening and to remind you about emulsion in use.

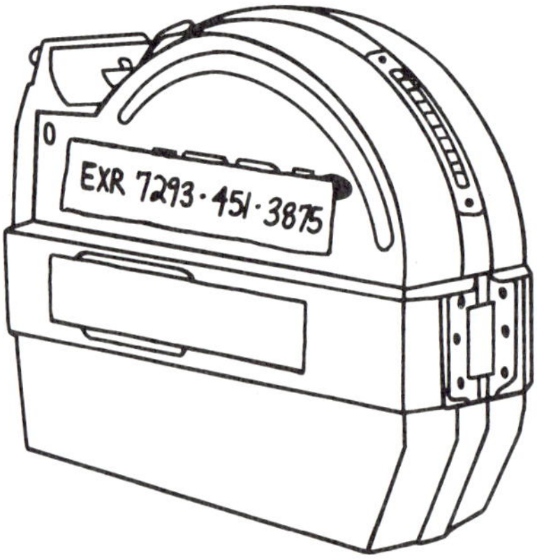

75. With many magazine cases, tape wound around the outside comes off too easily when pulling mags in and out. Use camera tape instead—one piece on the feed latch, one on the take-up latch, and a piece of the film identification tape on the take-up door to identify the emulsion.

76. Run the magazine drive gear in the direction of the arrow for 3 or 4 revolutions to feed film and make sure it runs smoothly.

77. Center the loop. Position film under the 4 side guide hooks. You don't have to count frames: just do it by eye.

78. At this point, do not try to rotate the main magazine drive gear without manually advancing the film along the throat with your fingers. This is vividly demonstrated by Jonathan Ercole in the Camera Prep film.

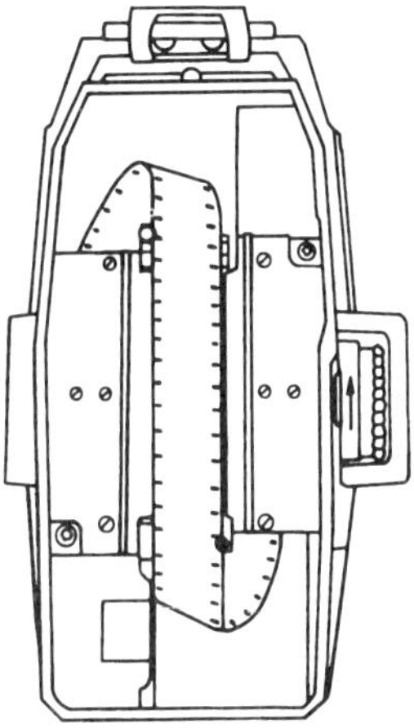

79. Attach the loop protector.

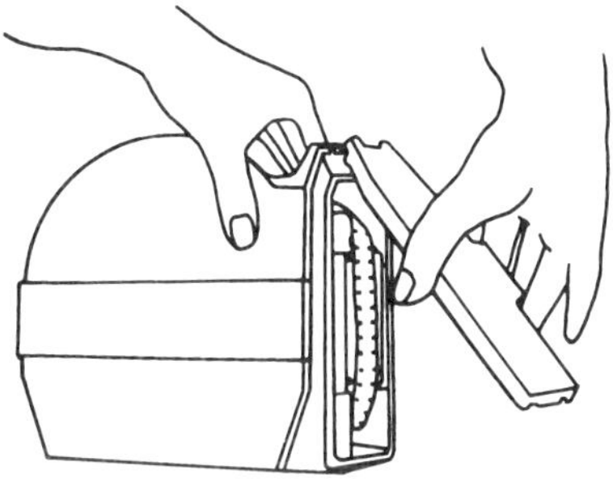

Core Slots, Cores & Collapsible Cores

You will hear a variety of opinions as to which way the film retaining slot on the core should face.

The safest, most foolproof direction is in the direction of rotation:

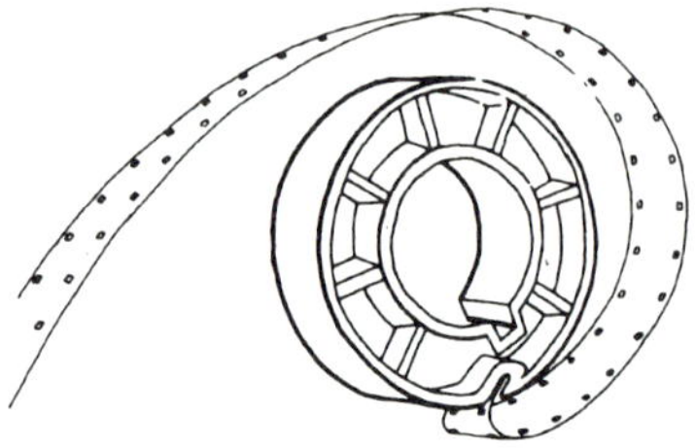

But the film buckles slightly, causing the guide roller to bump and make noise.

Therefore, because of the cut-out in the construction of the core, it is recommended that the slot face the film this way:

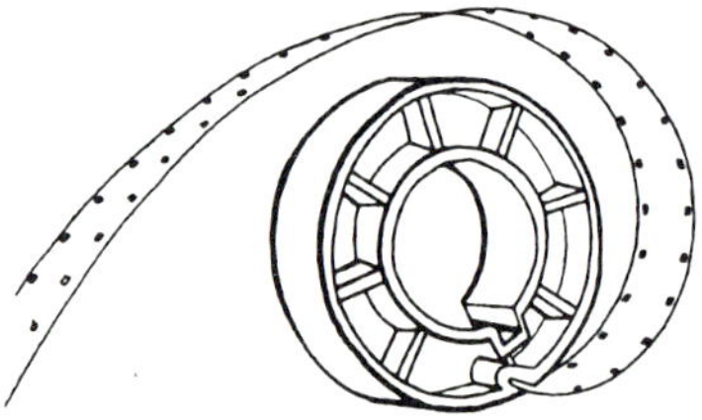

You will also hear different opinions on whether to fold or not to fold the film end.

The safest method is to fold the end straight, making sure that the edges do not buckle out from the sides of the core slot.

Not folding over the end is asking for trouble - if the film goes slack, you might lose take-up.

Never use tape on the end of the film. You could gum up a lab processing machine, or even your camera, assuming the worst.

Many Arriflex cameras are fitted with collapsible cores, as we mentioned before. They are handy because you don't have to remember about extra plastic cores or worry about short-ends. However, their disadvantages outnumber the advantages.

If you are using the collapsible core, the film is inserted into the slot without folding the end. The lever is pushed to bite down on the film end while expanding the core. Remember—be certain that the film end does not stick up above the collapsible core. If it does, it will make noise.

If you are using daylight spools (only up to 200'), remove the core holder from the take-up side. Do not lose the core adapter.

As mentioned, NASA has used slightly cut-down 400' daylight spools in SR cameras on the Space Shuttles. They have cut off 1/16th of an inch from the outside diameter of the 400' spool for them to fit.

On the take-up side, engage the film in the slot of the daylight spool, wind a few turns clockwise, and put the spool on the shaft. Tighten up the slack by turning spool and mag drive gear in opposite directions.

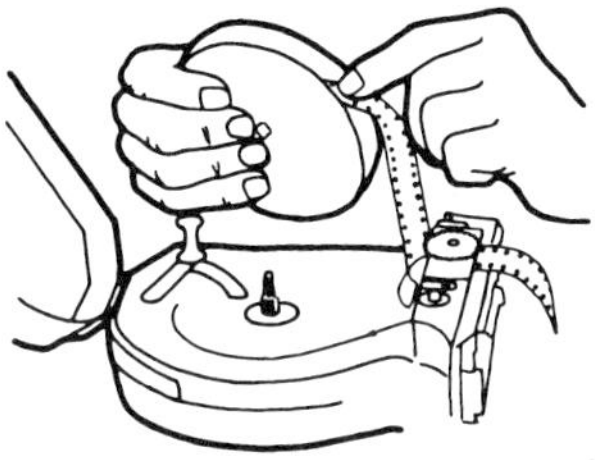

Keep the guide roller arm latched and away from the spool. You will be obliged to rely on the electronic footage counter.

Footage Counters

The 16SR has two footage counters: Film Remaining in the feed side of the mag (Magazine, top back).

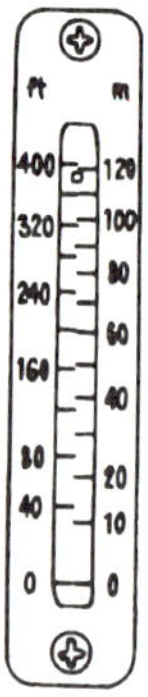

And an electronic counter in the main display.

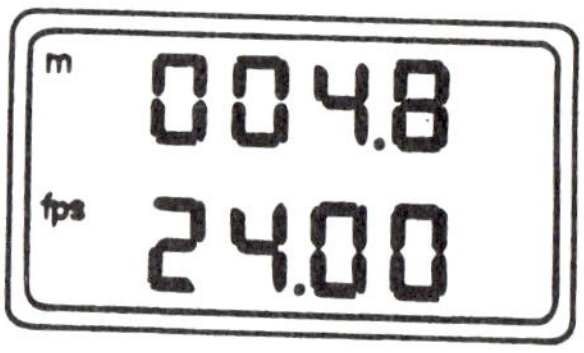

To reset the main display back to zero when you put a fresh load on the camera, see page 80.

There is no longer a mechanical counter on the take-up side, as on SR1 and SR2's.

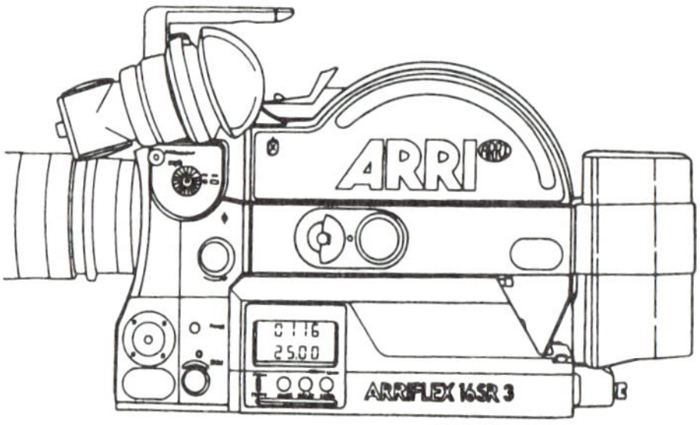

The counter there is now for timecode settings.

Do NOT reset it to "0" thinking you are resetting the footage!

If you are setting timecode sensitivity, look at the chart on page 195. Different films require different timecode settings. Changing the number allows more or less light to hit the film with barcode information.

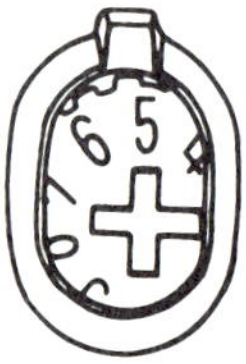

Loading An Exposed Mag

The cinematographer has just handed you a magazine which has been fully exposed—all 400 feet have been shot. The footage counter reads "O." There is no film visible. He tells you not to hurry, but as soon as you're out of the bag, he needs you to pull focus. Obviously, you should hurry as much as is safely possible.

RULE: Don't get into a panic situation, don't let yourself be rushed. But remember the entire crew can only go as fast as you go. Assistants who work often work fast, and without error.

1. Remove the loop protector.

2. Remove the camera identification tape. Many camera assistants save a piece, to tape to the outside of the exposed film can as identification of the emulsion.

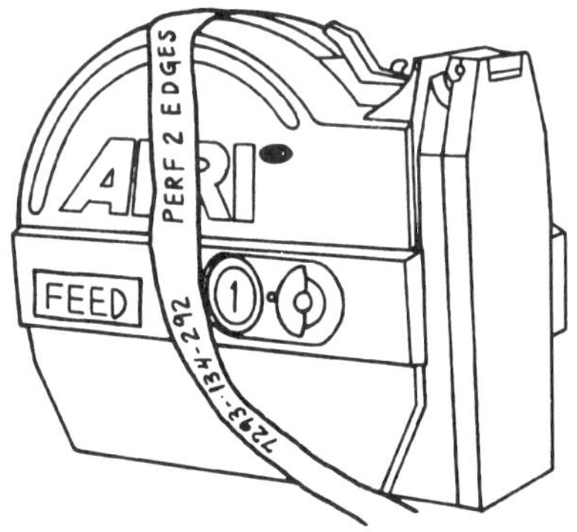

3. When the loop protector is on the right, you're looking at the feed side. The loop is also on the right. Remember: "FEEDS RIGHT."

4. It is helpful to put tapes marked "FEED" and "TAKE-UP" on the appropriate sides of the 16SR mag. This is not embarrassing— even the most experienced assistants mark them this way. In the heat of the moment, it is good to be reminded which side is which. Especially since Arriflex and Aaton magazines feed from opposite sides. Aaton cameras feed unexposed film from the camera left side; exposed film takes up on the camera right side.

5. What you are about to do is open the feed side, so it can be cleaned and blown out in daylight. You should be getting into the habit, essential when working with negative stock, of cleaning out both sides of the mag after every roll.

6. Rather than unload the film in the bag, cleaning the totally empty mag in daylight, and going back into the bag to load the new roll, you will be taking advantage of the coaxial feature of the SR magazine.

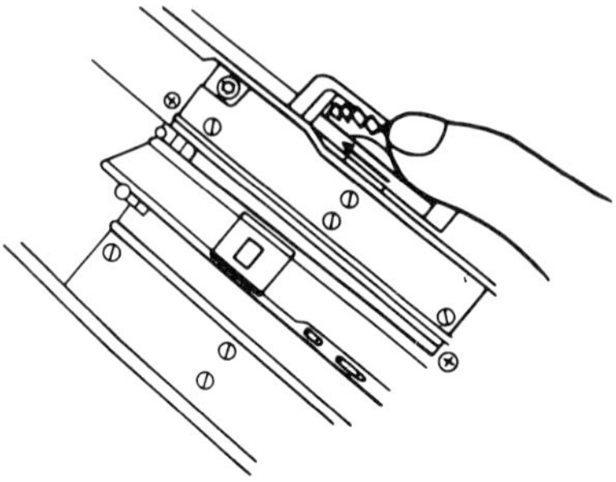

7. Reconfirm that you know which side is which. Spin the mag drive gear. You will be able to feel the exposed roll of film spinning around on the same side. Remember— exposed film is on the same side as the drive gear. DO NOT OPEN THIS SIDE.

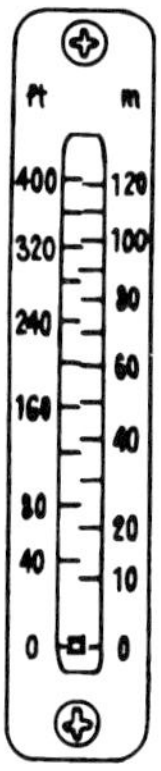

8. Check the footage counter one last time. It should read "0." If not, there is film inside the feed side. Check, and be sure.

9. In daylight, open the FEED side.

10. If for any reason you have fouled up at this stage, tell the cinematographer immediately— better now when things can still be reshot than a surprise in the screening room. Film exposed to light will have orange streaks, even if exposed for an instant. Incriminating evidence.

11. Clean out the FEED side with Dust-Off and a brush.

12. In the magazine throat, clean the chrome fixed gap, film channel and pressure pad with a well-washed chamois cloth, or even better, no-lint Selvyt.

13. Remove the old core left over from the expended roll of film. Save the core for use again later.

14. Take the ID tape off a can of unexposed stock.

15. Go into the changing bag or darkroom with the can and the magazine FEED side up.

16. Zip up both zippers of the bag.

17. Put your hands into the bag as far as possible. The elastic cuffs should be above your elbows.

18. Rotate the magazine drive gear away from you to be sure all the exposed film has cleared the sprocket rollers.

19. Open the film can. LOAD the FEED SIDE as we discussed earlier. Without turning the roll of film over, remove it from its black bag. Peel off the tape from head of roll. Place core on FEED core holder. Push down on the core, not on the film itself. Engage the film end in the feed slot. Rotate the mag drive gear a few turns. Slide the footage counter guide roller in place. Close the FEED door. Lock it. Check it. Double check it.

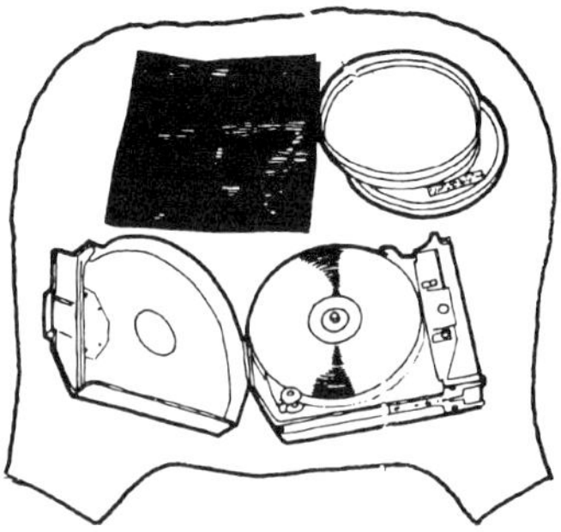

20. Turn the mag over, TAKE-UP side up.

21. .Open the cover.

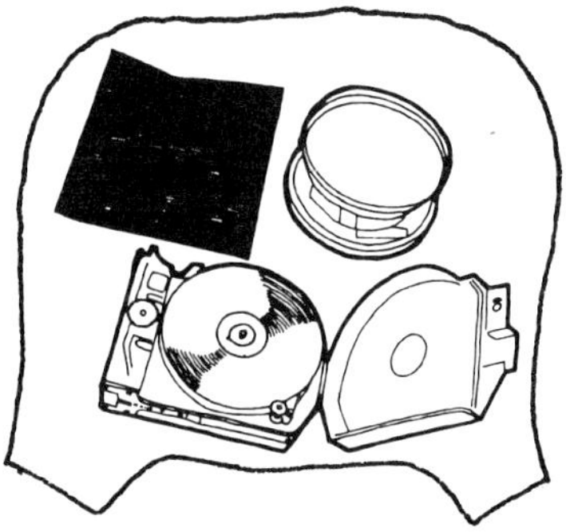

22. Slide the guide roller away to its open position. It will snap into place, and stay there. DO NOT LIFT UP ON IT.

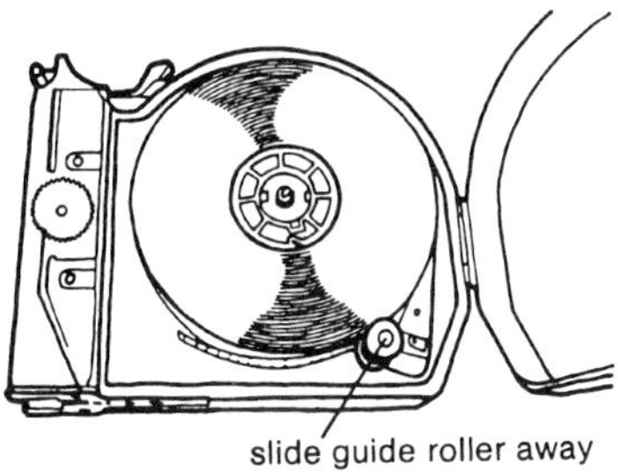

Plastic Core

23. *If the take-up side has a regular core:*, push on the spindle release lock.

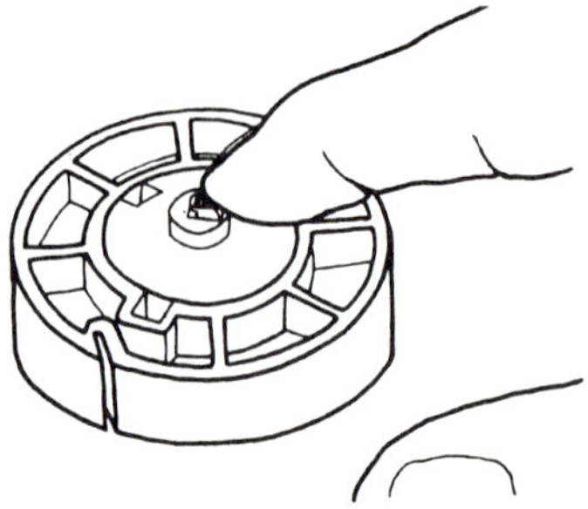

24. While holding the spindle lock with your right thumb, lift the roll of film up with your left hand. Push in while lifting—this will prevent coning.

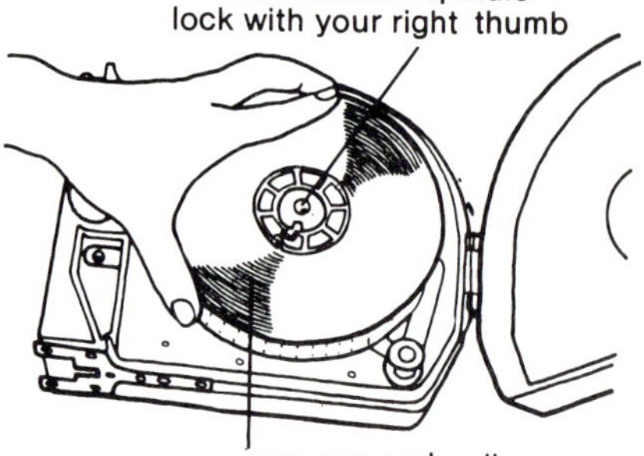

25. Since the core holder is still inside the core, and you don't want to send it to the lab, push it out from the core with the thumb of one hand, while holding the roll in both hands. Be careful, or you will push the core out as well.

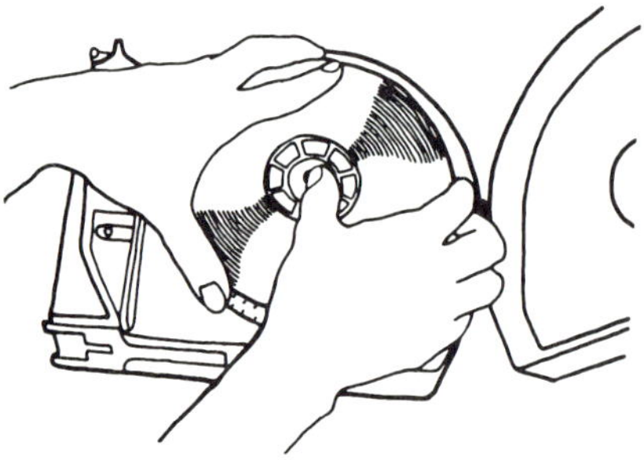

26. By holding the core itself back with the tips of your fingers, only the metal holder will come out leaving everything else in place.

27. ***If the roll of film is loose, NEVER tighten it. Leave it loose. Tightening will cause cinch marks to appear on the negative.***

Collapsible Core

28. If the take-up side has a collapsible core, leave it in the magazine.

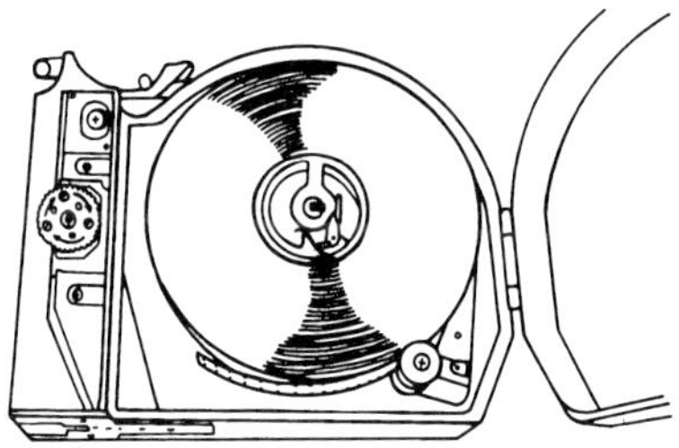

29. To remove the film, first pinch the small strip of film caught inside the core.

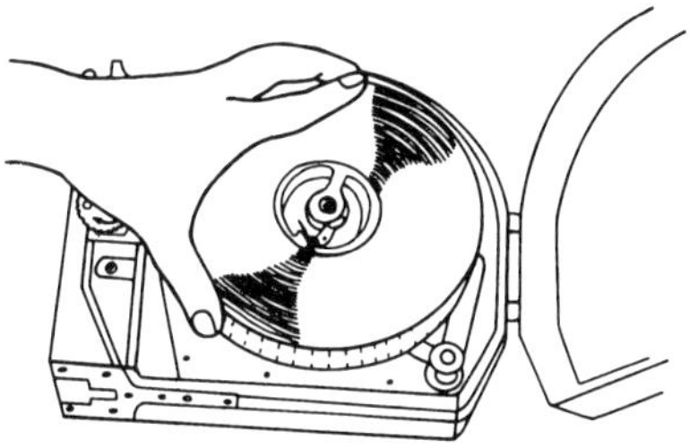

30. With your other hand, release the chrome lever. The core will collapse.

31. With one hand holding the circumference of the film, and the other hand guiding the center of the film roll, carefully pull up on the roll.

32. Immediately place a core inside the empty center of the roll of film to reduce lab handling, and to protect the film in shipment.

33. Problem: When you lifted the film up, the center coned out. Solution:

34. Wind it back into the hole: a frustrating and tedious procedure. Whenever an assistant has turned pale, with hands in the bag, back drenched with sweat- the assistant is without a doubt salvaging a collapsible core disaster.

35. When the film gets to the lab it can still cinch because the film is loose on the core, or it can cinch because there is no core and the lab has put their "best men" on the job. Risky business.

36. Put the exposed roll of film inside the black paper or plastic bag. Fold all the edges and corners in and down, so the bag is a circle around the roll of film.

37. Put the bag in the can, folds down. Cover the can.

Meanwhile, back at the plastic core

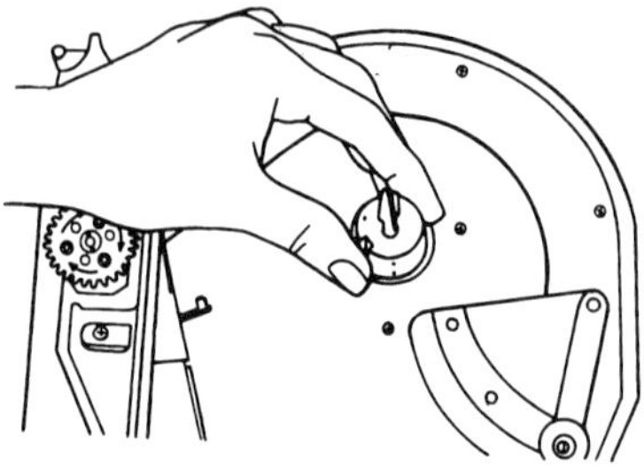

38. Return the core adapter onto its spindle.

39. This is easily done with your left hand.

40. Hold the mag drive gear with the palm of your left hand, to prevent it from rotating.

41. Slip the core adapter onto its spindle with your left thumb and index finger. You may have to jiggle it around until it finds its position. Then, it will just drop down and lock into place.

42. An immutable law of the film business: core holders sent inadvertently to the lab are lost forever.

Finishing Up

43. Time to come out of the changing bag. ***DOUBLE CHECK- EXPOSED FILM CAN SHUT. FEED SIDE SHUT. Check again.***

44. Pull your hands out of the changing bag. Tap the closed exposed can through the bag, to make sure it's closed.

45. While pressing on the can through the bag to keep it shut, Open the zippers. Take the can out.

46. Use camera tape to seal the can shut. Do NOT use the original can ID tape—it can be confusing.

47. This way, it is virtually impossible to mix up exposed film with unexposed.

48. If you were using a darkroom, now is the time to turn on the light.

49. Next, clean out the take-up side of the mag.

50. Finish up threading the take-up side. If you're using plastic cores, put one on the take-up core-holder, and proceed as described on page 144.

51. If you're using collapsible cores, proceed as described on page 143

52. Close the magazine lid and tape it up.

53. This system of loading works well in cramped quarters when you have to load with the bag on your lap.

54. When opening the bag, just be sure to hold the can of exposed film between your knees- protecting it from accidental opening.

55. The other advantage of this loading method is that the unexposed film goes directly from the can to the bag—and cannot pick up dirt or hairs from the bag.

Taping And Labeling Exposed Film

Most assistants use black camera tape along the edges of the film can to seal it shut and identify it as exposed. Others use camera tape that has been printed up: **"WARNING: EXPOSED FILM - OPEN IN DARK ROOM ONLY."**

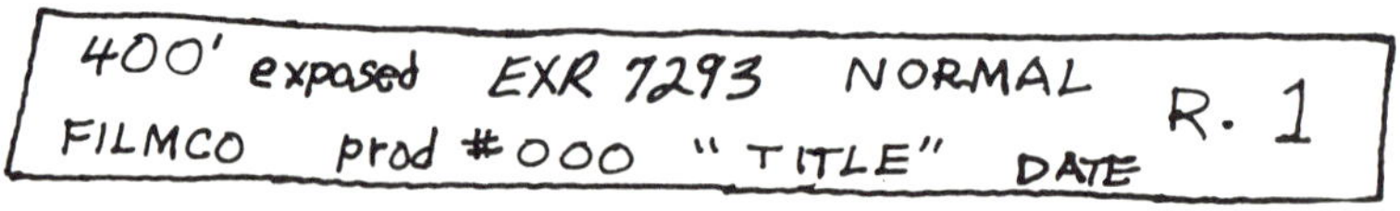

Label the exposed cans with white camera tape or labels. Stick to the information as shown. If you have pushed the film, or have special processing instructions, use a separate label.

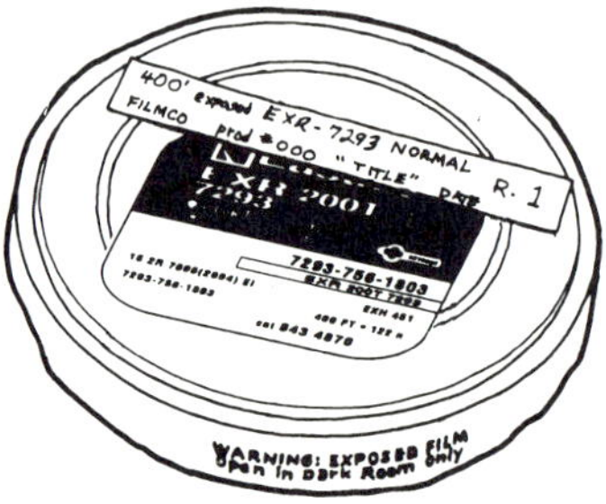

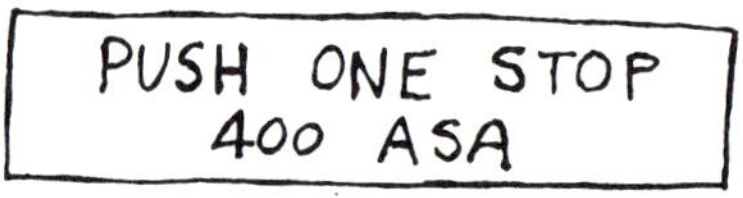

Store your exposed film in a special area. In hot climates, use a cooler. Do not put ice or dry ice in the cooler. Just keep the cooler and the film out of the hot sun, preferably in a cool, dry place.

When preparing film for delivery to the lab, tape the cans together in sequence. Only tape film with the same processing requirements together. Tape rolls for Forced Processing or Special Handling separately.

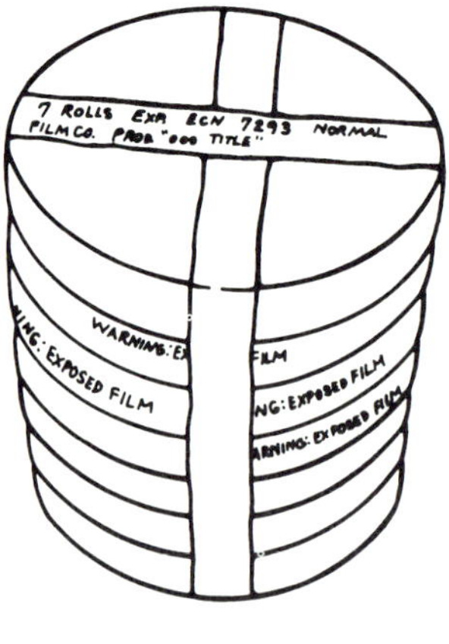

Flip top and bottom cans so they face inward. That way the labels won't peel off.

Write instructions, number of rolls, production company, job title and other information on the outer tape.

Loading a Mag with a Short-End To Be Discarded

If the magazine has some film left over which is expendable (usually fewer than 100'), open the feed door in daylight.

Swing the footage counter arm out of the way.

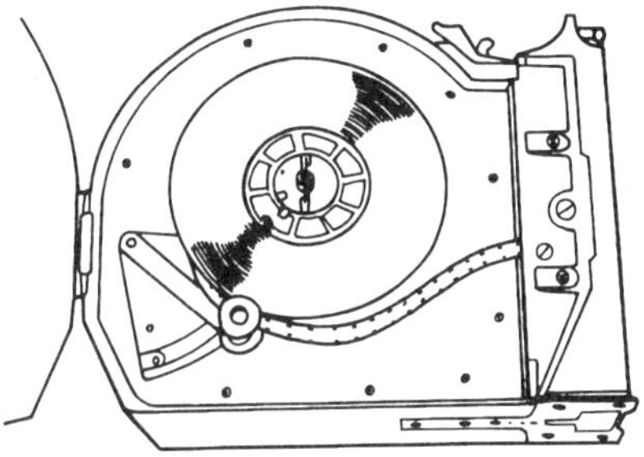

Cut the film off with your Swiss Army Knife, or tear it as indicated.

Lift the film off by applying equal pressure on both sides of the roll. Lift straight up. Do not wiggle from side to side, or you'll loosen the press-fit rivets. If it's tight, you'll have to release the spindle lock, and remove the core and core holder.

Since you might need the core for the take-up side later on, if you're using plastic cores on the take-up side, push out and discard the film. Or, hold the core, and let the film spool off into a waste basket or garbage bag.

Speaking of garbage, it's very helpful to tape up a large and heavy duty plastic garbage bag, in the area where you're working. It speeds clean-up and makes things neater.

Loading A Mag Where You Must Save The Short-End

If the feed side has a short-end which must be saved (usually over 100') you will go into the bag without first opening the feed side.

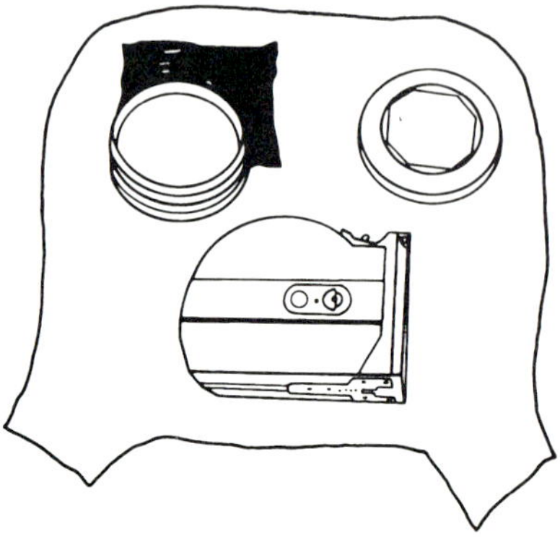

Into the bag or darkroom go: magazine, can of unexposed film, empty 400' can with empty black bag.

The can of unexposed film goes on the right.

The empty can to receive the short-end goes on the left.

The short-end comes out first. Open the feed side door. Break off the film, push the guide roller out of the way, lift off the short-end and can it.

If you have time, after making sure both cans are shut, open the bag, remove and tape up short-end can, and clean out the feed side of the mag.

Otherwise, stick to the system of short-end cans on the left so you won't get confused.

Tape up the edge of the can containing the short-end with white camera tape, and identify it as in this example, with footage, emulsion, date and your name:

250' unexposed	**EXR-200T**	**7293-755-1803**
short-end	**7/11/96**	**Otto Focus**

Then, proceed with loading as described earlier. Make sure a spare core is available for the TAKE-UP side.

ARRIHEAD II

The ARRIHEAD should ride in its case with all locks off.

To lift it out of the case, it is sometimes helpful to lock one of the tilt locks.

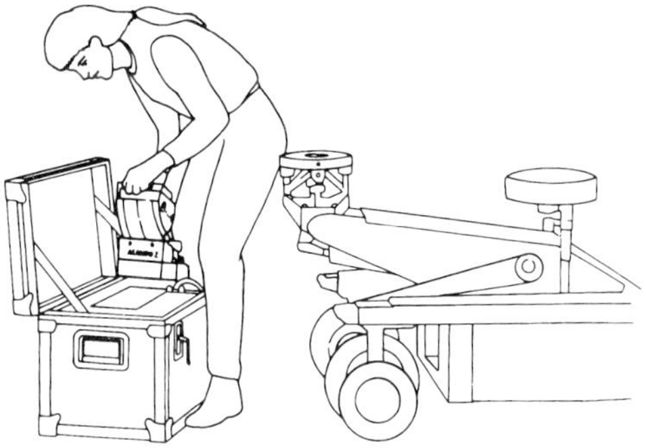

Figure 218 3-10.

Set the ARRIHEAD on the dolly.

Line up the keyway on the Head with the Mitchell base's slot.

Some dollies have very tight tolerances. Do not force a head onto any Mitchell mount. It is very difficult to remove.

Sometimes, in dire situations, you can unscrew the keyway bar—which simply prevents the head from spinning freely.

With enough weight, and with the tie-down screwed in tightly, the head will not spin anyway.

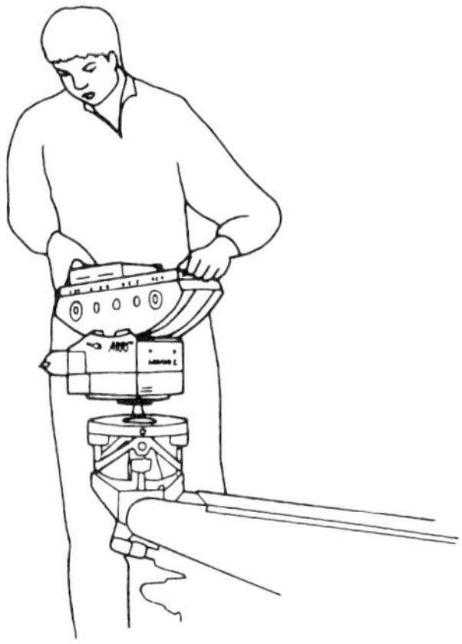

Figure 219 3-11.ti

Attach the tie-down screw to the bottom.

Tighten.

Attach the two handwheels.

Unlock the friction locks.

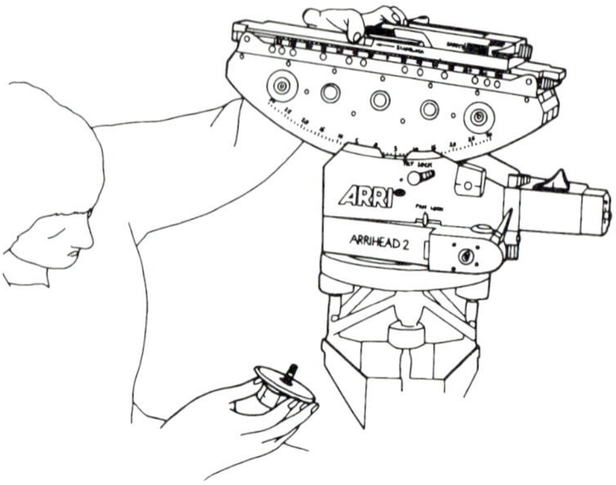

Release the safety LOCK lever on the camera left side.

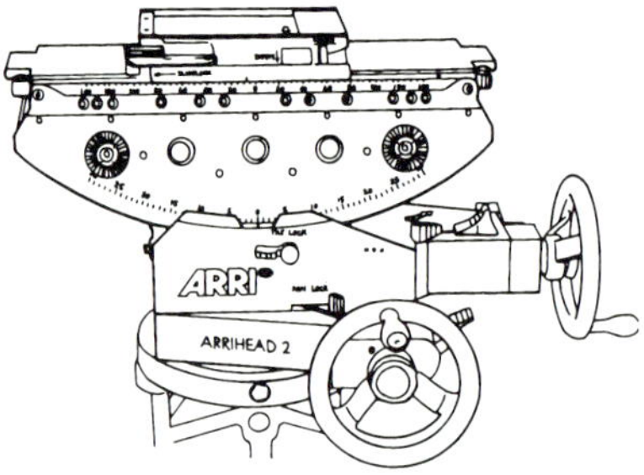

And release the safety LOCK lever on the camera right side.

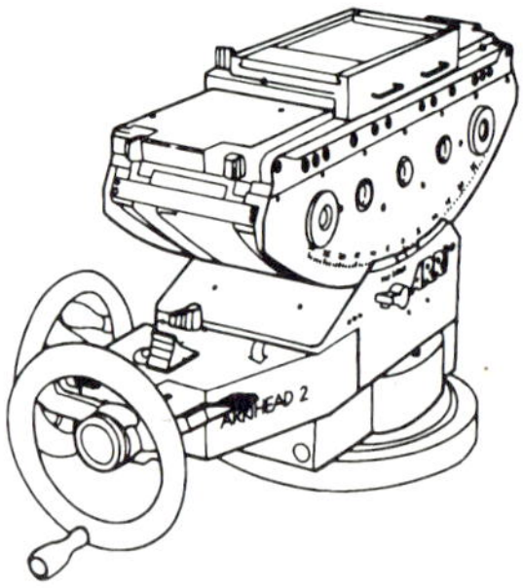

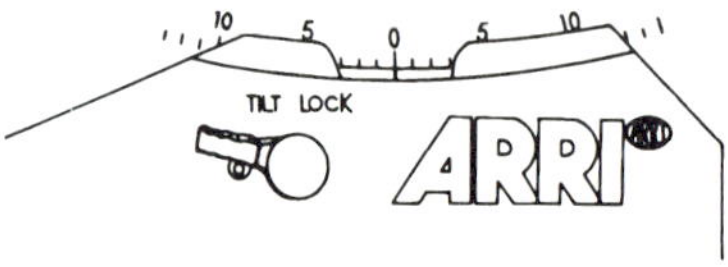

You can tilt the ARRIHEAD 90° straight up and down.

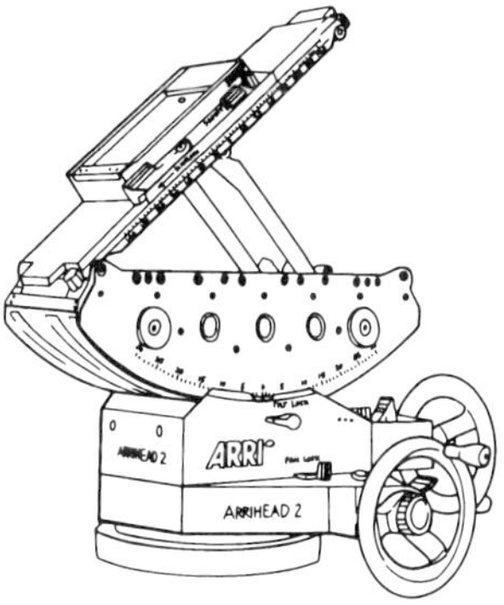

Organize your cables so they do not interfere with the dolly or smooth operation of the camera.

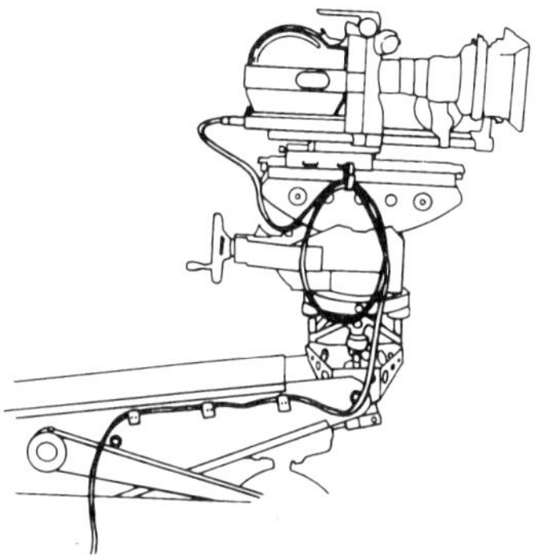

Head Saver

Remember to use a "head saver" when using a dolly—many dollies will boom down low enough to hit the handwheels.

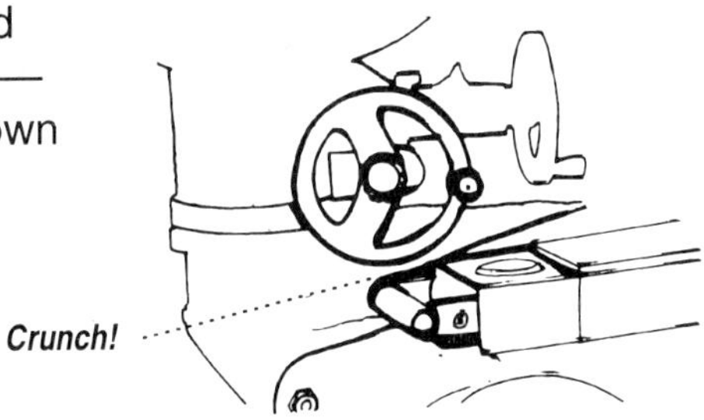

A small block of wood placed under the boom arm will prevent this.

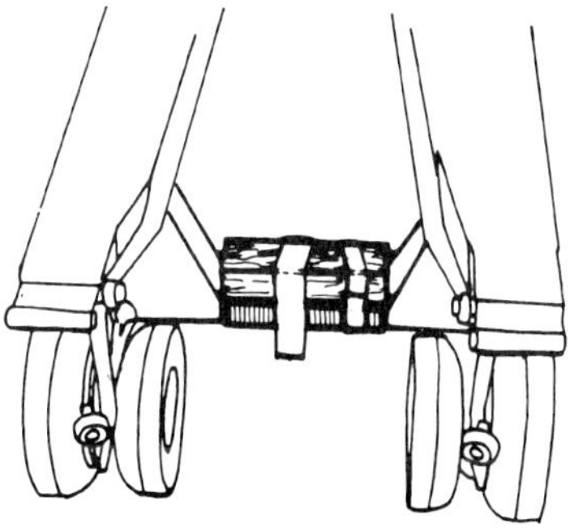

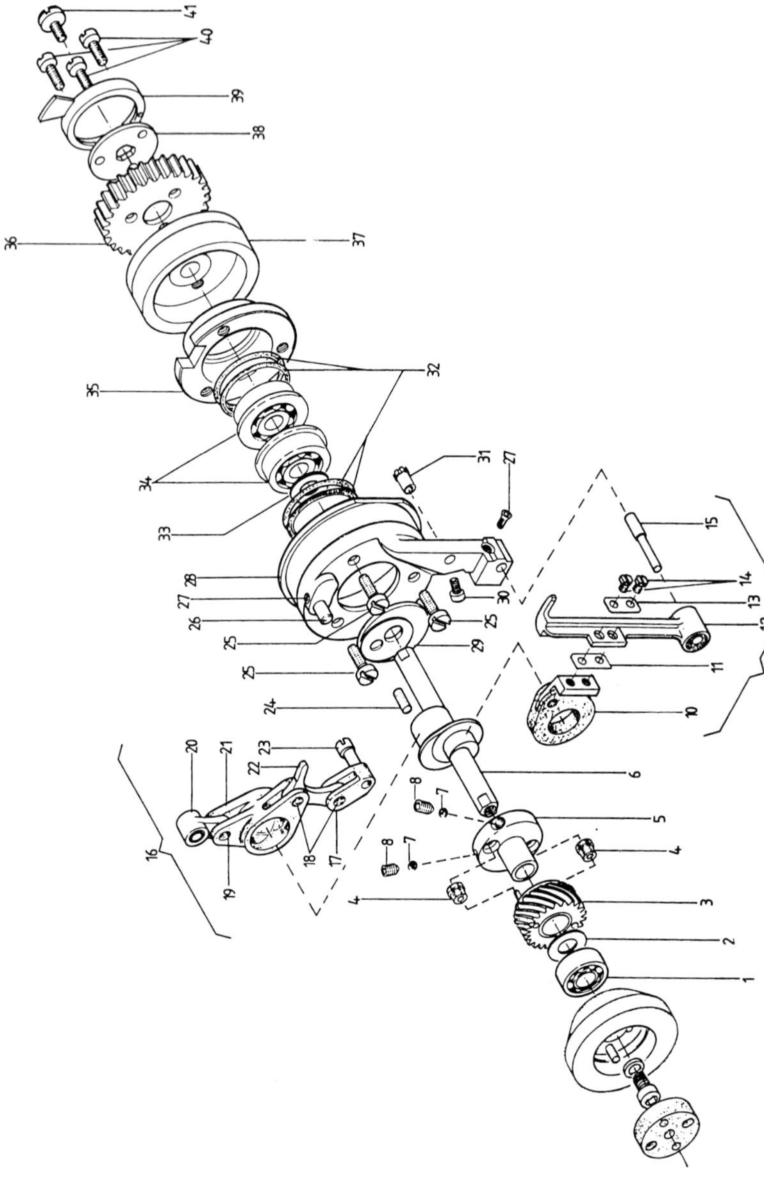

Exploded View of Movement

Electronic Accessories

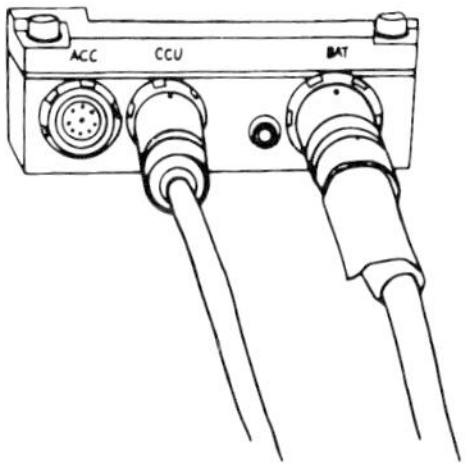

There are 3 receptacles at the back of the camera. The extreme right one is for power. The others are for electronic accessories and controls.

Most accessories plug into the **ACC** 9-pin Fischer Socket:

ICU Iris Control Unit
LCS Lens Control System
ESU External Sync Unit
RU Remote Unit—535 accessory, but works on SR3
VSU Variable Speed Unit—another 535 accessory
Timecode Input (jam syncing)
Timecode Output when camera is in standby (as a Master Clock)

Anything with a brain plugs into the **CCU** 8-pin receptacle:

CCU (Camera Control Unit)
LCC (Laptop Camera Controller – Mac Powerbook)
RCU-1 (Remote Control Unit)
Continuous Timecode Output

Color Coding and Labeling

With electronic accessories, you will be the guardian of more cables than the sound department. Two things will help.

Color code each accessory and its corresponding cables with a unique colored tape. For example, when using the ICU and RCU together, attach blue tape to all the cables and things associated with the task. Use red tape on the Lens Control System, cables and motors. Some components will have more than one tape.

Next, write down the function of each cable on the tape. For example: "RCU to 16 SR3 CCU." "ICU to 16 SR3 ACC." Etc.

Rental houses gain great favor by tagging each cable with self-laminating labels: 3M Write-On Tape Labels, ZipTape Rite & Wrap, or Brady Lasertab Cable Markers. See Appendix.

RCU - Remote Control Unit

The RCU handles most functions that formerly could only be done with a CCU or LCC.

You can operate the camera on a remote head with a 20m long (60') KC41 cable, and have the RCU display all data and control Start/Stop.

The RCU also controls speeds and speed changes, so you can continuously vary your frame rate while an Iris Control Unit adjusts the aperture.

In the **Arriflex 16 SR3 Intro** film, we filmed the Silverthorne horse sequence beginning at 24 fps, and continuously ramped up to 150 fps, while the iris corrected from T11 at 24 fps to T4.5 at 150 fps.

Functions on the RCU designated with the angle symbol ∢ are unique to the 535 and 435, which have electronically variable shutters. An error "no" displays when trying those features with a 16 SR3.

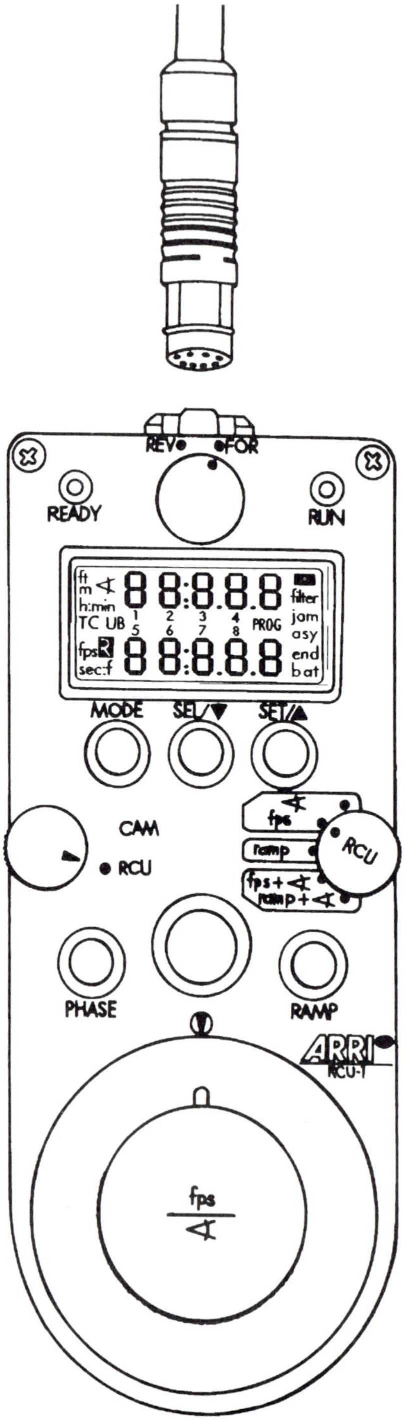

Connecting RCU

Turn off the main camera switch. Plug the RCU into the CCU receptacle at the rear of the camera (8-pin). The standard KC39 cable is 1.5m long (4 ½').

CAM Camera Setting

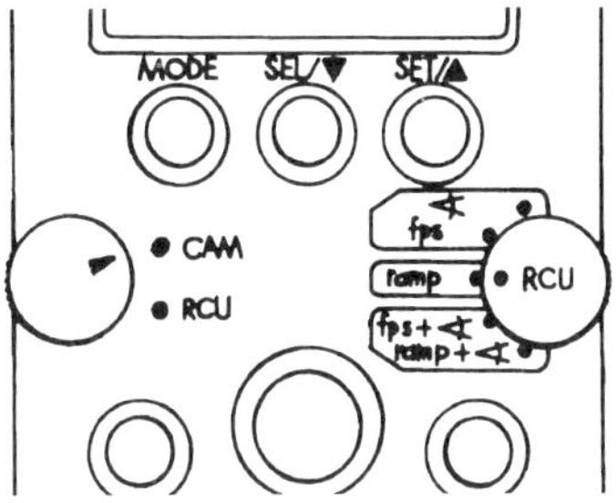

Set the CAM-RCU switch to CAM. That means the remote control unit's display will be the same as the camera's. If the CAM-RCU switch is set to RCU when you first plug in, you might re-program your Main Display to whatever values had been previously stored in the RCU. RCU settings override Camera Settings.

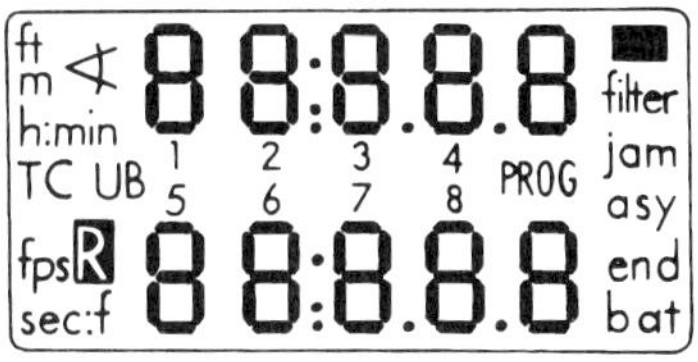

Turn the camera's main power switch ON. The Ready LED and the LCD display mimic the one on the camera.

One critical difference is that even if the **LOCK** slider on the camera is locked to the right to prevent changing speed or footage with the **SEL** button, pushing **SEL** on the RCU will
over-ride the mechanical lockout.

RCU Remote fps Speed Control

Turn the left-hand selector switch to the RCU setting. If you get a flashing warning "not PSCCU," you forgot to switch the slider from "NORM" to "PS/CCU" next to the MODE button on the camera.

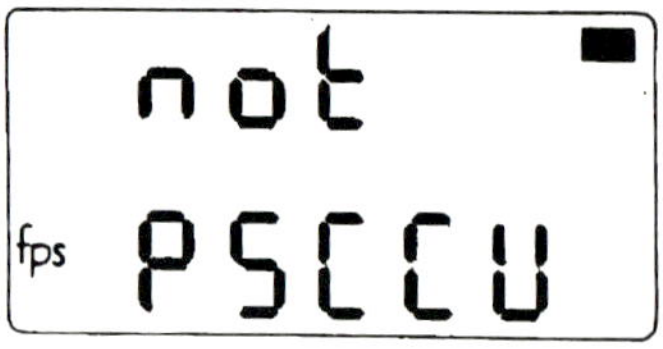

Turn the right-hand selector dial—**RCU**—to the **fps** position.

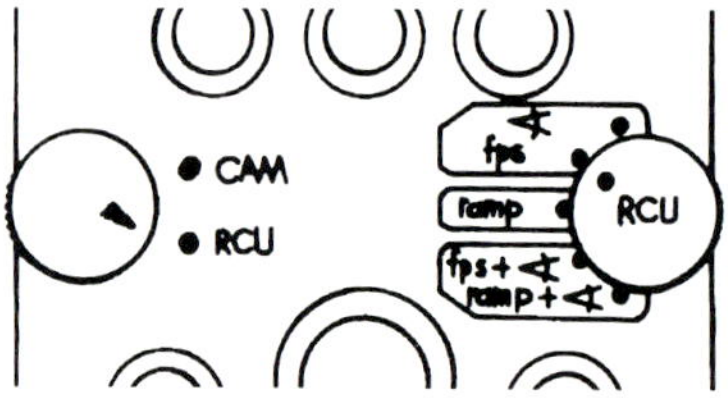

The top line of the display will display "**SPEEd**" and the bottom line will show the fps rate.

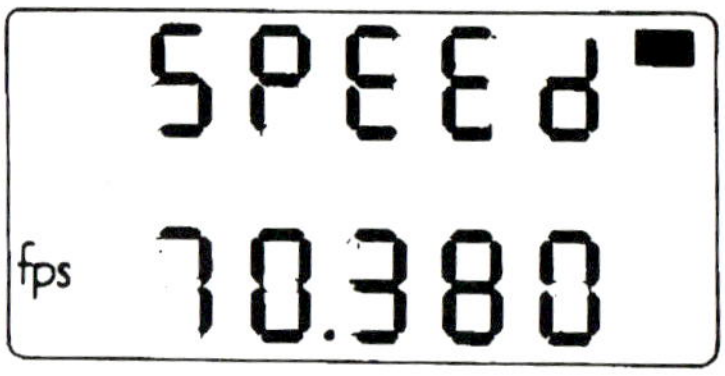

Since the RCU remembers its last setting, you may get an error message: "**SPEEd rAnGE**".

That means the previously stored setting is faster than the maximum speed of the 16 SR3 you are currently using. For example, if you set the speed to 150 fps for use on a Highspeed camera, and then use the same control on a regular one, you will get this error message.

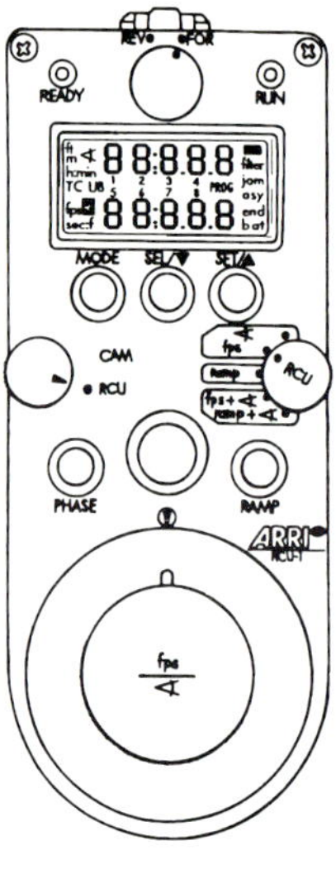

Turn the large **fps/**◁ dial until a valid speed displays.

The camera will run at that speed.

If you switch back to **CAM**, or unplug the **RCU**, the camera will continue to run at that speed until reprogrammed, or until you switch the speed select slider back from **PC/CCU** to **NORM**.

By the way, the black rectangle in the upper right corner of the display is the "home page" for each mode.

Setting fps end stops

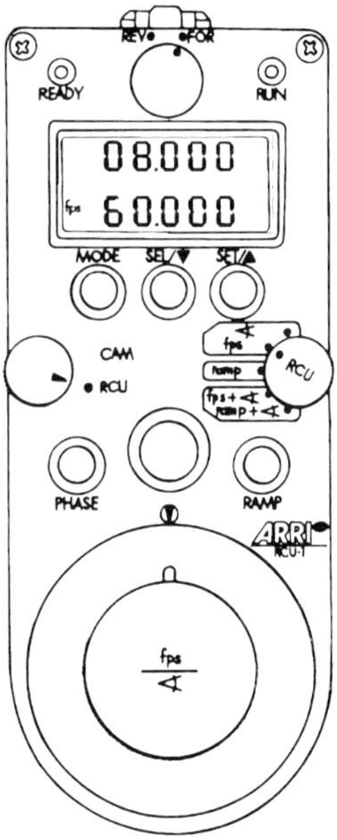

If you cannot access the entire speed range of the camera, electronic "end stops" have already been entered into your RCU. You can reset the end stops as follows.

Press **MODE** once. We're out of home page. The upper right black rectangle is gone.

Press **SEL** (select) for about two seconds—until the upper left digits blink. The top line is the low speed limit.

Turn the large **fps/**∢ dial to set your minimum speed. At this point, you can press **SET** to go directly to the high speed limit, or press **SEL** again to set 1/100ths fps. Press **SEL** yet again to go to 1/1000ths fps.

Either way, you get to the bottom row—the upper speed limit. Set it the same way.

Speed Ramp

Instead of dialing a speed change by hand, you can program the RCU to “ramp” up or down over a predetermined time period.

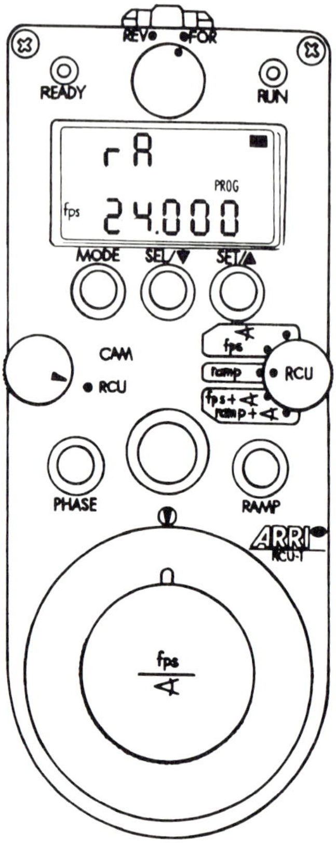

When you first turn the **RCU** selector to **ramp**, the home page (black rectangle) displays “**rA**” and the preset speed at which the camera will begin to run. To check or reset the ramping program, push **MODE** once.

Set the low and high speeds the same way as the electronic end stops. If you desire, you can set a high speed first, followed by a low speed.

Recap: Push **SEL** for about 2 seconds. Enter the speed with the dial. Press **SEL** or **SET** to enter each set of numbers.

After the high and low speeds are entered, push MODE again to view the ramp duration that has been stored.

To change the ramp duration, push **SEL** for 2 seconds. The lower line says **AUtO**. If you push **SET**, the shortest possible duration is automatically calculated and displayed. If you want that setting, press **MODE** again to view the screen time of the programmed ramp.

If you want to manually set a ramp (highly recommended), push **SEL** for 2 seconds when you see **AUtO** flash.

Enter a time in seconds by turning the dial. Push **SEL** again to enter decimal places. Push **SET** to lock it in.

Check the resulting screen time by pushing **MODE** again. Press **MODE** one more time to get back to the home page.

ICU (Iris Control Unit) + RCU (Remote Control Unit)

All these speed changes are pretty silly unless you have an Iris Control Unit or a very accurate wrist to compensate exposure. Setting up the ICU is pretty simple, made difficult only by the numerous permutations of cables available.

To cut to the chase, you only need 3 cables and 3 devices to use the ICU and RSU together for speed-iris changes on a 16 SR3:

> 8-pin female to 8-pin male cable (KC-39) connects RCU to 16 SR3 **CCU** receptacle (at rear of camera.)
>
> 16-pin male to 9-pin female cable (LC-D1) connects ICU to 16 SR3 **ACC** receptacle.
>
> 5-pin male to 5-pin male cable (LC-M1) connects ICU to either of the two receptacles on the Lens Motor (CLM).

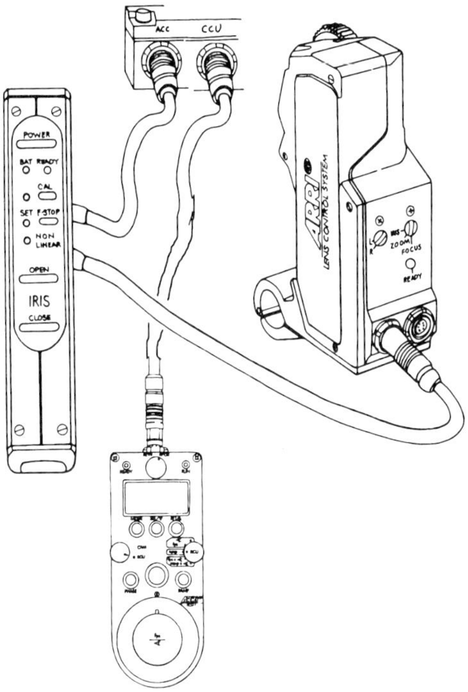

Setting up the ICU

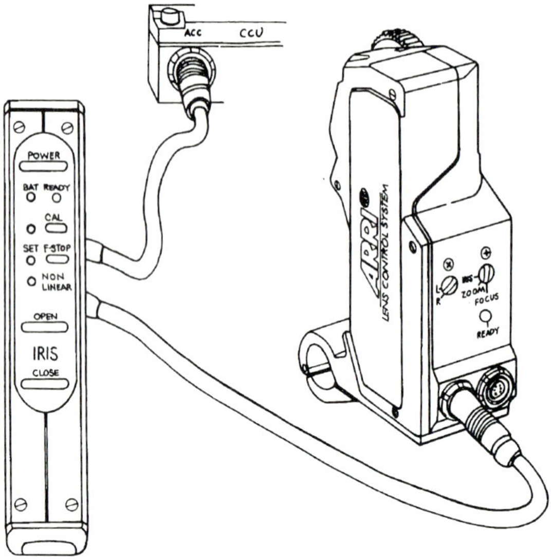

1. Turn the main camera power switch off.
2. Attach the cables.
3. Position the Lens Motor (CLM) on the lens rods.
4. Turn the **IRIS-ZOOM-FOCUS** switch to **IRIS**.
5. Set the other switch to **L** or **R** depending on whether you have mounted the motor on the camera left or camera right side.

6. Power up the camera. The RCU should be on, with a steady green **READY** light.

7. Push the ICU's **CLOSE** and **POWER** button simultaneously. The **SET F-STOP** and **NON LINEAR** LED's will slowly flash. Powering up the unit this way sets it to a slower feedback response time than just pushing the **POWER** button alone, and eliminates the disconcerting (but harmless) stuttering of the lens aperture.

8. The **READY** LED should slowly flash green.
The Lens Motor LED should glow a steady green.

9. Push the **CAL** button.
10. It sometimes helps to hold the motor against the lens: older EPROMS exert more force and the gears may disengage. The ICU calibrates the lens end stops.

11. Older EPROMS also do not have the slower feedback response option, so if your ICU exhibits stuttering or too much torque, have the EPROMS exchanged with newer ones.

Linear + Nonlinear Apertures

There are two types of lens irises: linear and nonlinear.

Linear irises have equal spaces between aperture settings. The Zeiss 11-110 is linear.

Linear

Use the **CLOSE** button to first close the lens all the way down, and then the **OPEN** button to set the lens to its widest full F or
T-stop. On the 11-110, set the lens to T2.8. (T2.2, the widest setting, is not a full T-stop—it is a fractional setting above T2.0). You close and then open to make sure the iris leaves work smoothly.

Next, press and keep holding down the **F-STOP** button while pushing **CLOSE** to stop the lens down 4 stops. On the 11-110, this would be T11.

If you overshoot, keep holding the **F-STOP** button, and adjust with the **OPEN** button.

When you're there, release the **F-STOP** button.

Nonlinear

To calibrate non-linear lenses, use the **CLOSE** and **OPEN** buttons as before to first close the lens down all the way and then open up to the widest full T-stop.

Keeping the **F-STOP** button held down, push the **CAL** button to memorize the first full aperture stop. The **NON LINEAR** green LED will flash.

Still keeping the **F-STOP** button held down, press **CLOSE** to set the iris ring to each full F or T-stop. Stop at each full setting, and briefly press **CAL**. Repeat for each full stop (minumum=2, maximum=12). The green **NON LINEAR** LED goes out while you press CAL, and flashes green until you release **F-STOP**, at which time it will remain a steady green if the procedure was done correctly.

Running the ICU and RCU

From now on, use OPEN and CLOSE to adjust your aperture. If you need to open all the way—to check focus, for example—press the blue micro-switch near the cable receptacles.

Now roll camera, and dial in your speed change.

Be aware that you cannot test the speed-iris operation unless the camera is running. You may want to check it out first by removing the magazine to avoid wasting film.

You have to plan ahead to know how fast you will be ramping, and wide open your lens will be correcting. You don't want to hit 150 fps and find out the iris motor has reached its end stop.

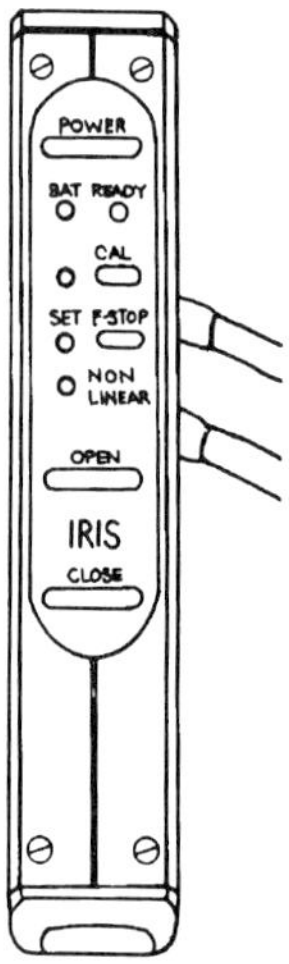

Also, remember that you must re-calibrate the ICU whenever you change lenses, lose power or unplug cables. Also, if the relationship changes between the gear of the lens motor and the iris gear on the lens itself (for example, you swing the motor away), you must recalibrate.

LCS - Lens Control System

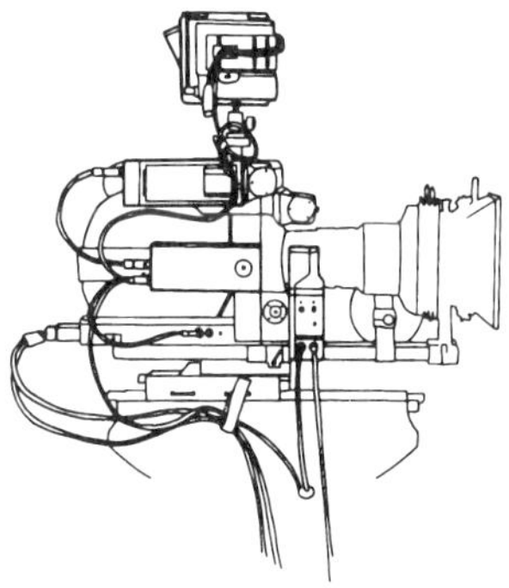

The LCS is a modular system for remote control of iris, zoom or focus in any permutation. A very useful feature is the modular, programmable memory unit, which can take some of the tedium out of very precise tabletop product shots. You can use it as a simple "motion control" device for blue-screen zooms, or hook the zoom motor up to an ARRIHEAD with gears instead of handwheels for repeatable pans and tilts.

Up to 3 lens motors (same as the ICU) attach to the camera's support rods. Keep your cables neat with Rip-Ties. And as we've noted, color code and label each cable.

Although ARRI prints a good instruction manual for the LCS, here's a quick five minute rental house rescue.

You've just opened up the case marked "LCS," and you are looking at more cables than you've ever seen before. Let's start with the simplest configuration: a zoom motor and zoom control.

LCS: Zoom Control Only

Pull all the cables out of the case, and look for these two: **LC-M1** and **LC-S3** (has a small metal box in the middle)

> **LC-M1:** 5-pin male to 5-pin male cable connects the Lens Control System ZMU (zoom motor unit) to the Lens Motor CLM.
>
> **LC-S3:** 5-pin male to metal box to 9-pin male cable connects the Lens Motor to the 9-pin **ACC** receptacle (rear of the 16 SR3), with another cable from the metal box to a 3 pin XLR to connect to a battery.

The Zoom Control plugs into the Lens Motor which plugs into the camera.

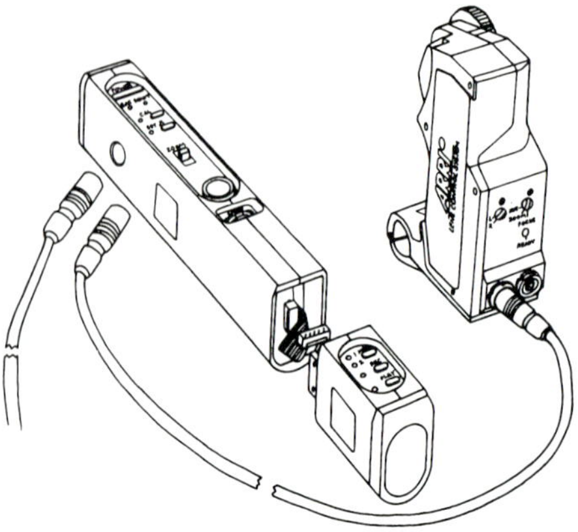

Set the zoom motor dials to **ZOOM,** and **L** or **R** for camera right or left, depending on how you have it mounted.

Turn the zoom control power ON.

Push **CAL** to calibrate the end stops. You should calibrate whenever you change lenses or power down. Calibrating the end settings prevents damage to the lens from hard mechanical stops.

If you must begin or end your zoom at critical focal lengths, program a reduced zoom range. Use the **ZOOM** lever to go to your first focal length. Press **SET**, and keep holding it in while zooming to your second lens setting. Release the **SET** button. The **SET** LED will glow green. To erase the setting, press **SET** for a couple of seconds.

To store zooms, a MEM memory module must be attached to the bottom of the ZMU control unit. Select a memory storage location **1** or **2** by pushing the **MEM** button.

Press **REC** to initialize. The green record LED flashes. Press **REC** again. The green REC LED stays on, meaning that you are recording. Do your zoom. Press **REC** one last time to stop recording.

To play back, select the memory location with the **MEM** button.
Press **PLAY**. The green PLAY LED flashes, and the lens moves to its first position. Press **PLAY** again to start the move. The move ends when the steady green PLAY LED goes out, or you hit **PLAY** one last time to end the sequence.

Zoom and Focus and Iris

When using more than one lens motor, use a different cable system than described above, because the combined load may be too much to run directly from the camera.

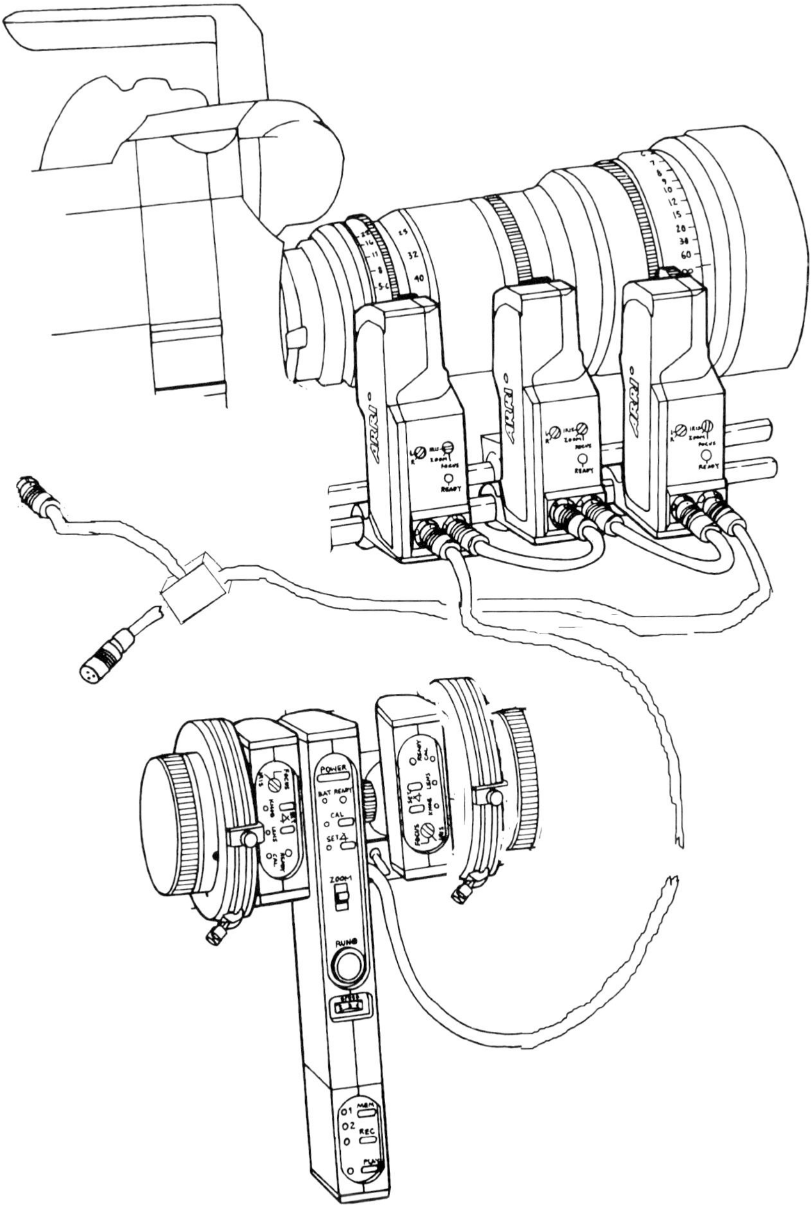

LC-S1 connects via a 3 pin XLR male to the 24 volt battery. The other end of the LC-S1 has a 5-pin male, which goes to the lens motor. In the middle of the cable is a box, to which you connect a LC-C1 6-pin male cable, the other end of which has a 9-pin male end to plug into the **ACC** socket of the camera for remote Start/Stop.

You can daisy chain up to three lens motors using various lengths of 5-pin male to 5-pin male cables (LC-M1 is 3 feet long, LC-M2 is a few inches) plugged into the 5-pin motor receptacles.

Use another LC-M1 5-pin male to 5-pin male cable to connect between the final zoom motor in the daisy chain and the ZMU Lens Control System.

If the camera is being used on a Powerpod, Hot Head or other remote head, there are longer cables:

LC-Z1	11½'	5-pin male to 5-pin male
LC-Z2	23'	"
LC-E1	246' extension cable	

Finally, you must connect a Focus/Iris Control dial (FIU) to the Lens Control System ZMU. Use the 10-pin male to 10-pin male LC-F1 cable. Use a second cable to daisy chain a second FIU dial. Make sure all corresponding dials, controls and motors are set to focus, iris or zoom.

Power up the ZMU. Press **CAL** to calibrate all the motors.

For finer adjustment of smaller focus ranges (i.e. a critical close-up on an actor from 3 to 6 feet), adjust the focus knob manually to the first setting—say 3 feet.

Press **SET LENS**, and keep holding while you turn the dial to the second position on the lens—6 feet in our example. The green LED flashes.

Release the button to save the range. The green LED stays on.

To erase, push **SET LENS** for a few seconds. The light will flash until you release the button, after which it should stay out.

If you have pre-calibrated focus disks—either for this unit or from your regular follow focus—they can be matched to the electronics of the Focus/Iris Unit.

Position the mechanical stops at the beginning and end positions corresponding to the disk.

Turn the dial clockwise to the first mark.

Press **SET KNOB.** The green LED flashes.

Keep the button pushed in while you turn the dial to the second stop.

Release the button. The LED should glow a steady green.

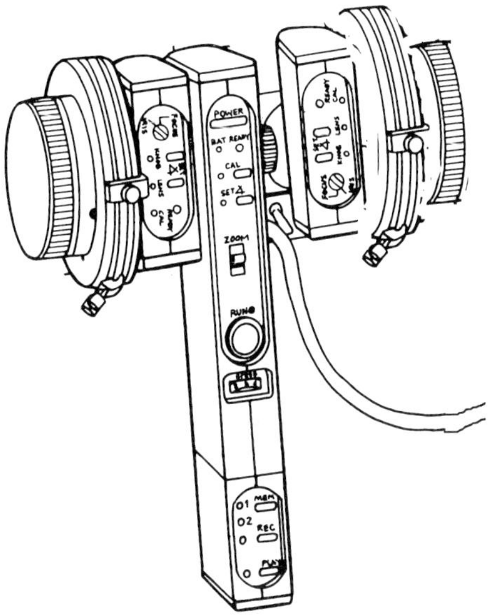

ESU - External Sync Unit

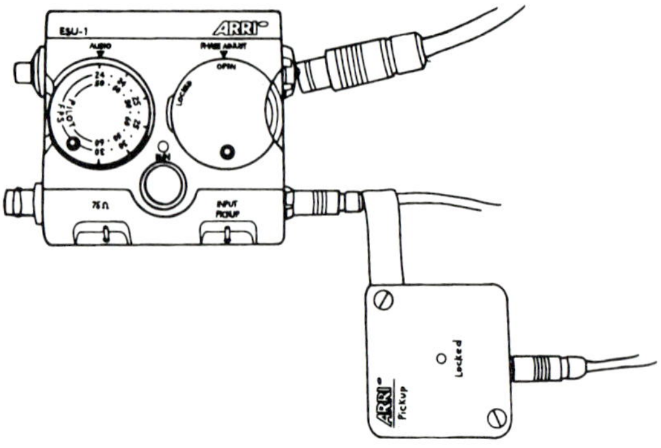

The ESU synchronizes the 16 SR3 (and 535, 535B, 435) to a video monitor to eliminate roll-bars.

Turn the main camera power switch OFF.
Plug the ESU into the camera's 9-pin ACC socket with cable KC-33 (9-pin male to 9-pin male).

Set the 3-position **INPUT PICKUP** switch to the middle position.

Plug the remote pickup into the ESU (4-pin male to 4-pin female—long, thin KC-32 cable)

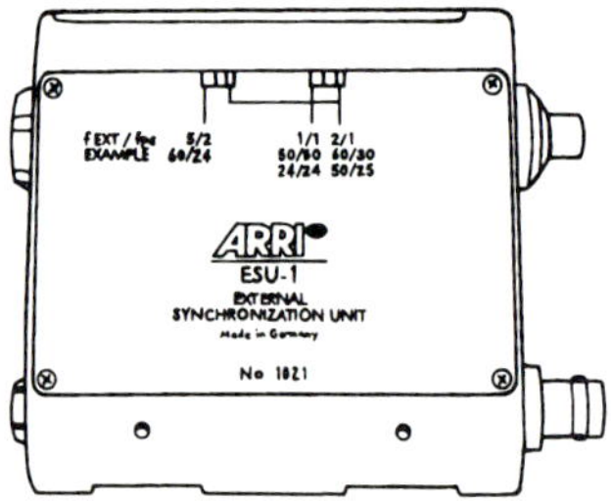

Turn the ESU over. The switches on the back determine the ratio of electronic fields to frame rate. An NTSC television monitor scans at 59.94, and you usually film it at 29.97. There are 2 electronic fields for every one field exposed on film (the other field is seen in the eyepiece). So, with a pointed tool, push both red slide switches to the right: to the 2/1 position.

PAL television is 50 Hz / 25 fps: the same 2:1 ratio.

Many computer graphics monitors have a scan rate of about 70 Hz., which you will shoot at around 35 fps. Also a 2:1 ratio.

Turn the main power switch ON.

Place the remote pickup on the video monitor you plan to shoot. Shielded computer monitors are tricky; you may have to move it around a bit. The red LED on the pickup will illuminate when it detects a signal. Often the rear or bottom of the monitor works best.

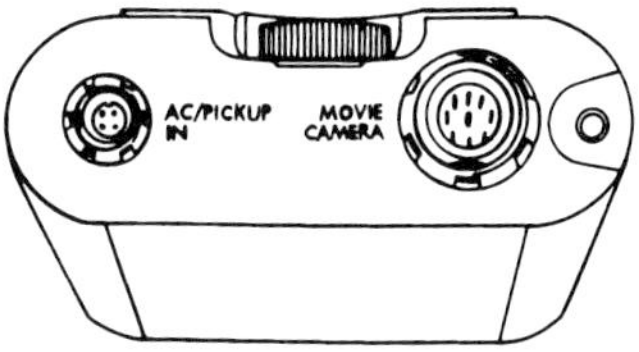

You do not have to switch the camera's NORM - PS/CCU switch to PS/CCU. It will work in either position. *ESU* should be displayed next to *FPS* on the bottom line of the camera's LCD display.

Press the MODE button once to go to 2nd Mode. *ESU* jumps to the top line, with the frame rate displayed on the bottom line. If the number jumps around wildly, play with the red slide switches on the back.

If there is no signal, the camera's main status LED will be red. The camera will not start. If the **INPUT PICKUP** switch points to
AC or **VIDEO**, the status LED will also glow red.

Next, remove the magazine so you do not waste film.

Rotate the PHASE ADJUST cover on the ESU open.

Run the camera. Look through the finder. You can start and stop the camera from the ESU.

Turn the PHASE ADJUST wheel until the monitor's roll bar is out of frame.

Rotate the PHASE ADJUST cover back to LOCKED.

Now you can start and stop the camera, and the roll bar will automatically be placed out of the shot.

You can also feed the video signal directly into the ESU via the BNC connector. Make sure the 75Ω terminating switch is set to ON.

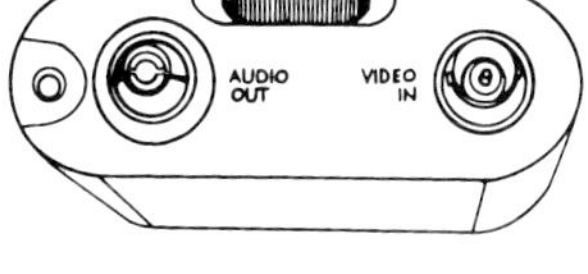

Filming Monitors without the ESU

NTSC Monitors (North America, Japan, etc.) can be filmed with a preset speed of 29.97 fps. PAL Monitors (Europe, etc) can be shot at 25 fps.

In the 1st Mode (Home Page), push SEL until 29.97 flashes: for NTSC (or 25.00 for PAL). Push SET.

Roll camera. Push PHASE until the roll bar goes out of frame. If you are having trouble, chances are that the monitor is being fed by an unstable tape deck (which is what determines the frame accuracy). In that case, you're better off with an ESU.

If you are filming a computer monitor, you can determine its frequency by holding a Cinematography Electronics Cine-Check against the screen. Set the frame rate in PS (Mode 2). Shoot. Push PHASE to eliminate the roll bar.

Cinematography Electronics Synchronizer

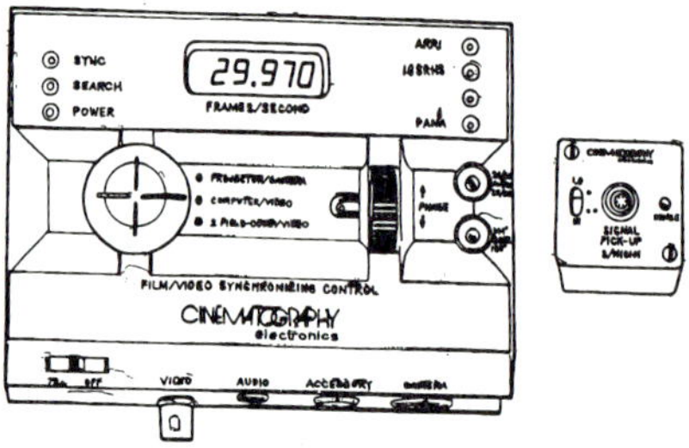

No discussion about filming monitors would be complete without mentioning Larry Barton's Cinematography Electronics Film/Video Synchronizer. It is so widely used that little explanation is necessary, unless of course, you want to read more about it in the ever popular ARRI 35 Book.

Its remote pickup has a high and low setting, making it ideal for filming well-shielded monitors.

CCU - Camera Control Unit

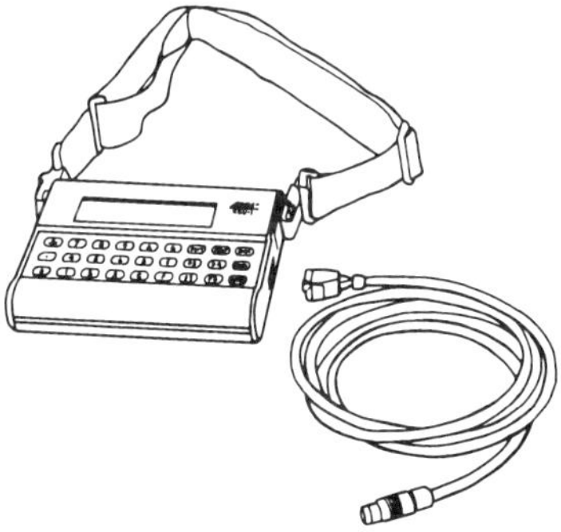

The Camera Control Unit is an older remote control unit that largely has been replaced by the RCU. One of the few areas in which the CCU outperforms the RCU is in its ability to set timecode and User Bits. User Bits can identify camera or date. For example, Camera "A" on August 3, 1996 could be displayed as:

08:03
96:CA

User bits may only contain the numbers 0-9 or letters A-F.

LCC - Laptop Camera Controller

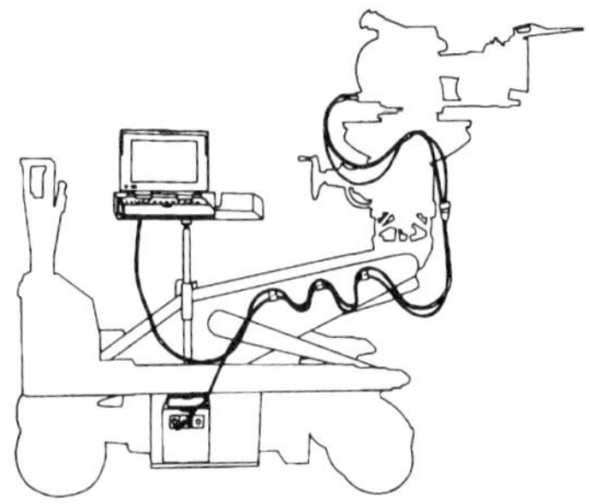

The Laptop Camera Controller does everything the CCU does and more—using an off-the-shelf Mac Powerbook. Arriflex distributes the software, cables and an excellent manual by Marc Shipman-Mueller, who also designed the software. Pictured at right is a place to put the computer—the RAM Desk, designed by Steve Ramsey and built by J.L. Fisher.

By the time you read this, a Windows version of the program should be out.

The program has a "virtual camera" function, so you can practice without a camera.

There are many useful features. One of the best is a graphical display of speed-change programs. You can set speed ramps over time intervals, have the iris compensate exposure, and store all the settings for use again at a later time.

The LCC also creates automatic camera reports. Plug the LCC into your 16 SR3, and every time you start up the camera, Scene, Take, Timecode, Frame Rate and other pertinent information will be recorded for later printout.

This is an example of what the display looks like.

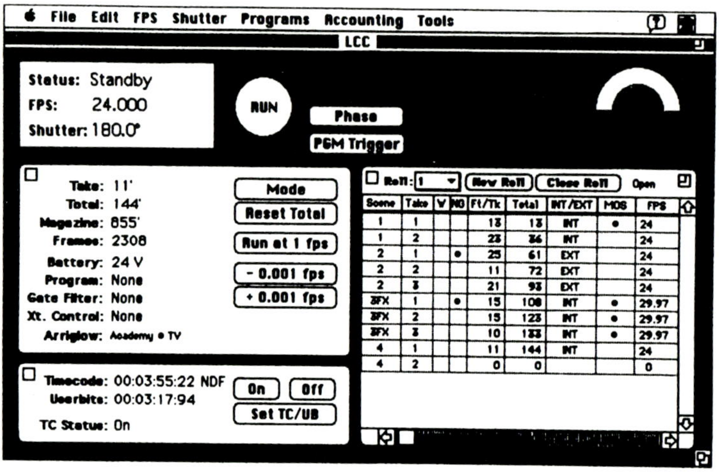

24 to 12 volt Adapter

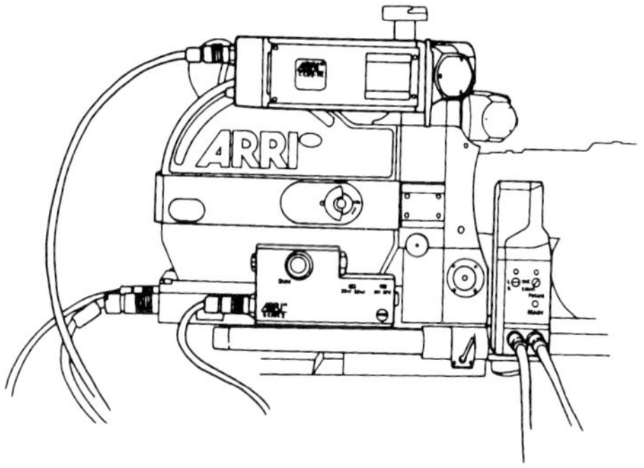

ARRI's DC/DC-2 plugs into the two RS receptacles on the camera right side, and attaches with a silver thumbscrew.

It provides camera right start/stop by pushing the green RUN button.

There are two 11 pin Fischer receptacles for 12 volt accessories (like Microforce zoom controls /motors, lens lights, and some video taps). Pin 1 is ground. Pin 11 is +12v. The ON/OFF slide switch controls the 11 pin Fischer receptacles only—not the 3 pins. A green light indicates on.

The two RS ports are replicated. Pin 1 is ground. Pin 2 is +24v. Pin 3 provides remote on/off functions when using a momentary switch .

The 22W - 60W slide switch limits output current to the 12 volt Fischer receptacles. When using camera electronics prior to E3/4 (your electronic vintage is engraved below the serial number on the camera right side) slide the switch to 22W (1.8 amps at 12 volts) . That will protect the camera's circuitry on earlier models. Running a video tap and an on-board monitor can draw over 2 ½ amps.

RU - Remote Unit

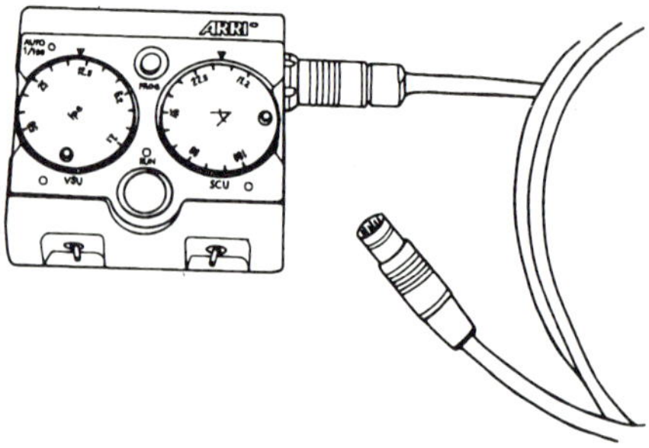

The RU-1, shown here, was built for the ARRI 535. You can probably find a used one very cheaply, since the RCU-1 replaced it. There are two dials. You'll only use the Speed Dial, with the toggle switch set to VSU (variable speed unit). Although the left-hand scale is calibrated to 50 fps, this device will control your 16 SR3 throughout its speed range—normal or Highspeed. You must watch the camera's LCD display, and re-calibrate the dial. The shutter control will not function.

VSU - Variable Speed Unit

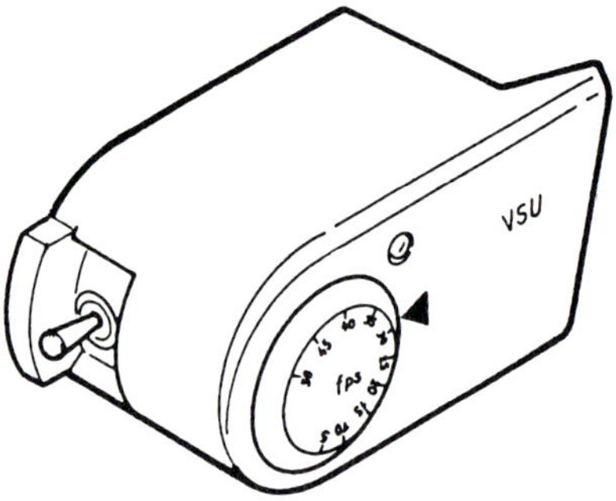

Another good used item (replaced by the RCU) is the VSU from a 535. This was a tiny dial that plugged into the back of the camera, and also controlled the speed. It was so small, most of us could never find it. Weighing just a few ounces, it should find a useful afterlife on documentary, expedition and wildlife shoots. If you find one, have an Arriflex service shop wire up a short cable, and Velcro the VSU to the side of the camera.

Other Accessories

This very lightweight French Flag, made of plastic, will not mash your mattebox, and is great for keeping lights and flares out of your lens. Made by the Clamping French Flag Company in Boulder, CO.

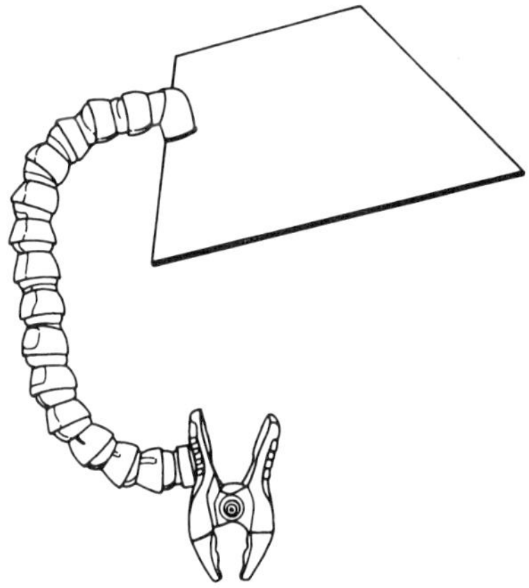

PACE and Hydroflex manufacture underwater housings for the 16 SR3.

No matter what housing you use, be sure to test it first: submerge it without the camera inside.

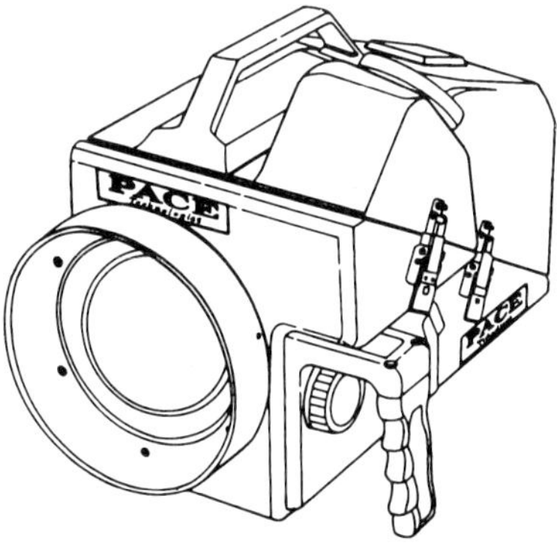

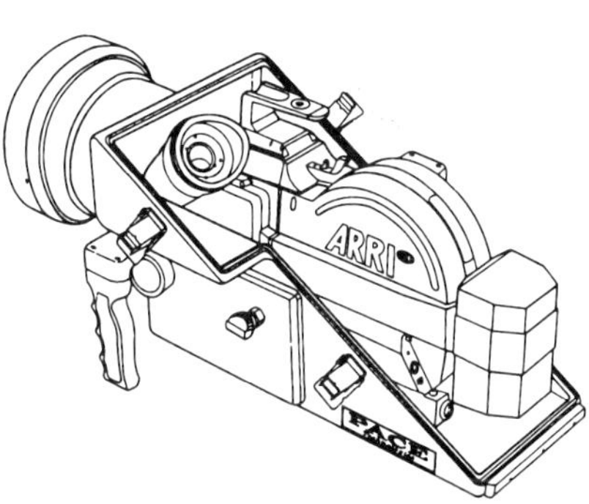

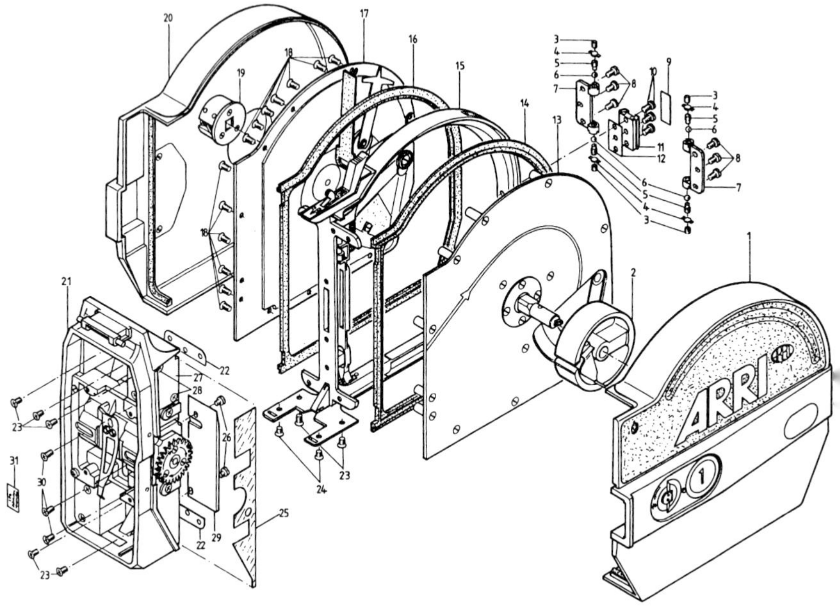

Exploded View of Magazine

Timecode

Jump Start

1. Set timecode sensitivity on the mag.
2. Set camera speed to 24, or 30, fps.
3. Set the sound recorder to 30 fps non drop frame.
4. If you are shooting at 23.97 or 29.97 fps, the sound recorder should be set to 29.97 fps non drop frame. If you are shooting at 25 fps, set the recorder to 25 fps non drop frame.
5. Connect the camera with the sound recorder by plugging the jam-sync cable into the 9 pin Fischer **ACC** receptacle at the back of the 16 SR3.
6. Wait a couple of seconds. Unplug.
7. You should see "*TC*" in the camera's LCD display.

Theory of Timecode

The notion of timecode for film is pretty simple. Every frame we shoot is assigned an hour, minute, second and frame—based on the time of day. An accurate crystal-controlled glorified wristwatch keeps the time. There's a timepiece in the camera, one in the sound recorder, one attached to the electronic slate and in anything else that runs concurrently and must be frame accurate: video recorders, script loggers, Avid Media Location Recorders, and Master Clocks. In the 16 SR3 (and 535, 435), timecode is optically exposed as a barcode on the film by an LED. In audio devices, timecode is recorded electronically onto the magnetic tape.

Why use timecode?

In-camera timecode identifies every frame of film as it is being exposed during production. This information can be used for logging, slaving, and syncing.

The script supervisor, equipped with a timecode display clipboard, can log timecode numbers. This is already commonly done in video production, but has not yet caught on in our film world. The clipboard is jam synced along with all the other timecode devices. It speeds up locating footage in the editing suite, where the editor simply types in a timecode number, and the Avid or other electronic editing device can automatically locate that frame immediately.

The script supervisor can still assign scene and take numbers on the script notes. However, production can be simplified since the camera assistant theoretically would no longer have to write down scene and take number on the slate, as long as it is an electronic one displaying the same timecode numbers as the camera and script logger.

Video assist can use the same timecode numbers, and editing can begin immediately from the video assist image. The editor can then replace the selected scenes with higher quality picture from the dailies when they arrive. Since only selected takes would have to be digitized, telecines suites equipped with Avid's Media Recorder can save on hard-drive space using the script supervisor's timecode numbers.

Timecode is can speed up editing and post production, because it can be linked to a computer for in-depth logging and identification of every frame. This can be very helpful in projects with many effects and opticals, where it is essential to keep track of every frame.

Since the timecode is a visible barcode which few of us could figure out without the help of a machine, information about each frame is obtained by passing the film under a "reader head" consisting of rollers and an optical sensor that "reads" the barcode on the film and converts it back into hours-minutes-seconds-frames.

Timecode can also help sync dailies automatically. When the film travels through a reader head in the telecine machine, the timecode of each film frame is read, and can be "chased" by the audio tape, which has the same timecode numbers, thus synchronizing automatically.

Synchronize your watches.

Remember all those scenes in action films, when the hero says "OK, let's synchronize our watches?" It's usually just before they blow up the bridge. Everyone pushes a little button on the trusty military watch when he says "On my mark, three, two, one, now." It is hoped that this synchronizing will enable critical things to happen at the same time.

Synchronize your cameras

But lip syncing and frame identification must be even more accurate than that—in fact, they should not waiver by one frame in eight hours.

Before synchronizing camera, sound, video, electronic slate and anything else, we determine that one device is the master clock—the known quantity, the reference standard. Often this is the sound recorder, because usually the sound recordist is the only one on the set who really understands timecode, probably the result of having read a manual by Mike Denecke (Father Time) or Manfred Klemme.

To synchronize the camera, we run a cable from the master clock (often the sound recorder) to the camera, plug it into the 9 pin **ACC** Fischer connector on the back of the 16 SR3 for a few seconds, and then unplug. The jargon for this is "jam syncing" or "jamming." All the other devices that must be jammed are connected in the same way.

Although the 16 SR3 is accurate for eight hours because it's crystal is temperature stabilized, you still should re-jam every few hours. Extremes in temperatures can make crystals differ. Nagras are usually as stable as the camera, but some DAT machines are less stable than others.

29.97002617 fps

That is the theory, and it is wonderfully simple in Europe where you shoot film at 25 fps and transfer to tape at 25 fps. Not so in the world of NTSC, where film shot at 24 fps (or any other rate) is transferred at a mind boggling speed of 29.97002617 fps.

Now we get into arcane and obfuscatory theory, like relativity, which can only be clearly explained by six people, but which is essential to everything we do.

Timecode probably would have been much simpler had the NTSC standard not been created by the ancestors of the infamous committee of television engineers who dreamed up the mysterious formula of 1.77:1 as the baffling standard for high definition television, which we would all surely be watching by now in a more practical format, had they only noted that never in the history of motion pictures has anything ever been shot in 1.77:1.

How does the NTSC system transfer film at 29.976 frames per second? What is a 976/1000th of a frame? Is it most of the frame—without the frameline? The film is running at 30 whole, complete, un-fractioned frames in 1.0008 seconds. That adds 3.6 seconds in one hour. And that is why television stations use "drop frame" code to reconcile the extra 108 frames per hour.

ARRI Code

ARRI Code is exposed along the edge of the film opposite the sprockets. It is a machine readable continuous barcode. When properly exposed, the barcode should be contrasty, with clearly defined spaces between the solid bars.

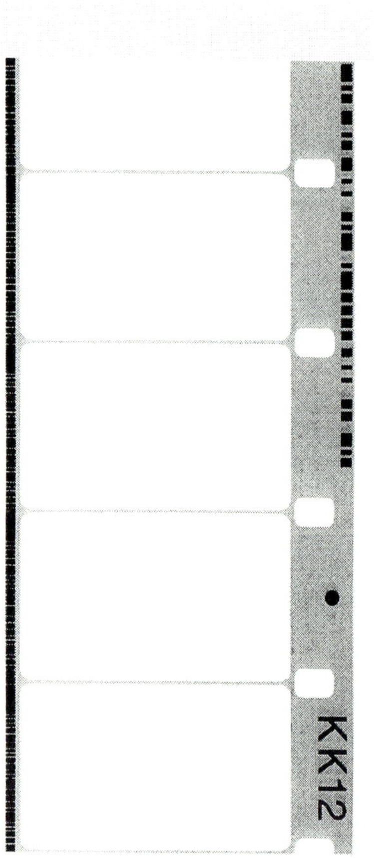

The barcode's binary information identifies each frame's hour, minute, second and frame number. For example, if you are shooting at 24 fps, the frames are numbered 0 through 23.

The barcode also has room for 8 bits (places) of user-entered information (8 numbers 0-9 or letters A-F). These 8 bits would let you enter the date and camera number, for example, as 08:03:95:C1.

The information on the other side of the film, along the sprockets, takes the form of regular readable numbers and machine readable keycode, which is exposed on the film as a latent image during manufacturing. (The information shows up when the film is processed.) The keycode appears twice every foot, and contains manufacturer identification, film type, footage and offset from a reference mark, which appears every foot. By the way, if keycode were readable during filming, we probably wouldn't need timecode.

Before using timecode, check with your the lab to be sure they have a timecode reader. It is also prudent to check with your lab to make sure they can read ARRICODE.

Timecode Preparation

Like the celestial bodies, a number of propitious events must be in your favor for timecode to work. There are 5 places gently conspiring against proper timecode.

Magazine Drive Gear

If there is any slop between the gear on the camera which drives the magazine, and the main gear on the magazine itself, the optically exposed timecode signal could be slightly blurred. Because timecode is "written" between the magazine drive gear and the take-up spindle, vibration or play between the gears may cause uneven tension in this area of the film.

If you are planning a timecode job, take the magazines to an Arriflex service facility. Have all your magazine drive gears adjusted to mesh tightly with the camera drive gear. If you have any chipped gears, replace them with the softer, honey-colored "Gummi Bear" consistency magazine drive gears. These replacement gears can be purchased, and will be less prone to chipping if the magazine is attached with inconsiderate force.

Clean Timecode Lenses, Glass and PSD

There are four remaining areas needing attention when using timecode. Clean with lens fluid and lens tissue in the following 4 locations:

1. Occasionally clean the timecode lens in the magazine, though it is quite difficult for the lens to become dirty in the first place. To clean it, swing out the little tray adjacent to where the film emerges from the throat into the feed side. In most instances, there is more chance of getting the lens dirty by opening it than just leaving it alone.

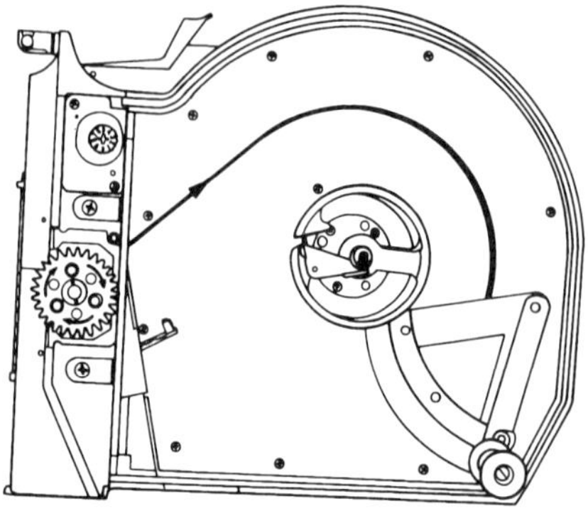

2. Clean the black infra-red glass at the bottom of the magazine. This passes light (at a frequency not sensitive to the film) from the Position Sensor Device (PSD): the LED's on the camera which measure the loop size and timecode offset from the gate.

3 & 4. Position Sensor Device (PSD). Below the gate, there are two green lenses. Keep them clean with lens tissue and lens fluid. They are the end-of-roll and timecode offset sensors. Infrared light (which is not exposed) measures the loop size of the film. Clean the LED emitter and the receiver.

Set Timecode Sensitivity on the Magazine

The timecode barcode is exposed onto the film by an LED in the magazine's throat. Since various film stocks must be exposed at different exposure levels, the LED must also be set to a proper exposure level.

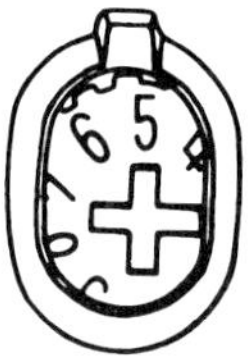

Use a small screwdriver to adjust the setting. This is where the mechanical footage counter used to be on SR1 and 2's. Setting "0" turns exposure off. The next page shows the timecode sensitivity number for each of the popular film emulsions.

Timecode Sensitivity Settings for 16 SR3

Film Stock Kodak	Name	Mfg's rec EI (ASA)	Type	Timecode Sensitivity Setting
7245	EXR 50D	50D	Color Neg	6
7248	EXR 100T	100T	Color Neg	6
7293	EXR 200T	200T	Color Neg	5
7287	EXR 7287	200-500T	Color Neg	6
7297	ECN 250D	250D	Color Neg	6
7298	EXR 500T	500T	Color Neg	4
7231	Plus-X	80D	B&W Neg	9
7222	Double-X	250D	B&W Neg	8
7240	Ektachrome	125T	Color Rev	6
7239	Ektachrome	160D	Color Rev	5
7250	Ektachrome	400T	Color Rev	5
7251	Ektachrome	400D	Color Rev	4
7296	EXR 7296	500T	Color Neg	5

Film Stock Fuji	Name	Mfg's rec EI (ASA)	Type	Timecode Sensitivity Setting
8621	F-64D	64D	Color Neg	6
8631	F-125	125T	Color Neg	6
8428		125T	Color Rev	6
8651	F-250	250T	Color Neg	4
8661	F-250D	250D	Color Neg	4
8670	F-500	500T	Color Neg	5

Timecode sensitivity chart as supplied by ARRI. Shoot a test to verify its accuracy.

Shoot a test that goes through the entire postproduction production as well, to verify that your code can be read all the way down the line, that the lab's reader heads are properly aligned, that the electronic timecode interfaces are working, that audio syncing can occur, and that enough pre-roll is provided on the audio tape for it to chase the picture in telecine. Finally, if you are shooting at 24fps, you want to be sure the telecine house has the appropriate box to convert 24fps timecode to video timecode

Jam Syncing the Camera

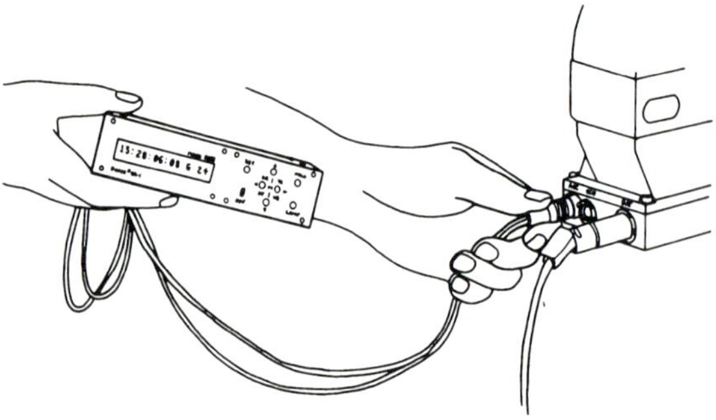

Here, a Denecke Dcode GR-1 Timecode Generator/Reader is working as a Master Clock to jam sync the camera with the same timecode as the sound recorder, the video assist recorder and the electronic slate.

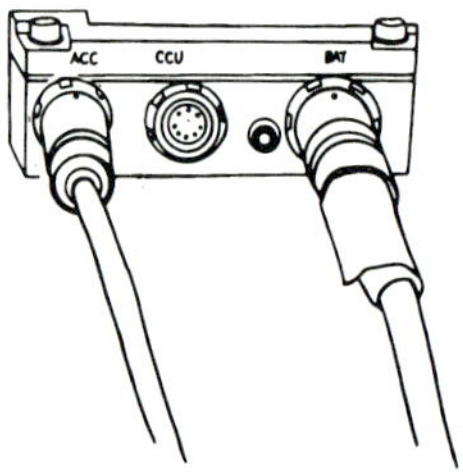

To jam the camera from an external source, such as a Master Clock or sound recorder, plug the jam sync cable into the 9 pin **ACC** receptacle at the back of the camera. Wait a few seconds, and unplug.

The cable usually has a 3 pin XLR connector at one end, and a 9 pin Fischer Male at the other.

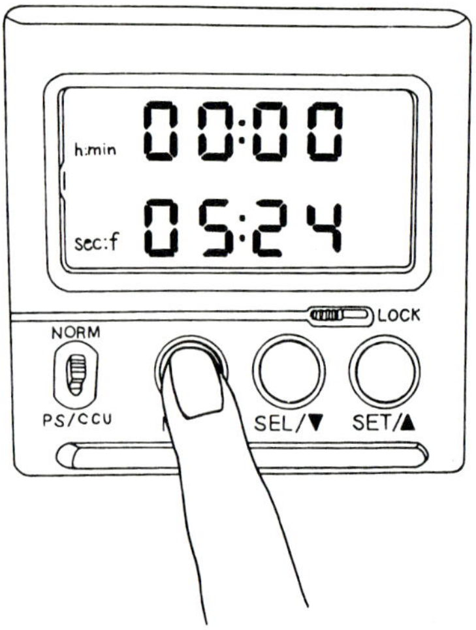

To check that the camera accepts the timecode, push the **MODE** button 3 times (from home position) to get to Timecode Mode 4.

When jamming, you will see TC EC for timecode external code.

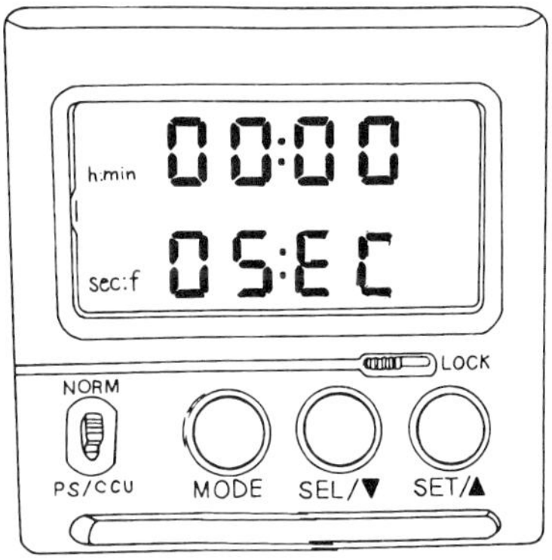

A few seconds later, you should see TC CC for Correct Code.

“*TC*” should be visible in the main camera display. If you do not see these letters, timecode will not be recorded on film.)

If “*TC*” flashes, try re-jamming because you do not have valid timecode.

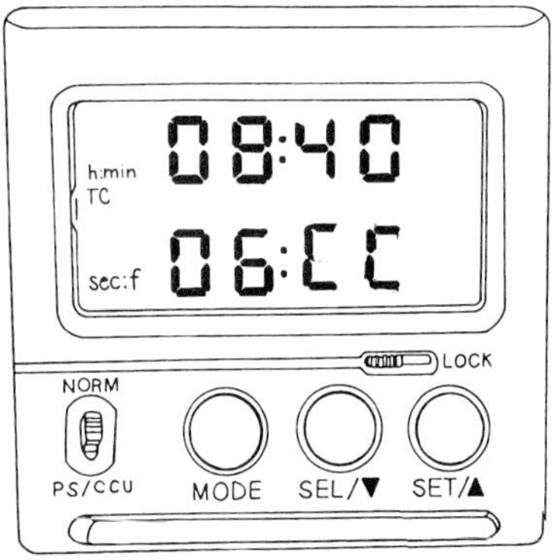

Confirm the following:

Is the magazine set to the correct Timecode Sensitivity Setting?

Go to Mode 6 (push 5 times from home page). The timecode sensitivity set on the magazine should be displayed after the “S”.

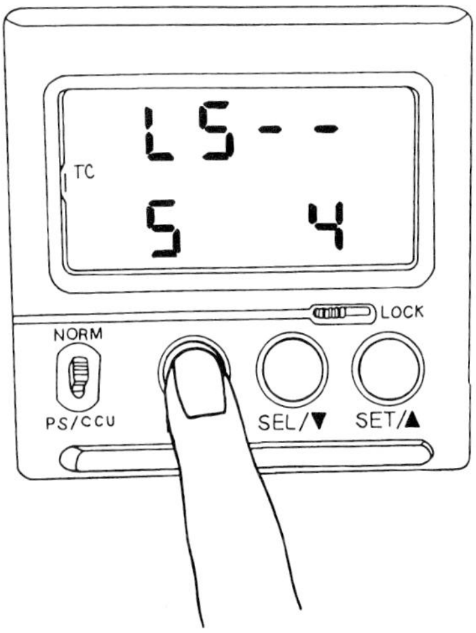

Electronic Slate

Because there are so many variables, I recommend using an electronic slate as backup. The slate can be left on continuous run. You simply have to pan over to it for an instant.

Also, shoot the electronic slate and use its built-in clapsticks at the beginning of the day so the lab can confirm timecode offset.

Turn off Timecode

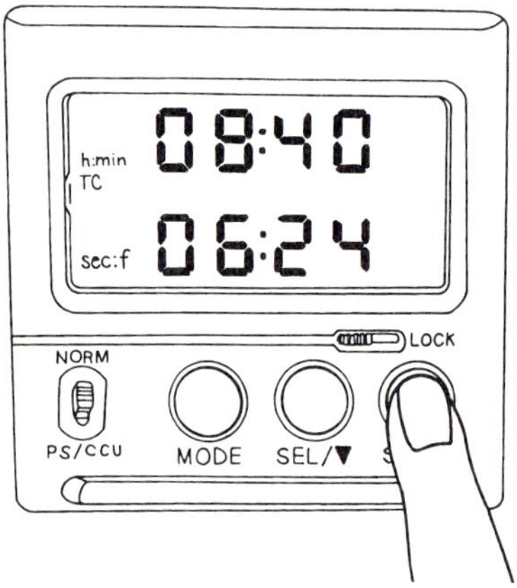

Let's say you are shooting sync material at 24 fps. You want to shoot some slow motion scenes. The best thing to do is go to Timecode Mode 4, and push **SET** for several seconds to disable timecode.

When you want to enable timecode, push **SET** again in Mode 4.

Changing batteries

Even if the main camera power switch is off, timecode memory is retained as long as a battery is connected, which means that the battery can eventually be drained unintentionally.

The timecode circuit retains memory for about 1½ minutes after unplugging batteries.

TCB - External Timecode Battery

If you are using block batteries, ARRI's TCB (Timecode Battery) uses a 9 volt battery to keep timecode memory for about a week when the main power is disconnected. Re-jamming is still necessary every eight hours. The TCB plugs between the battery receptacle and the power cable.

Fake Timecode

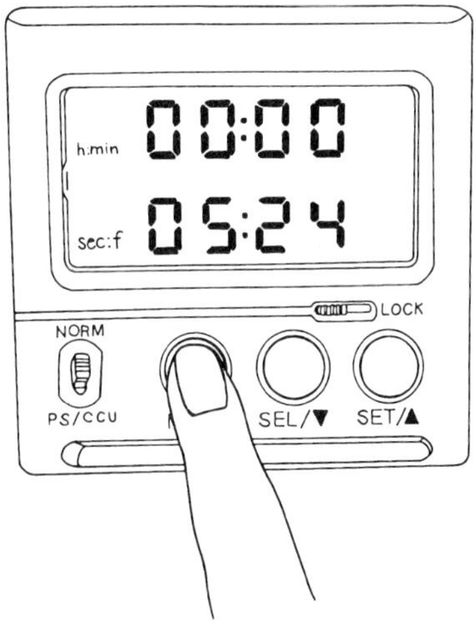

If you just turned the camera on, and cycle to Timecode Mode 4, the display is an arbitrary time-of-day read-out. The clock starts ticking when you first switch the main power switch.

In the example at right, the camera was turned on 5 seconds ago. ("24" is the timecode frame rate.)

Example of Real and Non-Real Timecode

You have jammed the camera, and are shooting at 24 fps. Your next scene involves dialogue in front of a television screen. You change camera speed to 29.97 (This is a good speed to have programmed in PS Mode 2)

The sound recordist must switch to 29.97 timecode as well, but the director is screaming to get the shot. No time to re-jam. What do you do? You must use an electronic slate until you can re-jam, so the editor can use the slate numbers.

With timecode previously enabled, when switching from 24 to 29.97 on the camera, the TC display will blink, and the camera usually beeps, indicating timecode error. The camera is telling you it needs to re-jam. This is because it was running at a real-time timecode speed (24, 25 or 30 fps), where one real second takes one second of timecode time. Now that you've switched to 29.97, you are running in a non-real timecode speed, where one second of shooting is actually 1.001 seconds of timecode. You can switch from 24 to 25 and 30 fps without re-jamming; but you must re-jam when going to and from 29.97 to re-establish sync.

To silence the camera beep, push **SET** briefly from any mode (briefly, so you do not reset the footage counter).

This will get you through the next 15 minutes, by which time you should have the chance to re-jam.

Timecode Errors

Flashing and Beeping

If the TC indicator flashes or the camera beeps, you are probably having a timecode problem. The camera is probably beeping, and you have to continue shooting.

1. First try re-jamming.

2. Silence the persistent beep for 15 minutes. In Mode 1- Home Page, press the **SET** button for a second (not longer—you will reset the footage.)

3. To silence the beep forever (not a good idea), go to Mode 6. From Home Page, press the **MODE** button five times. Press the **SEL** button once. Next, press the **SET** button until both dashes after *LS* are at the bottom position.

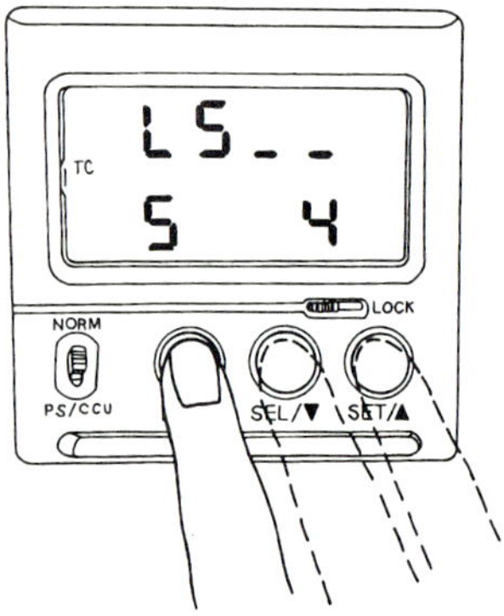

4. If that did not work, turn the timecode off: go to Mode 4. From Home Page, press the **MODE** button three times. Press **SET** for 3 seconds. The *TC* symbol goes off.

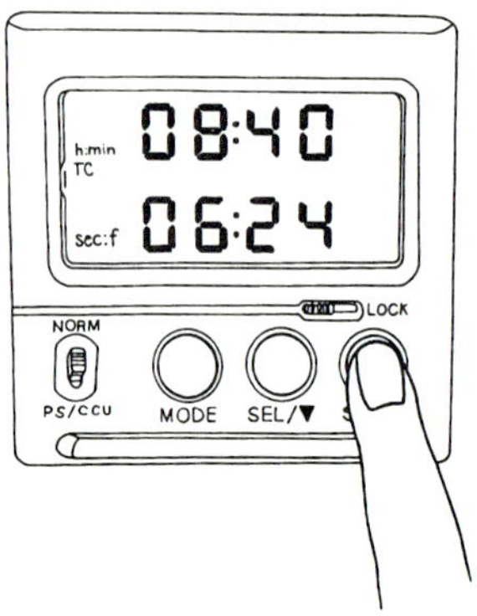

Timecode Error Messages

To find out the cause all the flashing and beeping, go to Mode 5 (User Bits) by pressing **MODE** four times from the Home Page.

Press **SEL** to display the error message. If you see all zeroes, all should be well.

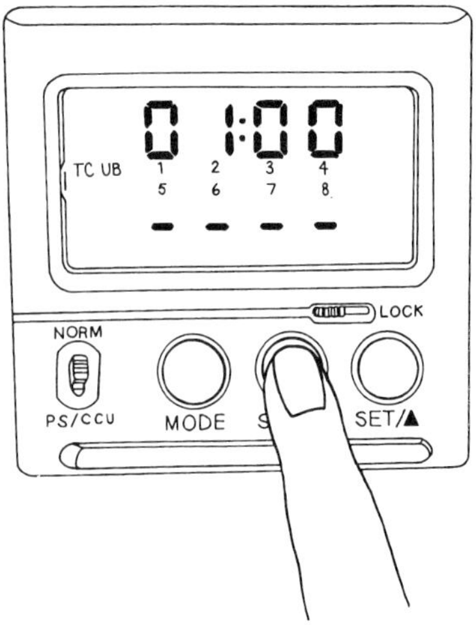

The error messages in the following pages refer to the four individual digits in the top line, starting at the left. In our example here, the error message is displayed by the second digit. Looking at the chart below (next page), we see that 01:00 (the numeral "1" in the Second Digit section) means that we must rejam timecode, since it has been over 8 hours since we last jammed.

Errors by Digits
First Digit from the left

Errors reported here mostly occur when timecode is switched on and the camera runs at a speed other than 24, 25, 30, 23.97 and 29.97 fps. Timecode will only record correctly at these five "valid" speeds.

0 OK
1 Invalid TC-frame rate
8 TC has not been recorded continuously
9 Invalid TC-frame rate and TC not recorded continuously

Second Digit from the Left

Errors in this section are usually caused when too much time has elapsed since you last jam synced the camera and sound, master clock, video or electronic slate.

0 OK
1 Time-Code was last set over 8 hours ago
2 Invalid TCS-value
3 Time-Code was last set over 8 hours ago and
invalid TCS-value
4 ESU frame rate varies too much from TC
5 Time-Code was last set over 8 hours ago and
ESU frame rate varies too much from TC
6 Invalid TCS-value and
ESU frame rate varies too much from TC
7 Time-Code was last set over 8 hours ago and
invalid TCS value and
ESU frame rate varies too much from TC
8 No TC with VSU possible
9 Time-Code was last set over 8 hours ago and
no TC with VSU possible
A Invalid TCS-value and
no TC with VSU possible
B Time-Code was last set over 8 hours ago and
invalid TCS value and
no TC with VSU possible
C ESU frame rate varies too much from TC and
no TC with VSU possible
D Time-Code was last set over 8 hours ago and
ESU frame rate varies too much from TC and
no TC with VSU possible
E Invalid TCS-value and
ESU frame rate varies too much from TC and
no TC with VSU possible
F Time-Code was last set over 8 hours ago and
invalid TCS-value and
ESU frame rate varies too much from TC and
no TC with VSU possible

Third Digit from Left

Errors here occur when you try to switch the camera speed from 24, 25, or 30 fps (real-time speeds) to 29.97 or 23.97(non-real-time speeds). You must re-jam whenever changing between real-time and non-real-time speeds.

0 OK
2 Mixture of real-time and non-real-time frame rates
8 TC could not be buffered
  (TC lost because battery change took too long)
A Mixture of real time and non-real-time frame rates and
  TC could not be buffered

Fourth Digit from Left

Errors from faulty external timecode when jamming: bad cables, incorrect values on master clock or sound recorder. Other errors in this section are caused when timecode is ON but has not been jammed. "PSD" (Position Sensor Device) errors are caused by a dirty LED emitter or receiver on the camera base or a dirty magazine glass. These measure the film loop for timecode offset from gate.

0 OK
1 Incorrect external TC
2 TC is on but not set
3 Incorrect external TC and TC is on but not set
4 Other TC warnings
5 Incorrect external TC and other TC warnings
6 TC is on but not set and other TC warnings
7 Incorrect external TC and TC is on but not set
  and other TC warnings
8 Incorrect PSD value
9 Incorrect external TC and incorrect PSD value
A TC is on but not set and incorrect PSD value
B Incorrect external TC and TC is on but not set
  and incorrect PSD value
C Other TC warnings and incorrect PSD value
D Incorrect external TC and other TC warnings and
  incorrect PSD value
E TC is on but not set and other TC warnings
  and incorrect PSD value
F Incorrect external TC and TC is on but not set
  and other TC warnings and incorrect PSD value

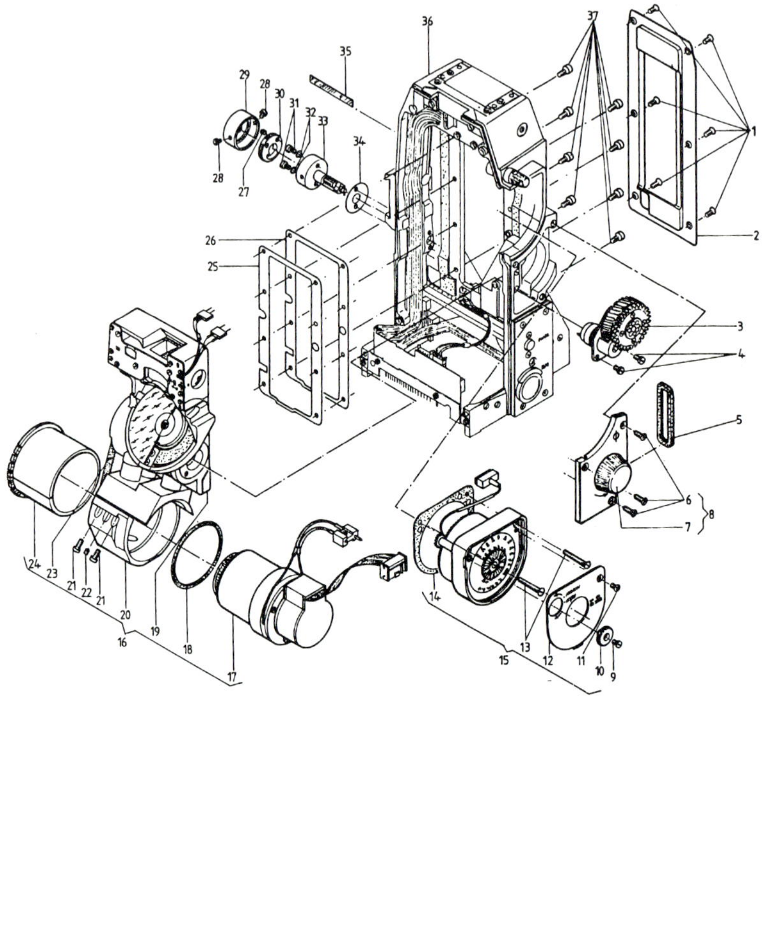

Exploded View of Motor, Mirror Shutter and Front Assembly

Super16

Super16 has been around for a long time. Originally suggested as a source for blow-up to 35mm for theatrical release, it is now gaining in popularity for television as well. Using the same size camera package, filmmakers can originate on the same size film stock, and be ready for future widescreen formats. Super16 is rapidly becoming the format of choice for documentaries and other productions that previously originated on video. It is also used for low-budget feature blowups, and for some TV movies.

The advantages: smaller, lighter and cheaper equipment than 35mm. Savings in film stock and equipment rental is estimated at 5% to 8% of the total film budget. The image area is 20% larger than standard 16mm. And, film is a universal standard as opposed to conflicting video standards.

There are disadvantages. For theatrical release and commercials, the quality is still 25% that of 35mm format (the picture area is ¼ the size). Super16 stock renders more pixels than most video formats, but is still grainier than 35. Using fast films is common in 35 for interiors, but many of us think twice before choosing any emulsion faster than 100 EI in 16mm because of the evidence of grain. To accommodate the slower stocks, we use much more light. So the savings in the camera department is often eaten up by the electric department: larger lights, and more of them. For theatrical, commercial or TV movie release, the 5% to 8% difference can often be made up from other areas in the budget. Finally, dirt or scratches are more evident than in 35.

Summary: if you were going to shoot the project on Regular 16, shoot on Super 16 instead—to be "future-proof."

A number of repair facilities (including ARRI GB, Cine Assist in Toronto, Axel Broda in California, and Denz in Munich) retrofit existing 16 SR1 and SR2 cameras to Super16. These cameras are switchable between Regular16 and Super16, have Super16 apertures, 172.8 shutters, new 54mm diameter PL mounts, and new viewing screens.

Old style magazines must be converted for Super16 operation--with modified rollers, film channels and pressure plates. Otherwise, there is danger of scratching the film on the non-sprocketed side.

Of course, the new 16SR-3 camera is ready for Super and Standard 16.

The Super16 SR aperture has the same height as the regular 16SR, but is 2mm wider, using what formerly was the left perf area on the negative (viewing camera from rear) for increased picture area. Single perf film must be used! The Super 16 aperture is 7.5mm x 12.3mm, while the aperture of Regular16 is 7.5mm x 10.3mm. This widening to one side requires repositioning the optical center axis of the camera: lens mount, viewfinder, threaded mounting hole and accessory holder all must shift 1mm to the left.

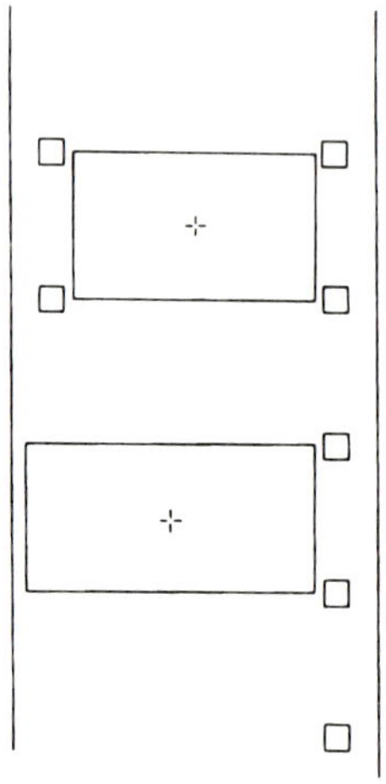

Regular 16 frame: 10.3mm x 7.5
2.82mm from each edge

Super 16 frame: 12.3mm x 7.5
0.82mm from left edge
2.82 from right edge

Because of the wider aperture area covered (20% more), some standard 16mm format lenses will vignette. More Super16 lenses and conversions are becoming available. All 35 mm lenses fit, and they cover the Super16 image area.

A quick optics refresher: Focal lengths stay the same no matter what format you're using. So, a 50mm lens designed to be used for 35mm still work will cover twice as much film aperture area as the same 50mm lens for 35mm motion picture work, which in turn covers roughly four times as much area as the 16mm format. As you go down in format size, the magnification of the image becomes greater because the aperture is that much smaller.

The 6 Steps of Super16 Conversion

There are 6 things to convert when changing formats between Regular16 and Super16:

1. Lens mount
2. Viewfinder
3. Viewing screen
4. Aperture (gate)
5. Baseplate and/or Lightweight support
6. Video

Lens Mount

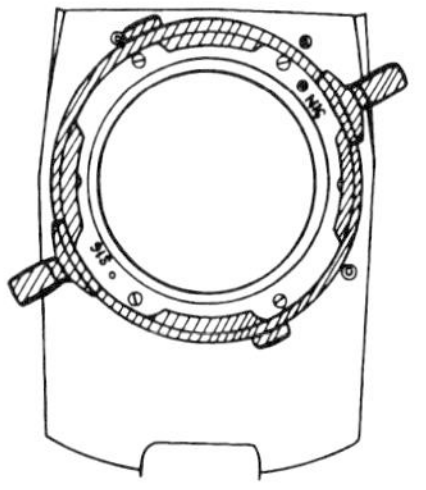

What we'll do in this step is to rotate the lens mount 180°, and move the lens locating pin from the Normal to the Super16 position. Since the PL mount is milled eccentrically, this 180° rotation will actually shift the optical axis of the lens 1mm camera left (to the right as you're facing the camera from the front).

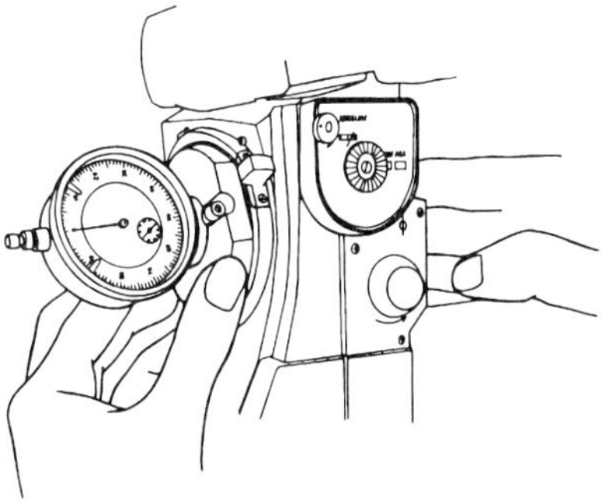

But first, check the flange focal depth of the camera before anything else—to make sure you bring the camera back to its original settings, and as a quick check to make sure nothing is wrong before you begin.

Magnetize a #1 (0.5 x 3.5mm) ARRI flat-head screwdriver (K5.26139.0). Don't use a regular screwdriver, unless you have milled it flat. Tapered screwdrivers will burr the screws.

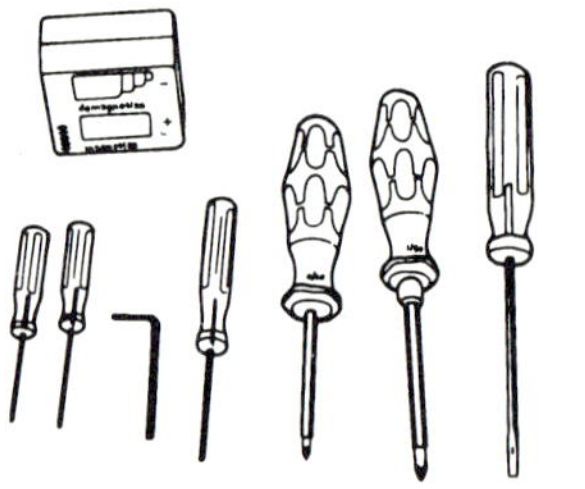

Unscrew the 6 black cylinder (cheese head) screws located on the PL mount. Magnetizing the screwdriver will prevent the small screws from dropping inside the lens cavity, which they surely will do otherwise.

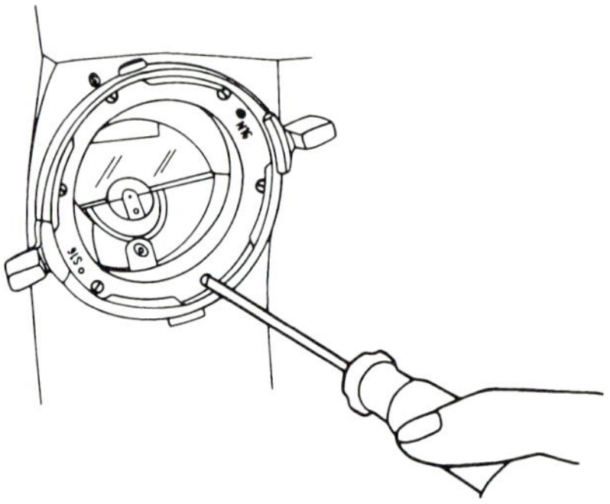

To access the two screws located at 3 and 9 O'clock, you will have to rotate the PL lock ring clockwise.

Gently remove the lens mount and its shims.

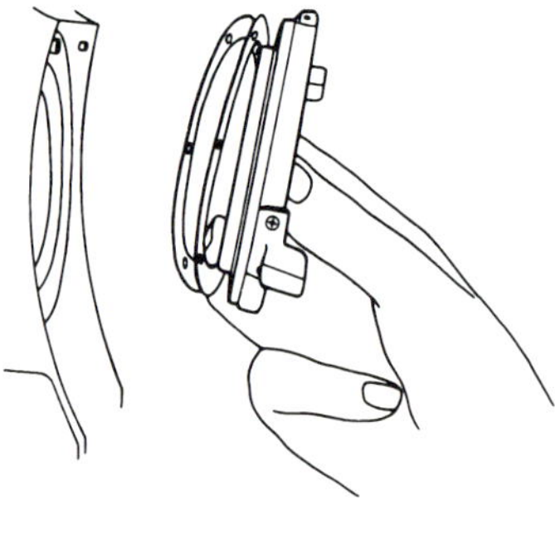

Be careful not to bend the thin shims, and put them on a clean, flat surface. Lens tissue or Kimwipes on a table top works well.

Magnetize a 1.5mm Hex key (05.02823.0). Remove the lens locating pin from the N16 position (marked in red).

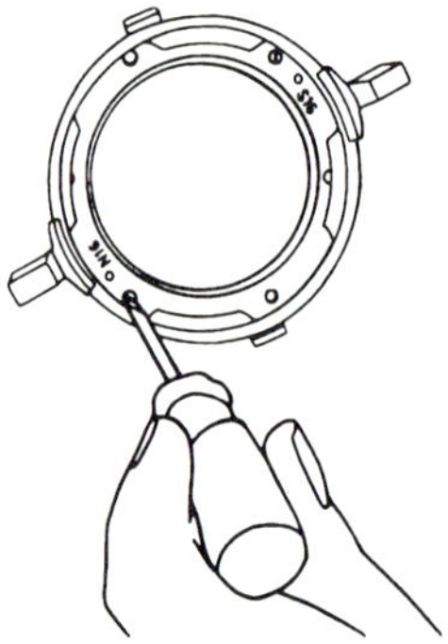

And screw the locating pin into the S16 position.

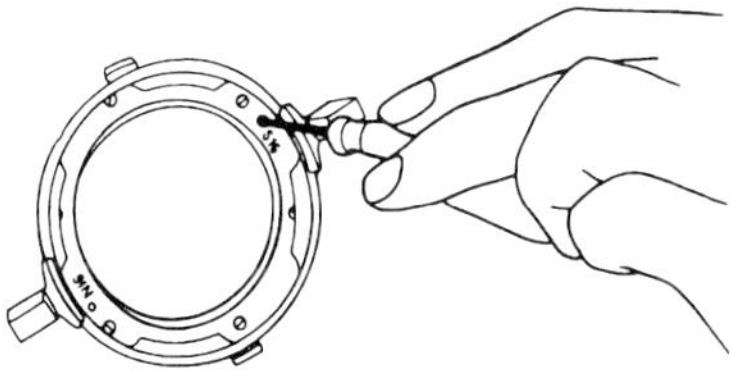

Next, we'll re-attach the mount. Notice how the S16 locating pin will be positioned at 1 o'clock.

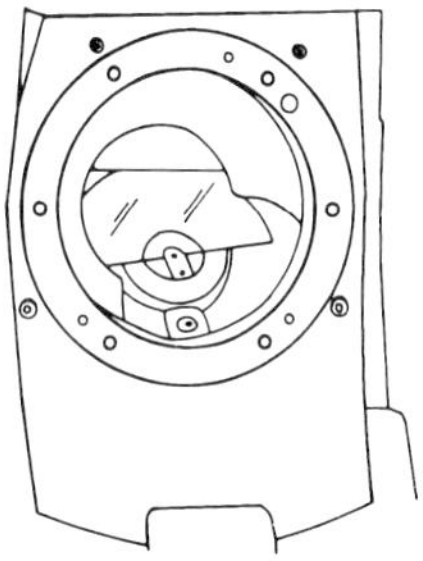

Take the shims from the table top, and stack them so the cut-out hangs on the back of the locating pin. Failure to do this will cut new holes in the shim by the locating pin, causing possible loss of depth.

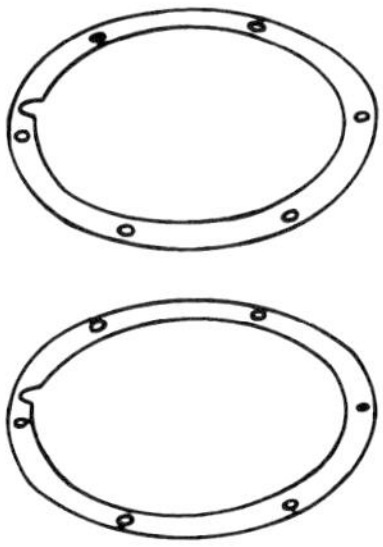

Put the mount back on the camera. Remember, the lens locating pin is at 1 o'clock. Be very careful not to wrinkle the shims.

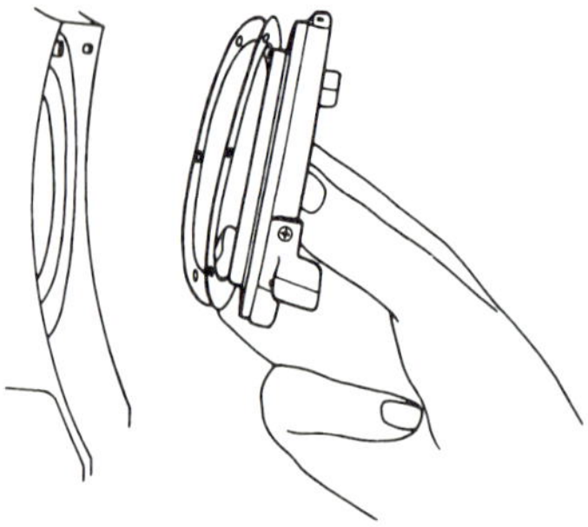

Sometimes it is easier to hold the camera between your knees, PL mount face up. Place the shims on the front, aligning them on the camera, followed by the mount.

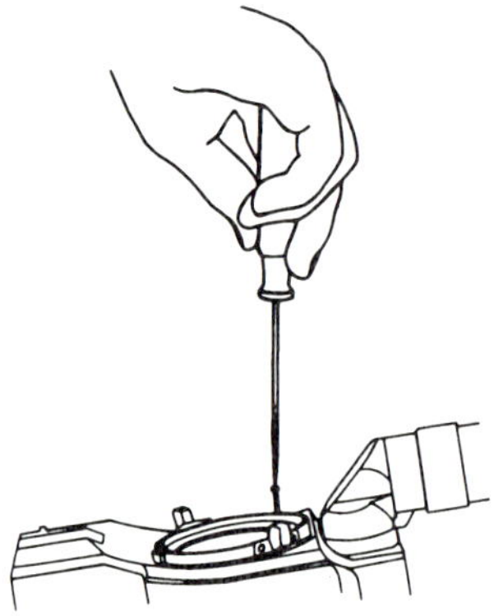

Gently tighten the 6 black cheese head screws until they meet with resistance. Now, turn each screw about 1/8th turn more until very tight. There are no torque settings, so it's a matter of experience.

Recheck the flange focal depth with a depth gauge.

As you can see, this operation is not for the faint of heart. Novices should not attempt. Nor should you do this on the beach. The best place is on the bench of your favorite rental house service technician.

Viewfinder

The viewfinder screws onto a collar that is also an eccentric, like the PL Lens Mount.

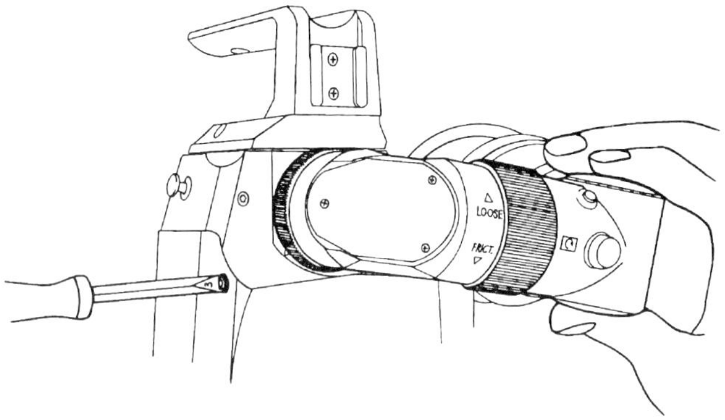

To remove the finder, back off the threaded bushing (camera right front) about 1/4 turn counter-clockwise, using ARRI Special tool A 16 SR-3 (K5.26129.0).

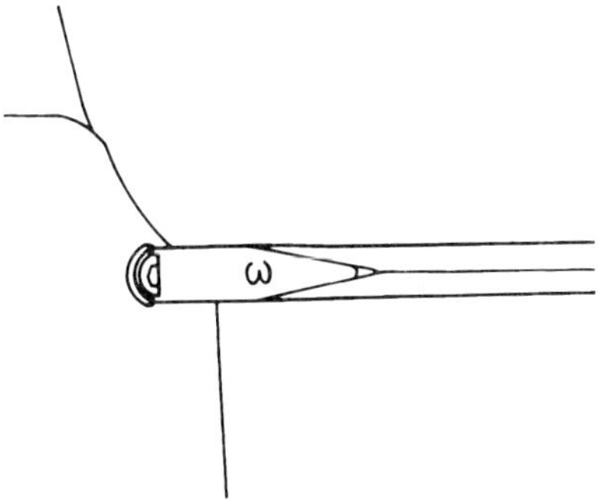

Next, use a 2mm Hex key (05.02431.0) to loosen the worm gear (counter-clockwise) about 10 turns.

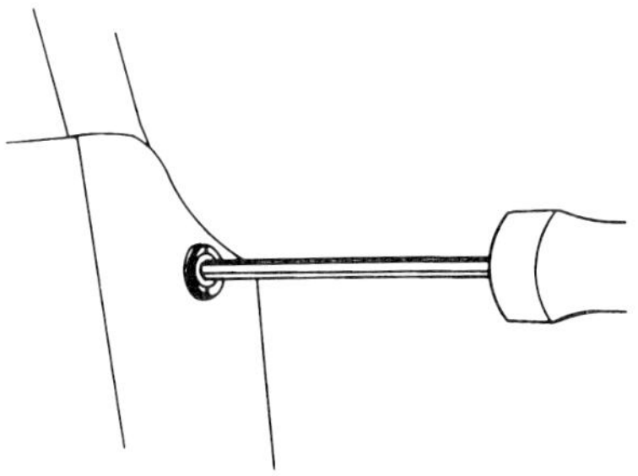

Remove the threaded bushing. It's easiest to use the special ARRI tool until you can grab it and unscrew it by hand. Hold the finder with your other hand.

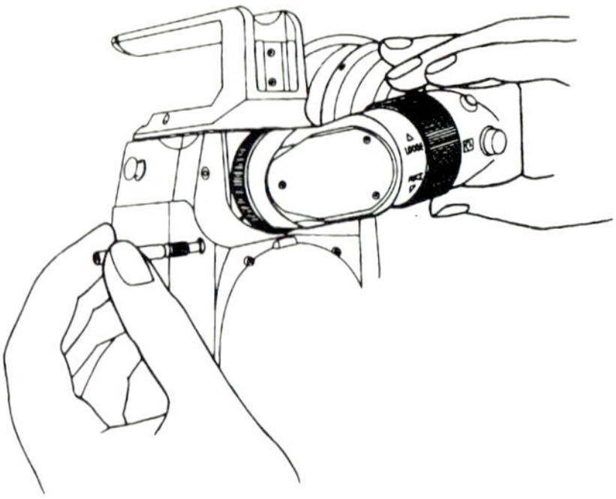

Unscrew the shiny knurled viewfinder ring. Turn it counter-clockwise. It requires quite a few turns.

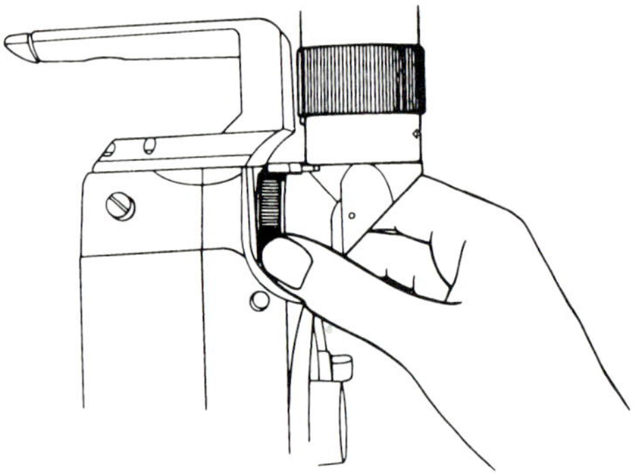

Remove the finder assembly. Make sure the brown phenolic friction disk comes off with it.

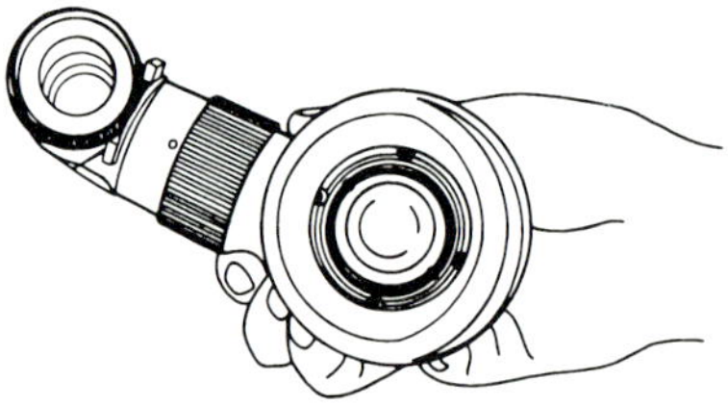

If the finder is positioned for Normal16, an "N" will be displayed through the round window at 6 o'clock.

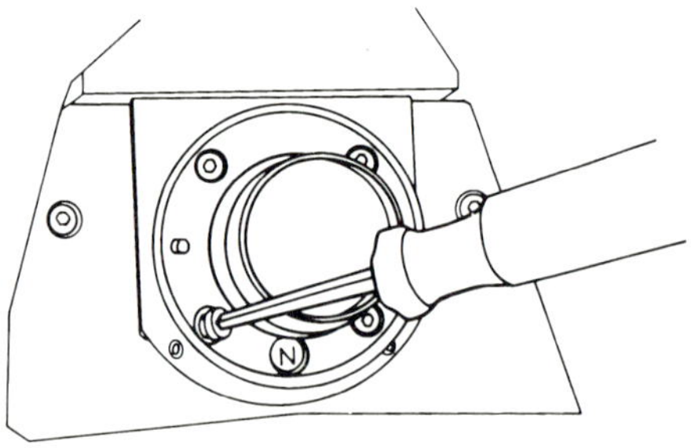

Unscrew the 4 black cheese head 2mm hex screws.

Remove the finder mount.

Rotate the mount 180°, so the round window faces up.

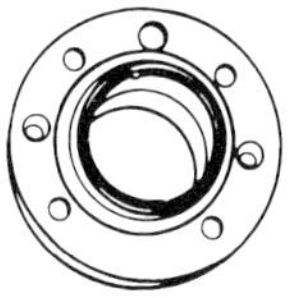

If there is any grit on the mount, clean it off with a mild solvent like denatured alcohol. Use Panchro lens fluid to clean the optical surfaces if they are dirty.

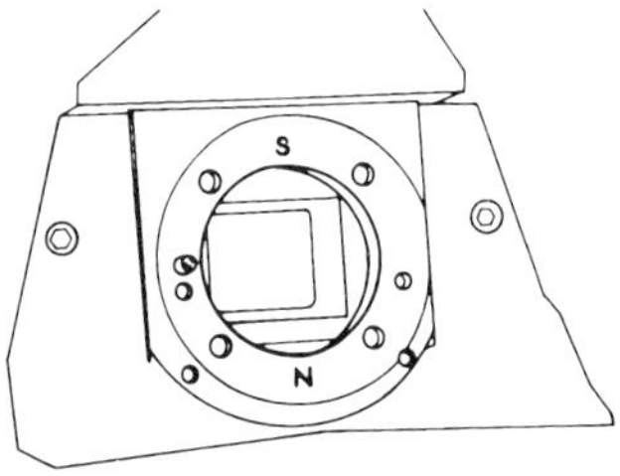

Put the finder mount back on the camera. The letter "S" should read through the window. Attach the 4 black screws. Tighten equally. Reattach the finder assembly.
Screw the shiny knurled collar clockwise.

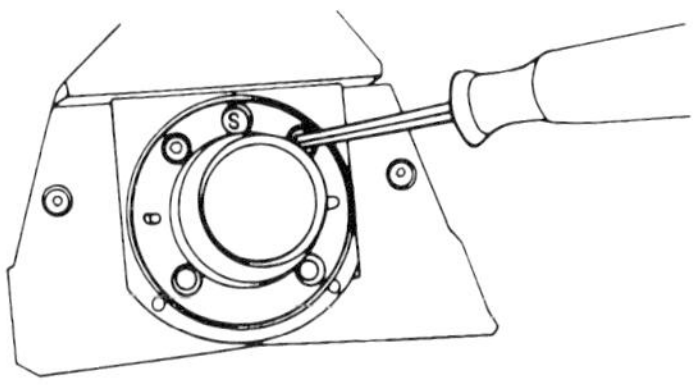

Insert the worm gear and threaded bushing. Tighten and check tension.

Viewing Screen

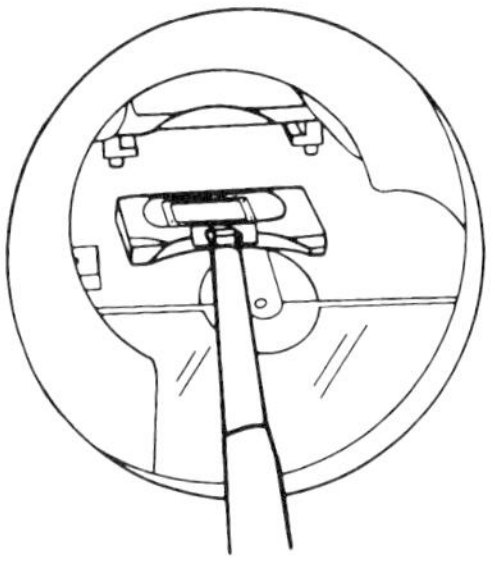

Clear the mirror shutter, and swap fiber optic viewing screens for one of the Super16 ones.

The Gate

Now it gets interesting.

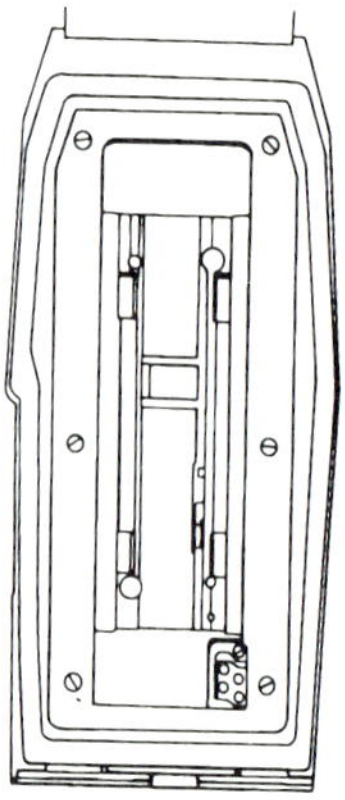

With a magnetized ARRI #1 flathead screwdriver (.5x3.5mm—K5.26139.0), unscrew the 6 black screws on the cover plate.

Some cameras have Phillips head screws. Use a small Phillips screwdriver Gr.0/60

Remove the cover.

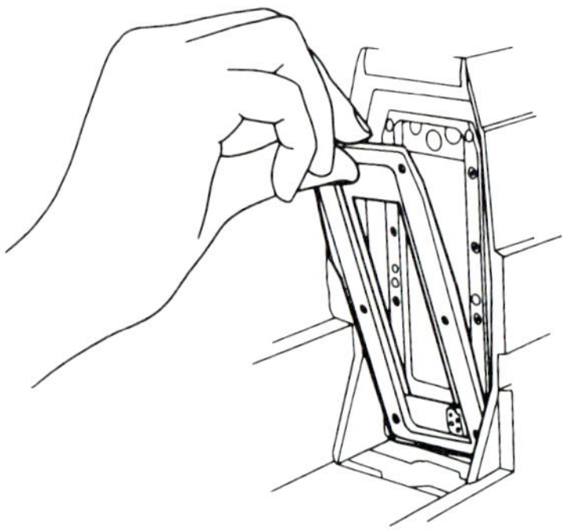

With the magnetized ARRI screwdriver #1, unscrew the 8 shiny flathead cheese-head screws holding the gate to the camera. Some cameras have 10 of these screws, and on the newest models, 2 screws are directly below the aperture instead of above.

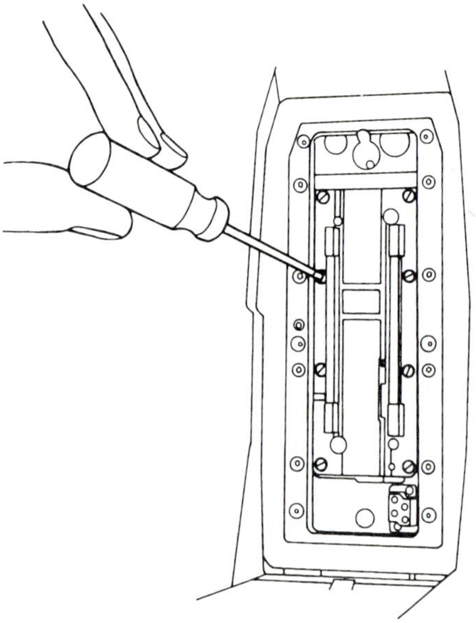

Do not remove the black Hex screws, or the black flathead screws.

Note—the frame line adjustment screw at the low left should not be touched.

Turn the inching knob until the registration pin (top pin) is fully retracted.

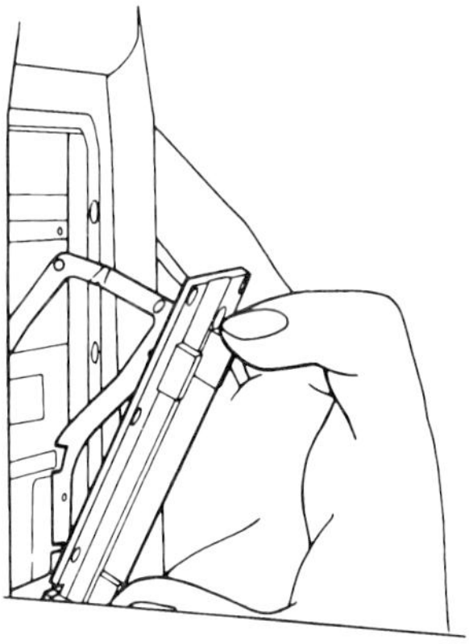

Remove the gate.

Be careful not to damage the shim behind it. Remove it if you want to. Often, it adheres to the camera. If so, leave it there.

The Regular16 Aperture has a small shiny rail covering the left edge of the frame.

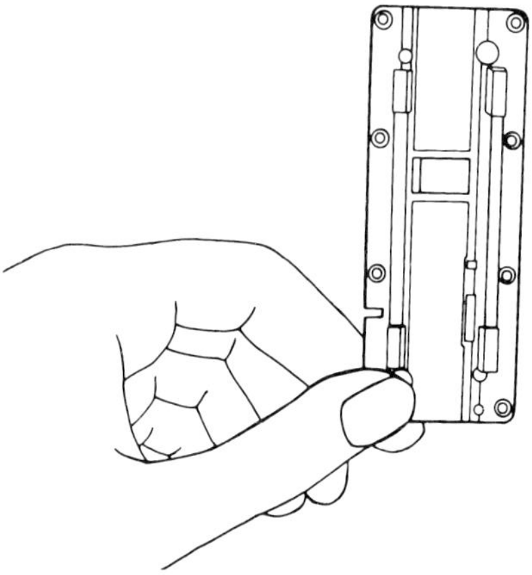

Turn the plate over, and pop out the Normal16 Rail.

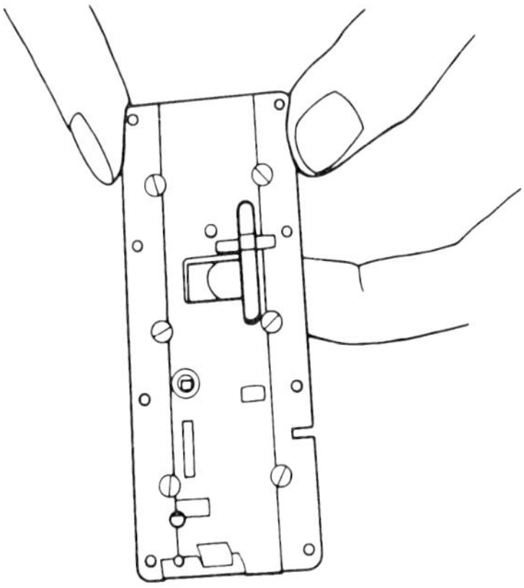

Now is a good time to lay the camera on its front, so the open gate area faces up. It's easier to complete the procedure this way.

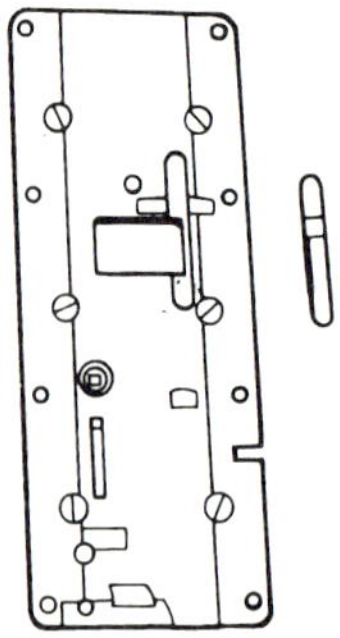

Carefully take the rail...

And insert it in its special foam-lined holder above the registration pin. The shiny side faces in.

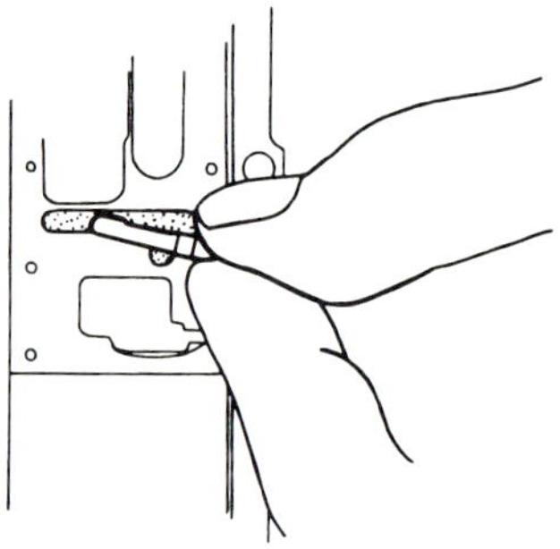

Replace Gate

With the camera face down, replace the shims, the gate, the 8 shiny screws, the cover, and the 6 black screws.

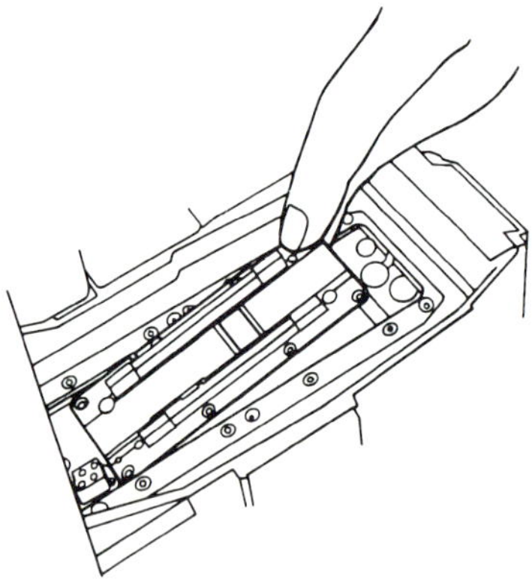

The 8 shiny screws must not be over-tightened. Use 2 fingers to tighten these screws.

Quick Time-out for Pitch Adjustment...

This has nothing to do with Super16 conversions, but it's an excellent time to point out how the pitch adjustment works.

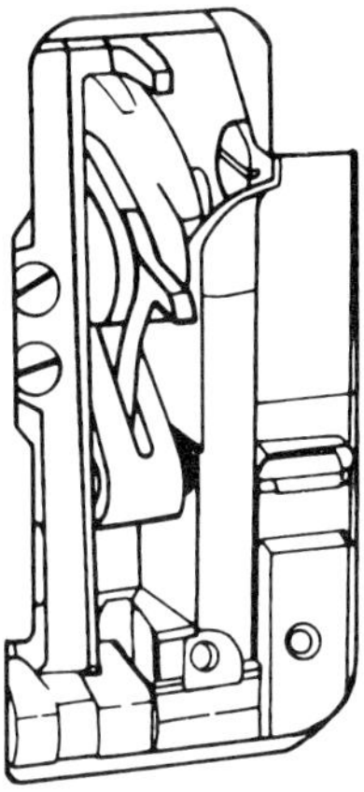

Since the camera is open, you can clearly see the pull-down claw and registration pin. If the film makes a chattering noise (film that is cold, old or very hot), you can adjust the distance between the pulldown claw and registration pin by slightly turning the PITCH ADJUST control on the camera right side with a 2mm Hex key driver.

The pull-down claw rides on an eccentric, and moves up or down in relation to the registration pin as you turn the Hex key while film is running until it makes the least noise.

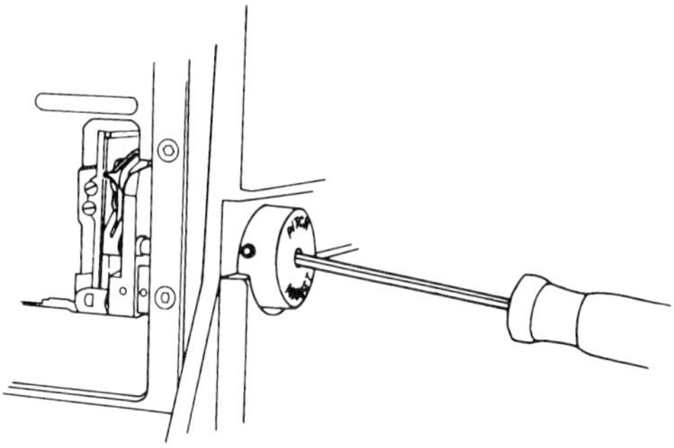

The registration pin remains in the same fixed position.

Converting the Baseplate

Unscrew the 3 black Phillips screws on top of the baseplate with the large screwdriver Gr. 1/80.

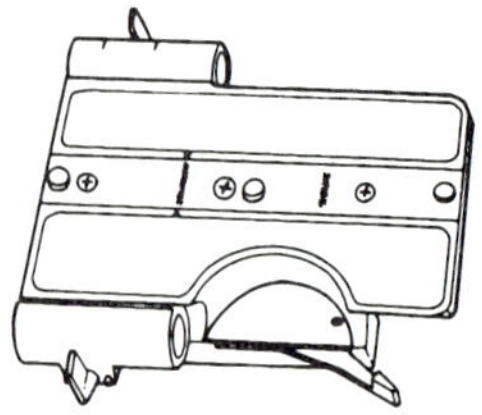

Remove the locating rail and turn it 180°. (It postions the 3/8 x 16 bolts and locating pins 1mm to the left). “SUPER16” should line up with the index mark in the front.

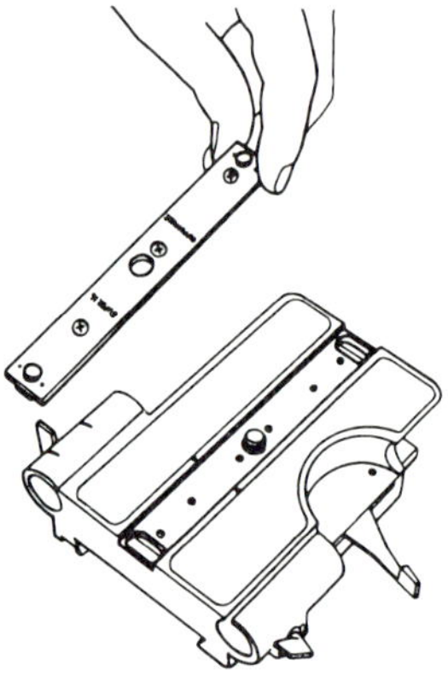

Tighten the screws.

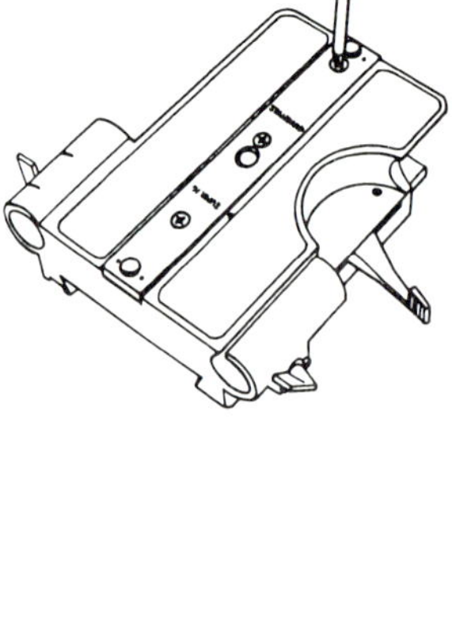

Lightweight Support

If you're using a lightweight support, unscrew the small setscrew with a jeweler's screwdriver. Rotate the square shoe 180° to the "SUPER16" position, and replace the screw into the shaft.

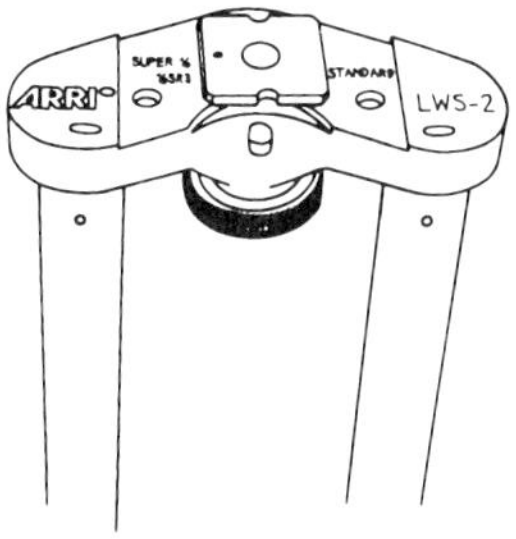

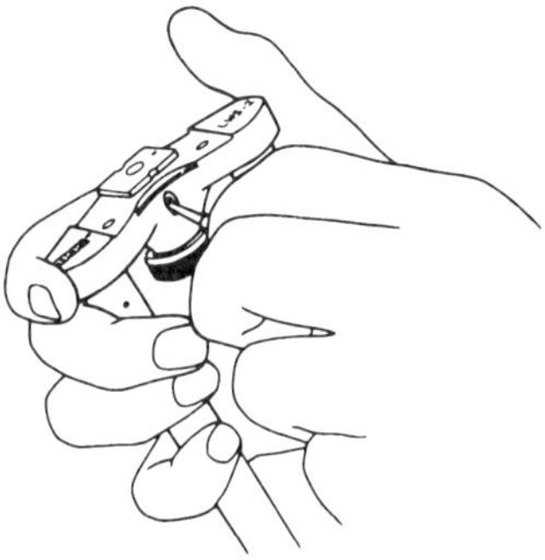

Video Assist

If you are using video assist, the Super16 image is wider than Regular16. So, the video assist camera must be moved further back to accept the larger area. To do this, you add a red spacer ring between the lock ring and the video camera.

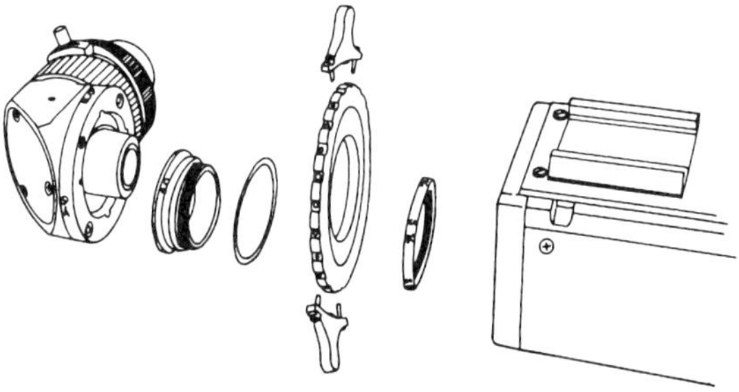

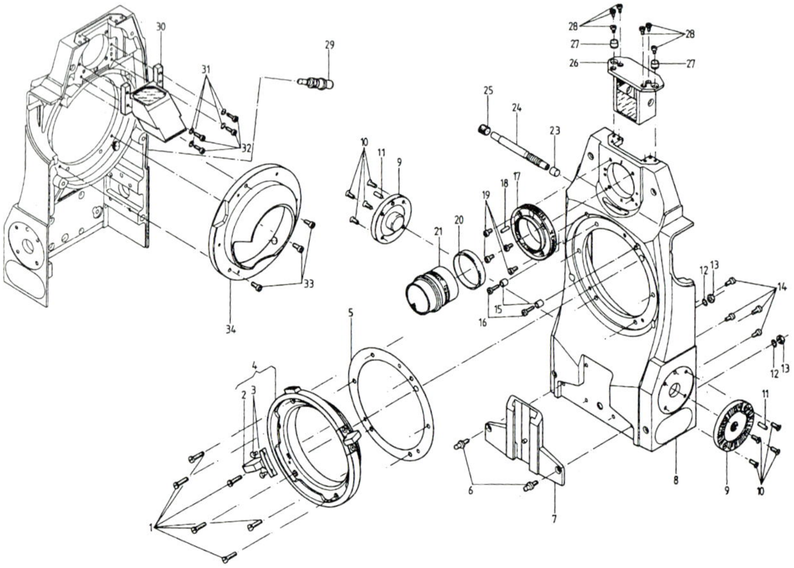

Exploded View of PL Mount and Front

Lenses

Super16 Zoom Lenses

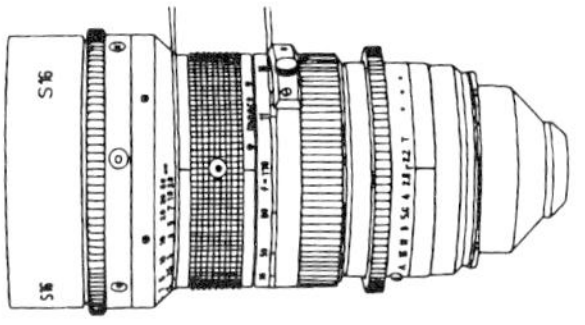

Zeiss 11-110

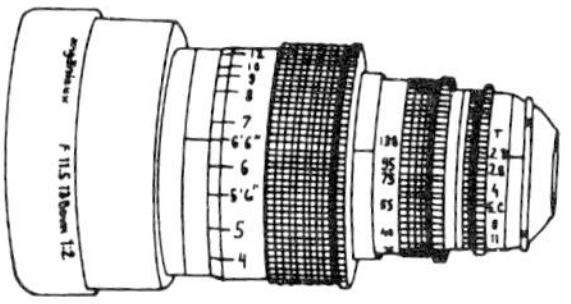

Angenieux 11.5-138

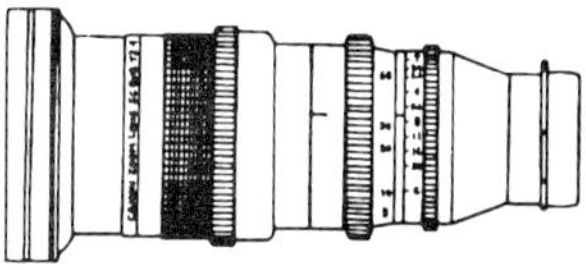

Canon 8-64

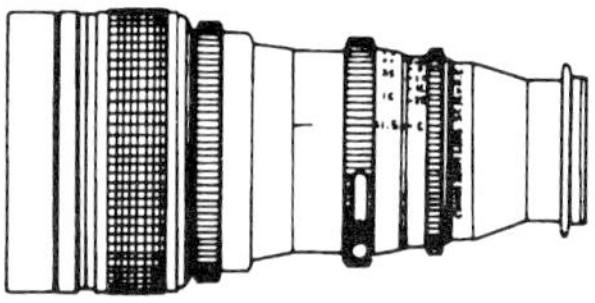

Canon 11-138.

Focal Length	Max. Aperture	Min. focusing distance
8-64mm Canon	T2.4	24"
11.5-138mm Canon	T2.5	3.5'
10.4-52mm Cooke	T2.8	18"
11-110mm Zeiss Vario Sonnar	T2.2	5'
11-66mm Angenieux	T2.6	2'
11.5-138mm Angenieux	T2.3	5'

Note: The minimum focusing distance of the 11-110 Zeiss is 5' at the wide end of the lens. The barrel will focus all the way down to 3'4", but will vignette around the corners. If you zoom all the way in to 110mm, you can fill a Super16 frame with an object 2" high x 3 ½" wide at a distance of 3'4".

Super 16 Zoom Lens Conversions

Optex modifies existing Zeiss 10-100 T2 zoom lenses into a 12-120mm T2.4, and the Cooke 9-50 T2.5 zoom into a 10.8-60 T3.

Century Precision and Optex install PL mounts on most lenses.

16mm format Zeiss Super Speed Primes for Super16

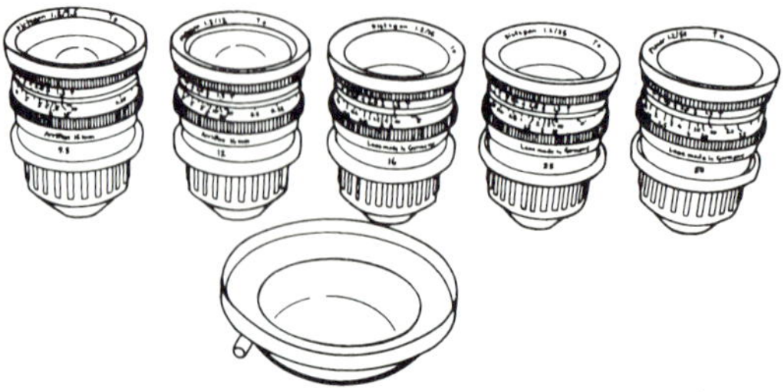

These Zeiss 16mm format Super Speeds cover the Super16 format:

Focal Length	Max. Aperture	Min focusinq distance
12mm Distagon	T1.3	8"
16mm Distagon	T1.3	8"
25mm Distagon	T1.3	10"
50mm Distagon	T1.3	28"

The following two lenses, designed for the Normal 16 format, may sometimes vignette around the edges of the frame, but often out of TV projection area.

Focal Length	Max. Aperture	Min focusinq distance
8mm Distagon	T2.1	8"
9.5mm Distagon	T1.3	8"

The ARRI/Zeiss Aspheron adapter clamps to the front of 9.5 and 12mm SuperSpeeds to convert them to 5.5 and 6.6mm respectively. There is no light loss. The corners will vignette slightly in Super16.

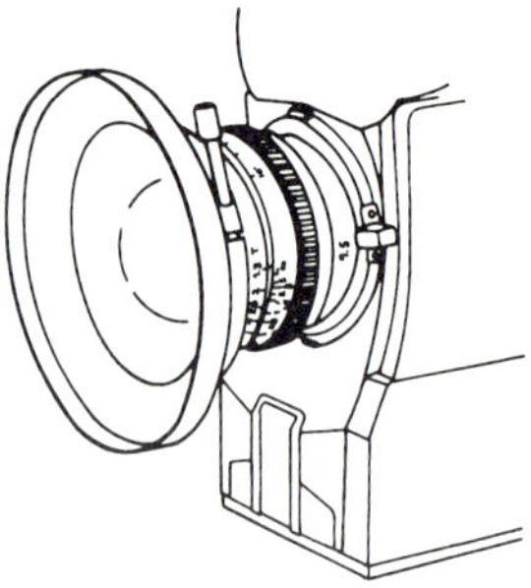

Original Lens	With Aspheron
9.5mm Distagon	5.6mm
9.5mm Distagon	6.6mm

Century Precision Optics Double Asphere

Century Precision Optics makes a Double Asphere wide angle adapter and a Fisheye Adapter. Slight vignetting in Super16.

Lens	w/ Double Asphere	with Fisheye
8mm T2.1	6mm	5mm
9.5mm T1.2	7mm	6mm
12mm T1.3	9mm	7mm
11-110 T2.2	7.3mm at wide end	5.7mm at wide end
10-100 T2.1	7mm at wide end	5.5mm at wide end

This adapter also works with 35mm format lenses:

Lens	w/ Double Asphere	with Fisheye
16mm T2.1	12mm	10.5mm
18mm T2.1	13.5mm	11.5mm

Century 6mm Super16 Format Lens

Minimum focus 12" from film plane, 6" from front of lens.
Internal focus.
40.5mm internal filter.

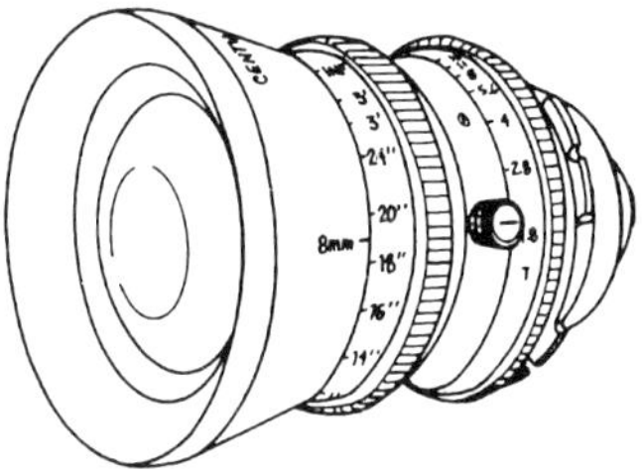

m	Max. Ap	horiz. view
6 mm	T1.9	81° Std 16
		92° Super16

Optex Super16 Super Cine Lenses

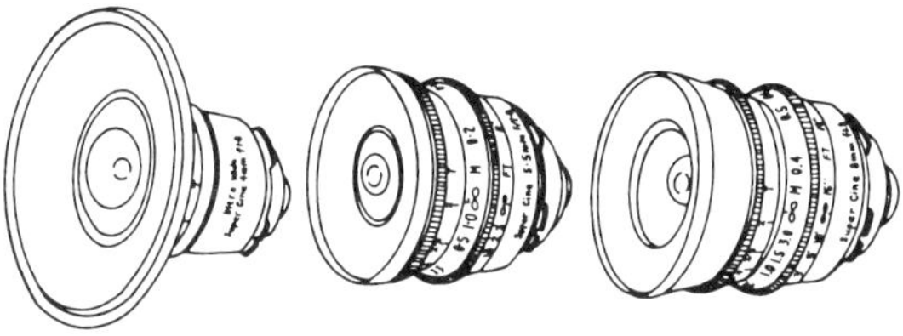

Focal Length	Max. Aperture	horiz. angle of view
4 mm	T1.9	118°
5.5 mm	T1.9	101°
8 mm	T1.9	78°

35mm Format Prime Lenses for S16

All the following 35mm format Zeiss and ARRI lenses will fit the 16 SR3 and will cover the entire frame without vignetting. A 25mm lens made for 35mm format will give you the same angle of view as a 25mm lens made for 16mm format. You are just carrying around a lot of extra glass, because the 35mm lenses must cover a wider area of film.

Zeiss Super Speed Primes (35mm format)

Focal Length	Max. Aperture	Min focusinq distance
18mm Distagon	T1.3	10"
25mm Distagon	T1.3	10"
35mm Distagon	T1.3	14"
50mm Planar	T1.3	28"
65mm Planar	T1.3	28"
85mm Planar	T1.3	3'

Zeiss Standard Primes (35mm format)

Focal Length	Max. Aperture	Min focusinq distance
10mm Distagon	T2.1	14"
12mm ARRI	T2.1	10"
14mm Distagon	T2.0	9"
16mm Distagon	T2.1	10"
20mm Distagon	T2.1	8"
24mm Distagon	T2.1	14"
28mm Distagon	T2.1	11"
32mm Planar	T2.1	2'
40mm Planar	T2.1	16"
50mm Planar	T2.1	17"
85mm Planar	T2.1	3'
100mm Planar	T2.1	3'
135mm Planar	T2.1	5'
180mm Sonnar	T3	5'
300mm Tele-Apotessar	T3	11'6"

Zeiss and ARRI Macro Lenses
(35mm format)

mm	Lens	Max Aperture	Min Focus
16	ARRI Macro 1:4	T2.1	6"
24	ARRI Macro 1:4	T 2.1	6"
32	ARRI Macro 1:4	T 2.1	8"
40	ARRI Macro 1:4	T 2.1	10"
50	ARRI Macro 1:1	T 2.1	8"
60	Zeiss Macro 1:2	T 3	11"
100	ARRI Macro 1:1	T3.0	14"
200	ARRI Macro 1:1	T4.3	23"

35mm Still Format Lenses

35mm Telephotos
Converted with PL or Bayonet mounts

mm Lens Aperture	min focus
200mm Optex/Canon f1.8	
200 Nikon f2	
300 Nikon f2	
300 Optex/Canon f2	
300 Nikon 2.8	13'
300 Canon f2.8	
400 Canon f2.8	15'
500 Canon f4.5	
150-600mm Century/Canon T6.3	
600 Nikon f4	
600 Canon f4.5	27'
800 Canon f5.6	45'
1000 Clairmont f4.5	60'

35mm format Zooms

All 35mm format zoom lenses will cover Super16. Cooke and Angenieux 25-250mm zooms are excellent lenses offering interesting visual possibilities. When fitted with a doubler, they become 50-500 T8 zooms.

Canon 150-600

The Canon 150-600mm lens comes in a number of versions. Century Precision makes two versions. The original 35mm format "TeleFx 2000" has two rectangular filter holders at the rear of the lens, which will hit the centrally located viewfinder assembly. You can request a dual 40.5mm filter holder, which clears the finder. The newer, and substantially lighter version (shown below) is highly recommended for 16mm shooting. Clairmont and Nemenz offer similar conversions of this lens.

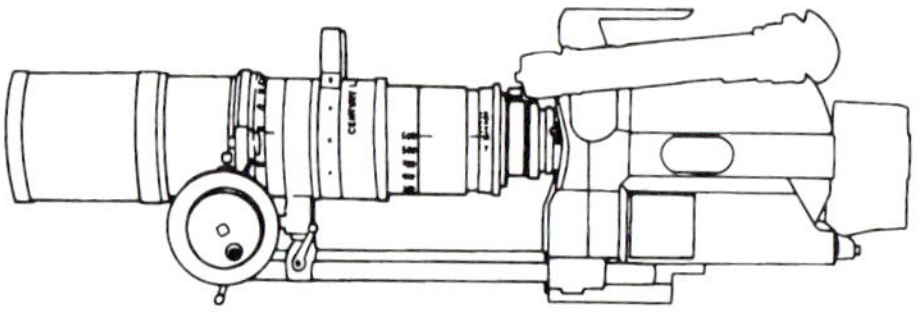

Depth and Collimation

A number of things must be in your favor to get a sharp image:

1. Lens must be seated properly on the camera flange.
2. Flange to aperture-plane depth must be 51.99 - 52.00 mm. (51.965 - 51.97mm on the High Speed Camera)
   Note: This distance is sometimes referred to as the "flange focal depth"—which is confusing. The jargon at most camera service departments is just "depth."
3. Lenses must be collimated to 52mm (flange-to-film depth).
4. A sharp image must be focused on the film which is "plastic" and moving, and buckles slightly away from metal film plane.
5. That same sharp image must also be sharp on the fiber optic viewing screen.
6. Tolerances must be accurate to 4/10,000 of an inch; 1/100 of a millimeter.

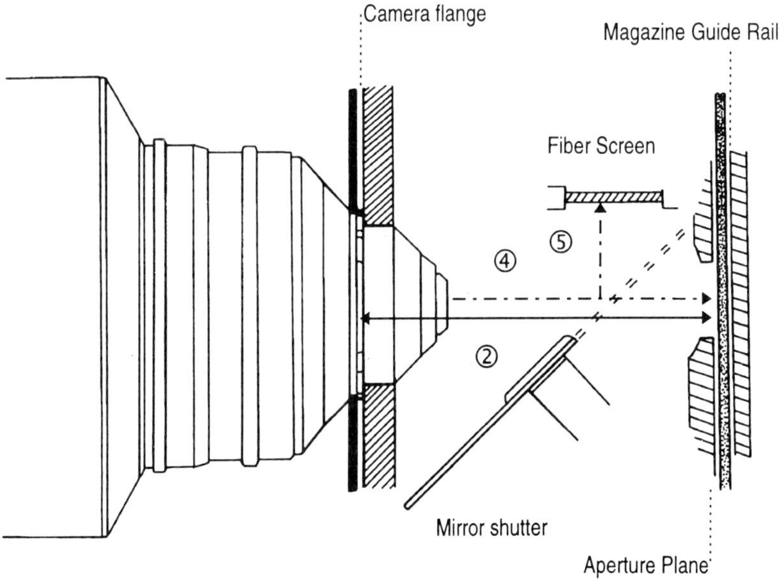

Most adjustments of lens and flange must be done by a skilled technician with proper tools. But, you can check the depth yourself.

To seat properly on the flange, both camera and lens mounts must be meticulously clean— free of dirt, grit or anything which could alter tolerances that are thinner than this piece of paper.

Flange-to-aperture depth is then measured with a Depth Gauge.

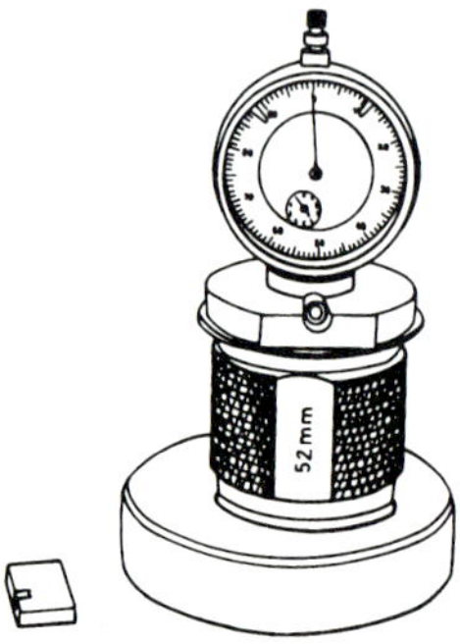

The Depth Gauge comes with a precision flat stainless steel base and a hollow steel tube or collar, both of which must be free of grease and spotlessly clean. The exact distance from top of tube to surface of steel plate is 52mm. This serves as a reference to zero the meter of the depth gauge.

You need the reference, incidentally, because temperature and environmental conditions would change the meter reading from day to day.

Measuring Flange Depth

Push in and rotate the inching knob of the camera counter-clockwise to clear the mirror shutter.

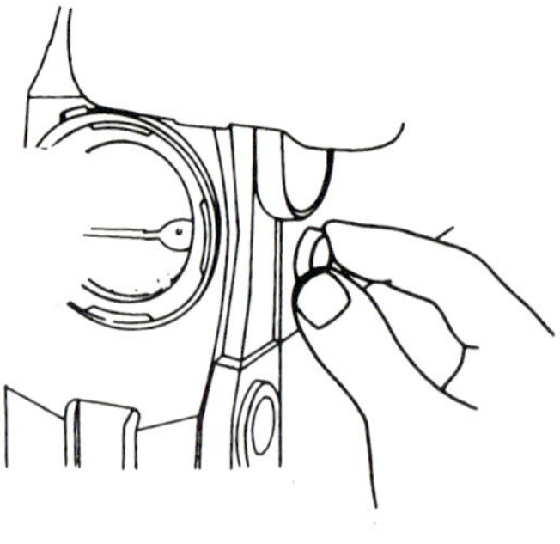

Look inside to double check.

You should be able to see the aperture from the front of camera.

IF YOU FORGET, YOU WILL CERTAINLY SCRATCH or BREAK THE MIRROR—a very embarrassing and expensive mistake.

Hold the small stainless steel aperture gauge plate over the camera aperture area. Be careful not to push in on the pull-down claw or registration pin.

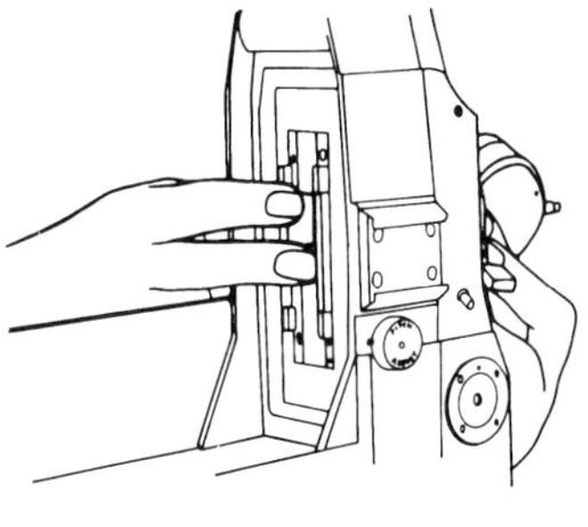

Insert the Depth Gauge. Push the gauge in against the camera flange.

The Gauge should read "1", one increment to the right (minus side) of "0", which translates as "-.01 mm."

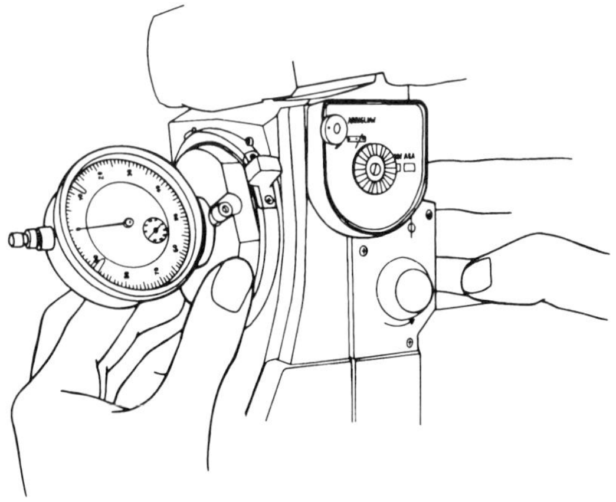

Depth on Standard 16 SR cameras is 52mm minus 0.01 mm, which translates to 51.99mm.

Tolerance is 52.00 minus .01mm, which means 51.99 - 52 mm. Flatness of flange focal distance—the variation as you check the center and all 4 corners—should be 0.005mm.

Depth on 16 SR Highspeed cameras should read 3 increments to the right (minus side) of "0", which translates to 51.97mm.

Tolerance is 51.965 plus .005mm, which means 51.965mm to 51.97mm.
Flatness of flange focal distance is 0.005mm.

If you are not getting these readings, return the camera to a service technician for adjustment with shims.

Collimating the Lens

The Depth Gauge simulates mechanically what the lens should do optically. But real film is not flat like the stainless steel gauge plate. Real film buckles slightly away from the emulsion side, away from the aperture.

That's why we set the camera-flange to aperture-plane depth at 51.99mm, and the lens-flange to film-plane distance at 52.00mm. That extra -.01 mm allows for the film buckling away from the aperture area. On other cameras, the difference may be even greater.

The 16SR has a small pressure pad behind the picture taking area to hold the film very flat. And the film runs through a fixed-gap channel just microns thicker than the film itself. ARRI "S" cameras are set at -.02mm, since the film is not held as firmly in the aperture gate.

Remember: the larger the number is on the minus side, the closer the lens is to the film, meaning that the film is buckling farther away from the aperture.

So, to check the "collimation" of the lens, an autocollimator is used. The lens is set up in a mount simulating the camera flange to film plane depth—at exactly 52mm.

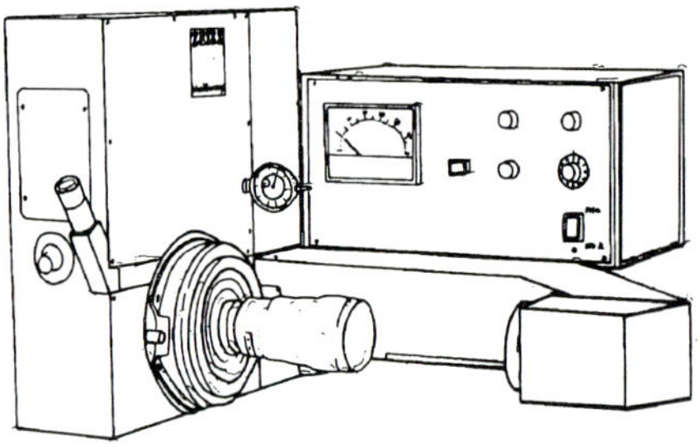

The lens is focused at infinity. A test target, also set at infinity, is projected by the collimator into the lens. The target is focused onto a simulated film plane. A micrometer is attached to the film plane, and moves it in and out to determine by how much the lens is in or out of adjustment.

Double Checking

So, the camera-flange to aperture-plane depth is OK—it's 51.99mm. The lens flange focal depth checks out at 52mm.

In the jargon of the industry, the "depth" is "minus one." The lens is "zero-zero."

Theoretically, every lens set this way will fit every Standard 16 SR camera.

Prudence dictates that the lens be put on the camera, the camera loaded up, and the collimation checked once again while the film is running. The test target should appear sharp and contrasty, and hold throughout the zoom range. This can be also be done with a pocket collimator.

Fiber Optic Viewing Screen

The camera's viewing system is reflex. What if the fiber optic viewing screen is out of place? Your film will not focus what you see.

First check that it is seated properly.

The fiber optic viewing screen can only be mounted one way. The mirrored, shiny side of the assembly faces up.

CLEAR THE MIRROR SHUTTER OUT OF THE WAY BEFORE REMOVING SCREEN.

Remember, only use the Hirschmann Forceps. (ARRI Part number 05.07238.0 — a mere $10.50.) Be very careful when removing. Do not touch the screen. Grab the "T" of the assembly holder with the Hirschmann Forceps. Pull gently, straight out.

Do NOT use DUST-OFF on the fiber screen. It leaves a residue. If smudged, use lens cleaner and lens tissue—gently. To clean, only use an air bulb syringe or pure compressed air.

DO NOT BLOW ANY AIR INTO THE LENS CAVITY WITH THE SCREEN REMOVED. You will blow the light-meter needle off its pins.

When putting the screen back in place, be sure it goes in all the way until it clicks in place. Otherwise, you will have a framing error. It only goes in one way: chrome side of holder up; black, ridged side down.

To check the fiber optic screen “depth,” use a traditional collimator. Remove the magazine. Use a lens which is known to be properly set to 52mm and has an accurate infinity setting. Run the camera. The collimator will only “see” the fiber screen through the lens, since there is nothing in the gate. The target projected by the collimator will be reflected by the mirror shutter onto the fiber optic screen, which should resolve at52.00 mm. Of course, the distance to the fiber optic screen is not straight, since the mirror deflects the light.

When properly in place, the fiber optic screen will render a sharp and contrasty target on the collimator.

If not, first check that it is seated properly.

If the fiber screen is out of adjustment, the remedy is a visit to a qualified Arriflex repair shop.

Maintenance

There is very little to maintain on the 16 SR3. Do not oil, grease or fix anything unless you know absolutely what you are doing. More damage is done to cameras by people who think they know what they are doing than by people who know their limits.

End Of Day Cleaning

While the rest of the crew is in the bar, the camera assistant has another hour of work ahead. Assuming the worst - salt water spray, wind, sand, rain, dust — here is a checklist:

- ❑ Unload and inventory Film.
- ❑ Camera reports current.
- ❑ Empty out Cases, Dry contents. (especially foam)
- ❑ Clean exterior surfaces of cases with commercial solvent (Simple Green).
- ❑ Remove ancient gaffers tape (hair dryer removes adhesive)
- ❑ Remove sand from "0" rings and hinges of cases.
- ❑ Wipe silicone on "O" rings with rag, and CRC 5-56 on hinges. Never spray - it gets all over the place. Do NOT use Silicone anywhere else
- ❑ Wipe tripod legs with wet rag. Clean points and spreader. Shower or tub is a good place. Dry with towel.
- ❑ Blow geared or fluid head with Dust-Off.
- ❑ Wipe metal surfaces of head and legs with CRC-556-impregnated cloth. Never use silicone on legs- they'll slip.
- ❑ Anything that got wet should be dried. A hairdryer on medium setting will help. Don't melt or overheat anything. If it's too hot to touch, it's too hot.
- ❑ Wipe off batteries with a damp cloth. Treat metal surfaces with CRC 5-56.
- ❑ Spray electrical connections and contacts with an electrical contact cleaner: CRC 2-26 or Contact Re-Nu.
- ❑ Charge Batteries. When the room lights are turned off, are the batteries still on?
- ❑ Batteries should never be charged inside a shipping case. (Unless they are one-piece units) Ensure adequate ventilation.

- ❑ Remove foam eyepiece. Wash with soap and water. Let dry overnight.

- ❑ Separate camera parts and lay out on table:
  mags, body and accessories
- ❑ Remove eyepiece, lenses, finder extender.
- ❑ Clean gate.
- ❑ Clean fiber screen, if necessary.
- ❑ Use lens tissue or foam Q-Tip (no cotton Q-Tips!) to wipe lens mount dry with alcohol or lens fluid.
- ❑ Insert cavity plug.
- ❑ Clean mag guide rails and aperture area with skewer. Wipe with Selvyt or chamois.

- ❑ DO NOT USE CRC OR ANY LUBRICANTS in aperture, gate, lens cavity or magazine throat. Use alcohol or lens fluid if emulsion has built up anywhere or if exposed to salt water. Don't wipe black enameled area of magazine pressure pad with solvent—the enamel could come off.
- ❑ Dab CRC in mag latch area. Attach mag cover.
- ❑ Wipe external camera body surfaces with a cotton cloth which has been very lightly sprayed with CRC 5-56:
- ❑ Wipe external surfaces of magazine (not the throat area)

- ❑ Wipe external surfaces of lens barrels - only if exposed to salt water. Be VERY careful—DON'T GET CRC ON ANY GLASS SURFACES. It is extremely difficult to remove.
- ❑ With a foam covered swab impregnated with CRC 5-56, dab screw heads and hard-to-reach places.
- ❑ With the same type of foam swabs and CRC 5-56, wipe the threads of filter rings, the eyepiece, and finder extender.
- ❑ Pull off the rubber eyecup, and wipe it with soap and water. The bearings inside the eyecup holder should be dabbed with CRC.
- ❑ Apply one or two drops of lens fluid to lens tissue and clean eyepiece, finder extender, and optical surfaces.
- ❑ Clean lens front and rear elements with lens fluid
- ❑ Open the mags. NO CRC OR LUBRICANTS INSIDE. Brush out and blow out with Dust-Off.
- ❑ Remove core holders and dab CRC on core holder bearings (which press against core).
- ❑ Check that screws aren't loose underneath core holders.
- ❑ Mag doors are tight?
- ❑ Electrical connections sprayed with CRC 2-26 or Contact Re-Nu — at back of camera, handgrip side, cables.

Lens Cleaning

There is really only one way to clean a lens or camera optical surface. Blow plain air with a hand operated air syringe. (Dust-Off is more convenient, but will leave a chemical residue which smears). If the dust is gritty, gently brush it off with a fine camel's hair brush which you have reserved for lens use only.
If the lens is smeared, dirty or fingerprinted, squirt one or two drops of lens fluid on a crumpled lens tissue. Wipe the lens in a circular motion. Dry the lens immediately with a dry piece of lens tissue. Also wipe in a circular motion - but don't scrub. If the lens is really dirty, you will have to repeat this process a number of times until the residue disappears.

Magazine Door Hinges

In time, the hinges of the magazine doors may loosen up.
Tighten the six screws on the outside of the hinge first (K).
If the door still wobbles and does not close and mate smoothly, remove Hex set screws (L) with a 1.5mm Hex hex driver.
With tweezers, carefully remove spacers (M).
Now, tighten equally the Hex screws (N), which push down on ball bearings (O), which press indent on lower hinge casting.
Remember to tighten equally on top and bottom.
Replace spacers (M) and set screws (L).

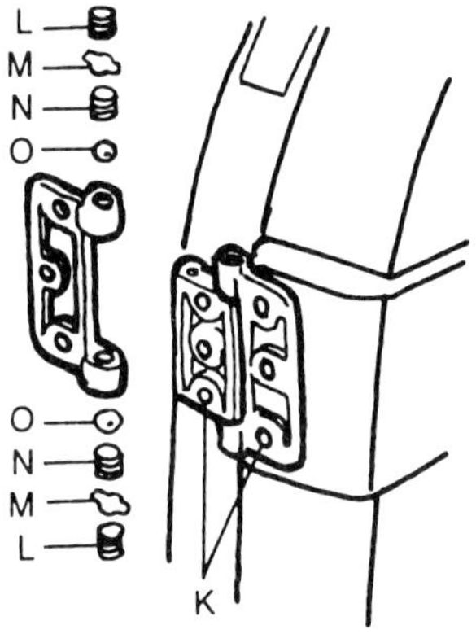

Checking Magazine Take-Up Tension

Advanced Users Only.

Use an ARRI "Spring Scale" (US part 339227, ARRI part K2.26100.0) to measure the magazine take-up tension. Too much tension will snap film. Not enough tension will wind it too loosely.

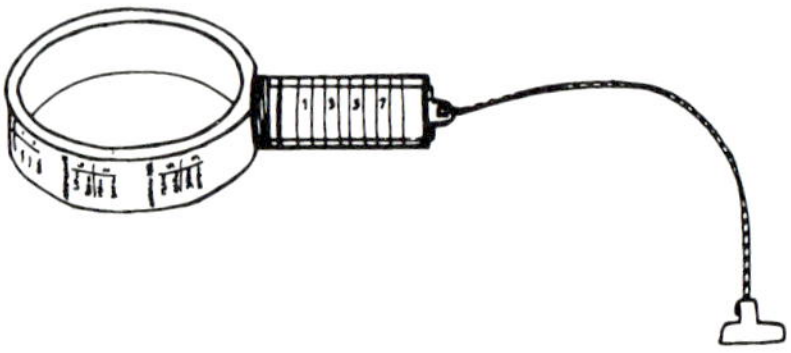

Open the take-up side. Insert the hook at the end of the Spring Scale's string into the take-up or collapsible core's slot. Hold the gauge in your left hand.

Wind the take-up core in the direction of the arrow to take up slack. Now, run the camera at 24 fps. The gauge should read "2."

If not, remove the take-up core. You will see a tiny hole at 7 o'clock, just below the take-up spindle. Insert a tiny jeweler's screwdriver, gently push down while turning the inching knob until the screwdriver enters a hole in the disk beneath the surface.

Turn the inching knob clockwise for more tension and counter-clockwise to decrease take-up tension.

Oops

I always approach this section of the book with a little trepidation. There seem to be an overabundance of overzealous film students everywhere who see pictures of an open camera, and immediately dig in and try to match their perfectly fine cameras to the exploded views in the book. Like they say in the commercials, "DO NOT ATTEMPT."

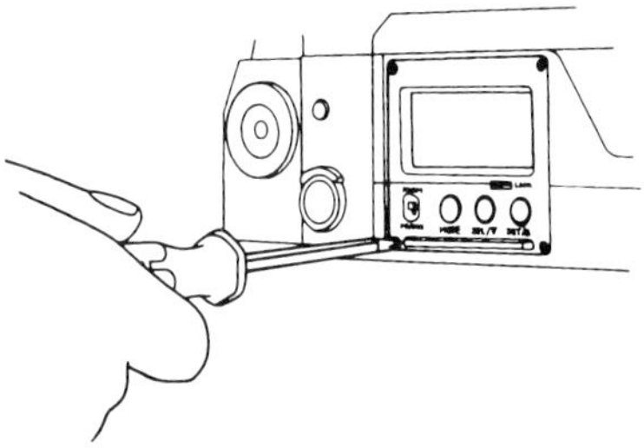

You just dropped the camera into a puddle of salt water, and you're three weeks by dugout canoe from the nearest ARRI service technician. You get on your Iridium satellite phone, and your friendly service manager talks you through a few delicate procedures.

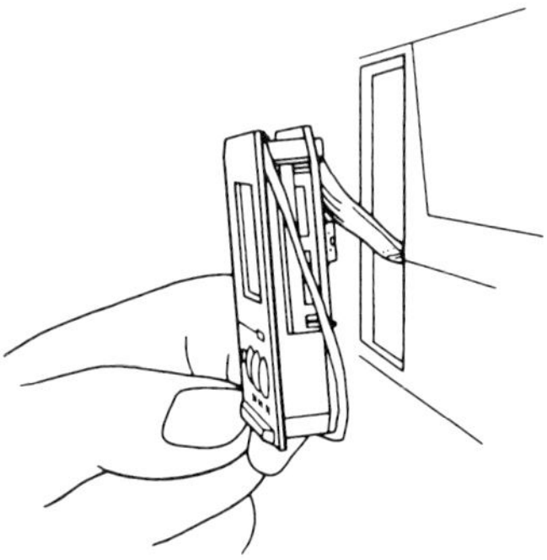

Of course, the spare parts have been air-dropped to you, along with this book.

To remove the main camera display, unscrew 4 Phillips screws, gently pull the display out, and unplug with tweezers.

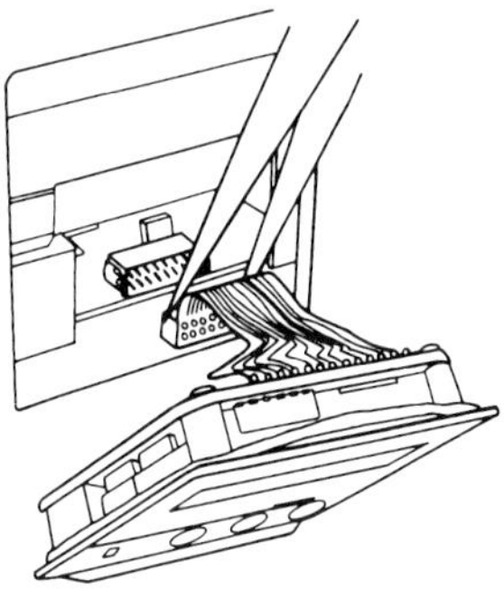

To remove the electronics base cover, use a 2mm Hex driver on the rear 8 recessed hex screws.

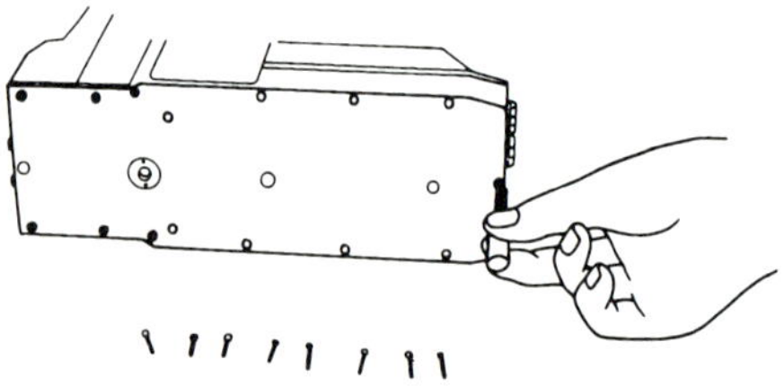

Gently lift the cover up.

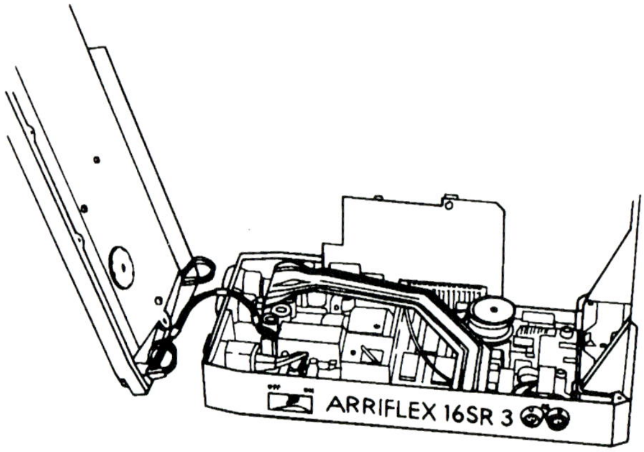

Assistant's Tools

Belt Pouch

Many camera assistants like to wear a nylon belt-pouch with the following items readily available:

- ❑ Lens tissue
- ❑ Panchro Lens fluid
- ❑ Plastic skewer
- ❑ Chamois or SELVYT cloth
- ❑ Swiss Army knife with all the goodies
- ❑ Illuminated magnifying glass
- ❑ Black, indelible, fine-tipped markers (Pilot Ultra-Fine)
- ❑ Ball-point pen
- ❑ Dust-Off Junior with plastic hose
- ❑ Jeweler's screwdriver
- ❑ Depth-of-field charts
- ❑ Roll of drafting tape
- ❑ Brush for cleaning inside of mags
- ❑ Tape measure
- ❑ And a roll of camera tape hanging from your belt, attached with a nylon strap.
- ❑ Sears Stubby Screwdriver for baseplates

Other Tools

Radio Shack makes a simple $25 Digital Fold-Up Multimeter to check batteries, cables and all things electronic. The test leads and probes store in the cover. Radio Shack Part #22-179. You don't need to carry this around in your belt pouch, but it's very useful.

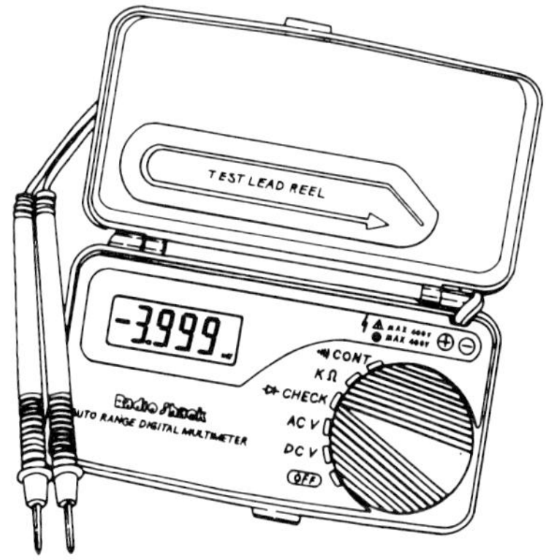

Tool Case

The belt pouch can fit into your larger assistant's case or shoulder bag, along with:

- ❑ Changing tent
- ❑ More Dust-Off (1 can for every 3 days on the job)
- ❑ Screwdrivers
- ❑ Metric and SAE hex key sets
- ❑ Vise-Grips (small)
- ❑ Needle nose pliers
- ❑ Soldering iron (fine tip)
- ❑ Solder
- ❑ Small digital multimeter
- ❑ File, tweezers, wire strippers, spare wire
- ❑ Wrench
- ❑ Gaffers' tape, black tape, camera tape
- ❑ Camera reports
- ❑ More lens tissue and fluid
- ❑ Flex-Light
- ❑ Battery powered fluorescent lantern
- ❑ ARRI depth gauge
- ❑ Nylon webbing for securing equipment or yourself
- ❑ 3/8"-16 bolts and eyebolts, nuts, washers
- ❑ CRC 5-56, CRC 2-26, (in 3 oz. and 12 oz. aerosols)
- ❑ Cotton rag, towel
- ❑ ARRI Spring Scale Magazine Tension Gauge
- ❑ Wiha #40010 Tool magnetizer / demagnetizer

ARRI TOOLS

	Tool		Part No.
❑	Hirschmann Forceps		05.07238.0
❑	1.3mm Hex driver		05.02825.0
❑	1.5mm Hex driver		05.02823.0
❑	2mm Hex Key		05.04454.0
❑	2mm Hex Driver		05.02431.0
❑	Small Phillips Driver	Gr. 0/60	05.02682.0
❑	Large Phillips Driver	Gr.1/80	05.02687.0
❑	Slotted Screwdriver	ARRI #1	K5.26139.0
❑	Special Bushing tool (ARRI #3 modified)		K5.26129.0

ARRI Tools

This pouch comes with new 16 SR3 cameras.

You can buy the tools individually.

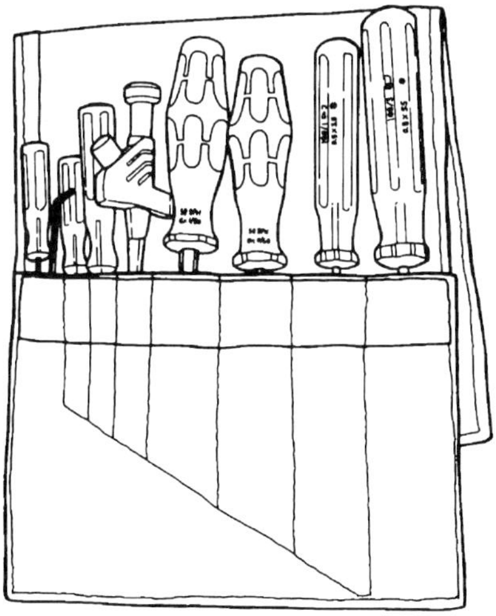

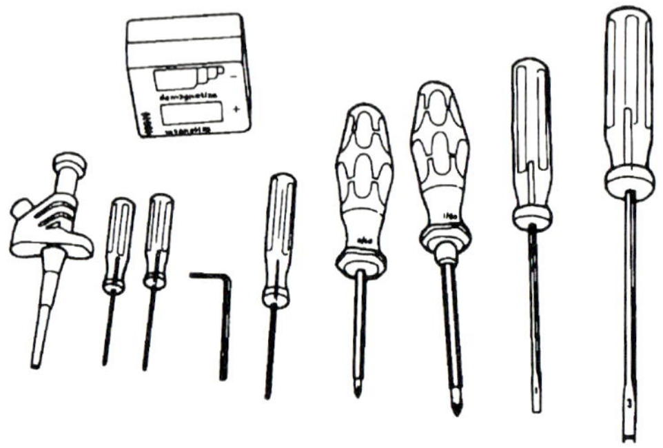

Tools: left to right:

Hirschmann Forceps		05.07238.0
1.3mm Hex driver		05.02825.0
1.5mm Hex driver		05.02823.0
2mm Hex Key		05.04454.0
2mm Hex Driver		05.02431.0
Small Phillips Driver	Gr. 0/60	05.02682.0
Large Phillips Driver 05.02687.0	Gr.1/80	
Slotted Screwdriver	ARRI #1	K5.26139.0
Special Bushing tool	ARRI #3 modified	K5.26129.0

top row: Wiha Magnetizer / Demagnetizer #40010
available from Griot's Garage and Jensen Tools

Crash Course for Camera Assistant Test

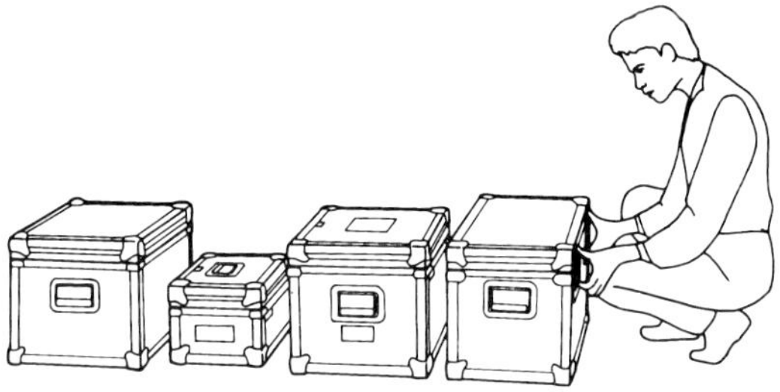

The Test for Camera Assistants is *tomorrow*. You just bought this book today.

Here's an outline of the key things to know about the Arriflex 16 SR3. You will probably be tested on many of these topics. Most camera assistant tests are run by the camera unions, rental houses and workshops. It usually involves putting the camera together, talking about it, and answering a few questions. However, learning a camera for a test is often quite different from actual location experience. Your graduation diploma will be your first paycheck, and the knowledge that you haven't trashed a piece of highly advanced electro-mechanical-optical machinery worth more than most houses. Put the book under your pillow tonight. Good luck.

- ❑ When the test begins, assemble the cases. Organize your workspace. Pretend you know what you're doing.
- ❑ Attach base to body (15 or 19mm rods)
  Standard or Super16?
- ❑ Attach Camera to Head w/ quick release or dovetail
- ❑ Camera off
- ❑ Remove PL cap
- ❑ Check mount
  Standard or Super16?
- ❑ Inch manually
- ❑ Check shutter angle (Adjust shutter angle)
- ❑ Check fiber optic viewing screen
  Standard or Super16?
- ❑ Plug in on-board battery or block battery
- ❑ Camera on

- ❑ Status light--red warning for a second, then light goes out
- ❑ What happens if you use the wrong battery or battery cable-- (Panavision)? Nothing. Camera shuts down. Turn it off.
- ❑ Wait a minute or two. Camera should reset. Check fuse.
- ❑ Check gate from rear: Standard or Super16?
- ❑ Attach magazine
- ❑ Inch with PHASE button or manually
- ❑ Mount lens
- ❑ Mount rods, zoom motor, follow focus, mattebox
- ❑ Check camera display functions
- ❑ Check speed and footage counter
- ❑ Check timecode sensitivity on magazine
- ❑ Check battery voltage
- ❑ Check timecode display
- ❑ Run Camera
- ❑ Program speed selector can be switched while camera runs
- ❑ Set pitch adjustment--camera right
- ❑ Set lightmeter ASA
- ❑ ARRIGLOW
- ❑ Install finder extender
- ❑ Set finder diopter
- ❑ Attach Leveling rod
- ❑ Heated eyecup
- ❑ Friction adjustment for eyepiece rotation and swing out
- ❑ Attach video assist camera and flicker reduction unit
- ❑ Adjust video camera. Align with monitor.
- ❑ Check lens--eye focus vs. tape. If lens doesn't have exact footage scale (Zeiss zoom), check with a prime which has exact witness marks, then use chart tape on the zoom.
- ❑ CCU (Camera Control Unit)
- ❑ LCC (Laptop Camera Controller) Mac Powerbook.
- ❑ RSU
- ❑ RCU
- ❑ ESU
- ❑ Iris Control Unit
- ❑ Timecode
- ❑ Magazines: loading.
- ❑ auto loop size correction for timecode
- ❑ film run out shut-off
- ❑ You can use SR1 and 2 mags on 16SR3 cameras

- ❑ But not High Speed mags on a Regular Camera
- ❑ And you can't use Normal mags on a High Speed Camera
- ❑ maintenance in the field
- ❑ End of day cleaning--fibre screen, gate, mags, lenses
- ❑ Pack up to go. Wrap loose objects so they don't become damaged from banging around in the cases.

Two Minute Refresher Course

For experienced camera assistants who are old hands with 16 SR1 and SR2's, here's a quick chart comparing features of the previous models with the new 16 SR3.

	16 SR1	16 SR2	16 SR3
voltage	12	12	24
mirror shutter	180	180	45, 90, 135, 144, 172.8, 180
mount	bayonet	bayonet	PL
analog dial on magazine	footage exposed	footage exposed	timecode sensitivity
video	change finder	change finder	integral video assist
format	Standard 16	Standard 16	Standard / Super16
			ARRIGLOW
			Timecode
			Computer Interface
speeds	24/25 external variable	24/25 external variable	Direct input of all speeds, crystal accurate to 1/1000 fps
weight body+mag	12lb (5.5kg)	11lb (5kg)	13.5lb (6.1kg)
sound level	28 db	24 db	20 db
finder xtndr	10x	10x	10/17x magnifier
standard model	5-75 fps	5-75 fps	5-75 fps
finder	symmetrical	symmetrical	symmetrical
magazines	black	black	grey w/ black grip
highspeed model	10-150 fps grey mags	10-150 fps grey mags	5-150 fps grey mags with black rubber grip + "HS"
size (l x h x w) (viewfinder horizontal)	264 x 195 x 160mm 10.4 x 7.7 x 6.3"	264 x 195 x 160mm 10.4 x 7.7 x 6.3"	264 x 195 x 172mm 10.4 x 7.7 x 6.8"

- Some 16 SR1 and 2 cameras have 144° shutters.
- Some 16 SR1 and 2 cameras have been modified to Super16 with 172.8° shutters, and PL mounts.

The Ten Minute 16 SR3 Refresher Course

How to tell which camera is which?

(there are two models:)

- ❑ Regular Speed 5-75 frames/sec:
  below 20db at 24/25fps

- ❑ High Speed 5-150 fps:
  marked with Yellow "HS" on body and mags
  20 to 23db at 24 fps

- ❑ Do not use regular mags on high speed cameras

- ❑ Do not use high speed mags on regular cameras.

Some important facts:

- ❑ Runs on 24 VDC

- ❑ Different pin configuration than previous accessories and cables. If there is any problem with voltage (incl. reverse polarity) camera will not run. Has auto cutout circuitry.

- ❑ 400 ft magazines: ARRI 16 SR2 mags will fit but are less quiet. 16 SR3 mags will fit on SR1 and SR2.

- ❑ 19 mm wide baseplate system. 15 support available.

- ❑ Quick Release or Dovetail Mounting

Setting up the Camera

- ❑ Connect power with power switch off. Switch camera to "on". Light above "RUN" button turns red, then goes out indicating system check sequence "passed" and camera is OK. No light indicates a voltage problem—possibly reversed polarity. Auto cutout circuit shuts down camera to prevent damage. Turn power off; wait a minute or two for it to reset (make sure you correct the problem). Light turns green when camera runs at speed.

- ❑ Steady red light above run button indicates a problem found during check sequence. Camera will not run with red on.

PL Mount

- ❑ Lens mount is same as 535, 535B, and 435. Two tabs on either side. Turn clockwise to secure the lens. "CLOCK to LOCK." Counter-clockwise to remove.

- ❑ Red lettering at 1 o'clock shows whether mount is set to Standard or Super 16.

Mirror shutter adjustment

- ❑ 180, 172.8, 144, 135, 90, 45 degrees

- ❑ Only use special 2mm Hex driver with rubber-covered shaft to adjust. Hold inching knob. Gently push special tool into receptacle, and turn to adjust shutter angle.

Fiber Screen

- ❑ Do not use compressed air on fiber screen. Use Hirschmann clip only to remove screen by "T" handle. It only fits in one way—shiny side up. Do not blow compressed air into the cavity—you could blow the lightmeter needle away.

Camera Left Side

❑ Backlit LED display panel. Backlight goes off after 30 sec.

❑ SIX MODES on the Main Camera Display
- Home Page: total footage(or take) and frame rate
- Programmed Speed
- Take (or total footage) and Battery Voltage
- Timecode — Hour:Min:Sec:Frame
- 8 User bits
- Timecode sensitivity and warning beep control

❑ PHASE Button = electronic inching of camera (runs the camera at 1 frame/sec)

❑ Push PHASE briefly to advance mirror shutter ½ way for gate check. Push again to return to viewing position

❑ Push the PHASE button when shooting monitors or computers (at any speed) to get "phase the roll bar out of the shot.

❑ Mechanical inching knob. Push in and turn counter-clockwise to advance the film (not while the camera is running!)

❑ Rosette mount is same as previous models—but only on camera right side

❑ Light Meter is coupled to electronics of camera. If you change frame rate, light meter automatically calculates change. Of course, you have to do something about it. The meter is a center-weighted, match-needle system. The middle dot is correct exposure. Each dot is one stop under or over—the plus is over, the minus is under.

❑ Select ASA. Set ARRIGLOW-Meter switch to desired function. You cannot have both at once. Turn the rotary switch all the way in one direction or the other. Middle positions do not work.

Viewfinder

- ❑ Red LED glows in viewing system when out of sync, low battery, or film has run out. Note: Camera stops on film roll out.
- ❑ Finder and extender are not compatible with previous models.
- ❑ Eyepiece has a lever to close light trap shutter
- ❑ Finder extender has 2x magnifier (10x=normal / 17x=2x)
- ❑ Rotate prism when changing between short and long eyepiece. Push silver button and turn black knob until it stops to rotate prism. You can set any intermediate prism position to reposition the horizon.
- ❑ Friction adjustment for eyepiece up-down tension can be adjusted with FRICTION-LOOSE knob.

The Rear

- ❑ Accessory connector: plug in speed controls: RCU-1, RU, Timecode jam sync cable, ESU
- ❑ CCU/LCC connector: same as 535, 535B, 435 to set speeds, speed ramps, timecode, etc. with a Mac Powerbook, RCU or CCU .
- ❑ Two side-mounted running lights.
- ❑ Connector to power heated eyecup. Light above indicates when it is on. The heated eyecup is thermostatically controlled.
- ❑ Above heater connector is the storage compartment for special rubber-covered 2mm hex mirror shutter adjustment tool.

Video Assist

- ❑ Two styles of handles: regular or video
- ❑ Regular handle supplies 100% of light to eyepiece
- ❑ Video assist handgrip has optics for video assist in it (80/20 or 50/50 beam splitter—80% and 50% of light to eyepiece respectively) . Handgrip swivels out of the way with push of locking button.
- ❑ Threaded mount for CCD video camera
- ❑ Video "elbow" with focus ring (with lock) and iris.
- ❑ Mechanical centering of video image (x-y.) Plug in a monitor. Loosen ring of CCD mount slightly. Use a 1.3mm Hex driver to adjust the x and y adjustment screws. Loosen the "F" screw at the bottom to extend the distance. Snug it back up again when the crosshairs are centered. Rotate the video camera if image is off level. Tighten the knurled ring.
- ❑ More drastic procedure: If the video image is way off, or this is the first time video elbow and video camera have been assembled, turn your video monitor 90° onto its left side to help in your orientation. Loosen ring of CCD mount and use 1.3 mm Hex driver to back off the two x-y adjustment screws. Back of the "F" screw if necessary. Move the CCD Camera until the crosshair is close to center. Tighten the ring gently. Fine tune with the 1.3 mm Hex screws. Snug up the "F" screw. Tighten the knurled ring.
- ❑ 24 v DC to 12 v DC converter screws into the two RS receptacles to provide 24 and 12 volt ouput and a camera right on/off switch.

Magazine

- ❑ Similar to previous models. Do not use High Speed mags with standard camera.
- ❑ What used to be a Footage Exposed dial on the take-up side is now a timecode sensitivity dial. If you are using timecode, you must set it to the proper setting. A common mistake is to set it to "0", thinking you are resetting the footage counter.
- ❑ Timecode magazines have an LED lens that should be cleaned every few rolls.
- ❑ Be careful not to bend the pins of the electronic connector on the bottom of the throat of timecode mags.
- ❑ Clean infrared glass on bottom of mag and the LED's themselves below gate area. The LED measures film loop size and determines timecode offset adjustment. It also stops the camera when film runs out.
- ❑ Rarely needed, but you can adjust pitch while camera is running.

Appendix

Camera Electronic Pin-outs

These are electronic pinout diagrams for "dummies."—all of us mortals without degrees in electronic engineering. These charts are simplified renderings, and are not meant to be use by anyone designing accessories for the camera.

CCU

1 RS-232 transmit
2 RS-232 receive
3 +24 v (max .4A) accessory output
4 accessory ground
5 LTC timecode output
6 input/output (I/O)
7 accessory ground

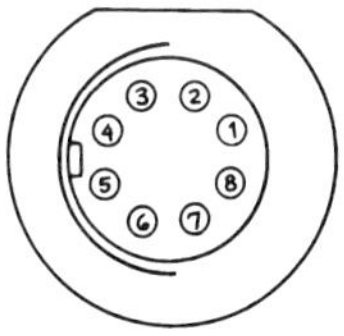

ACC

1 Remote Start. Momentary
Connection to pin 4 starts/stops camera.
2 Motor Tachometer signal out
3 +24 v (max .1A) accessory output
4 accessory ground
5 accessory identifier
6 accessory identifier
7 timecode out
8 timecode in
9 Startmark

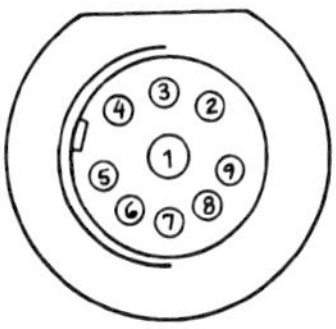

Pins 5 and 6 are used to identify the device being plugged in by various combinations of bridging that pin to ground.

If pins 4 and 5 are jumpered together, timecode in and out on pins 7 and 8 is enabled. Pins 7 and 8 have different functions depending on how pins 5 and 6 are wired.

RS

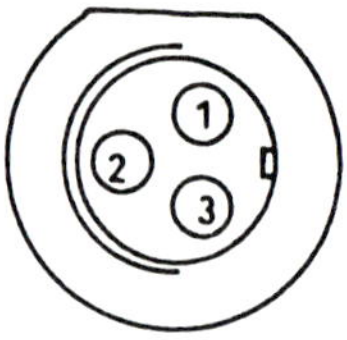

1 Ground
2 +24 v (max 1A)
(2.5A with new electronics E3/4 and new DC/DC converter)
3 /E-Run
Also output for shutter pulse when camera runs

11 Pin Fischer on DC/DC converter

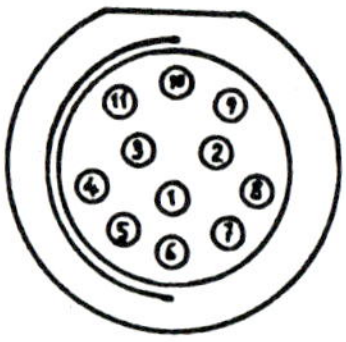

9 Ground
11 +12v (max 2.5 amps on E3/4 electronics, 1 amp on older)

Heater

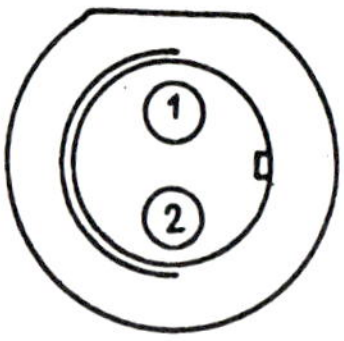

1 Ground
2 +24 v (max .4A)

Resource List: Tools, Parts, Supplies

Arriflex Corporation 617 Route 303 Blauvelt, NY 10913 914-353-1400 Fax: 914-425-1250 600 North Victory Blvd. Burbank, CA 91502 (818) 841-7070 fax: (818) 848-4028	Hirschmann clips, ARRI tools, and of course, you can buy an entire 16 SR3 package for your very own use.
Pelican Products 2255 Jefferson St Torrance, CA 90501 310-328-9910 800-824-9733	King Pelican Cases
Markertek large selection in catalog: 800-522-2025	Chemtronics Electronics Cleaner/Degreaser #ES1601 Chemtronics Contact Clean 2000 #ES 1602 Chemtronics TF Pad (electronics cleaner/degreaser pad in individual foil pouches) #C430 Foamatips Pro double ended urethane foam swabs #CFP50 Lint Free cloths #LFC-C50 Chemswab foam swab premoistened with isopropyl solvent in foil packs #CS25
	Brady Lasertab Markers (LAT-19-361, LAT-18-361)
Radio Shack 800-THE-SHACK	Wire & Cable Markers 1"x2.5" cat # 278-1616

Satter Inc Denver, CO 80207 303-399-7493	Tundra Cases SK518 Waterproof Attache Case Satter does not sell direct, but can provide a list of dealers
Griot's Garage 3500-A 20th Street E. Tacoma, WA 98424 800-345-5789	European Tools, Tool Demagnetizer
Pace Technologies 911 Washington Street San Carlos, CA 94070 415-802-8373	Underwater Camera Housing
Clamp Flag Company 1630 30th St, Ste 300 Boulder, CO 80301 800-547-FLAG.	Clamping French Flag
Jensen Tools Inc. 7815 S. 46th Street Phoenix, AZ 85044 800-426-1194 602-968-6231	Domestic variety of Hirschmann Forceps. Spring Loaded Grabber AC83. More expensive than ARRI. #317B533 Jewelers Screwdrivers, Tool cases. 3M Write-On Cable Tape System #649B333 Rite & Wrap II Cable Markers ¾ x 1¼" #518B510 ¾ x 3" #518B515 WIHA Bondhus 40010 Tool Magnetizer-Demagnetizer #289B013 ($7.95)
Automated Media Sys. 8 Holton St. Allston, MA 02134 617-787-4313	Lithium Expedition Batteries
Birns and Sawyer 213-466-8211	Accessories and Supplies
Camware 800-422-6927	Camera Assistant Supplies
NRG Research Inc. 840 Rogue River Hwy. Building 144 Grants Pass, OR 97527 503-479-9433	Norton Rodriguez Battery Vest

Super16 Conversions of 16 SR1 and 2 Cameras

Pierre Careau
CineAsst
332 Dupont Street
The Annex Center
Toronto, Ontario
M5R 1V9 Canada
ph: (416) 975-2565
fax: (416) 975-0895

Axel Broda
Arriflex Technic
29340 Surrey Way
Tehachapi, CA 93561
phone/fax: 805-821-6725

Praezisions-Entwicklung Denz
(089) 431-6047
fax: (089) 431-6967
Josephsburgstrasse 81-83
D-8000 Munich 80 Germany

ARRI GB Ltd
The Movie House
1-3 Airlinks, Spitfire Way
(Off Southall Lane)
Heston, Middlesex TW5 9HR
England
ph: (081) 848 88 81
fx: (081) 561 13 12

Suppliers

A & J Manufacturing Co.
11121 Hindry Avenue
Los Angeles, CA 90009
213-678-3053
800-537-4000
fax: 310-216-2694

Alfred Chrosziel Film-Technik GMBH
Regerstr. 27
D-8000 Munich 90
West Germany
phone: 089-448 03 39
fax: 089-447 08 61

Alan Gordon Enterprises
1340 Cahuenga Blvd.
Hollywood, CA 90078
(213) 466-3561

American Society of Cinematographers
1782 North Orange Drive
Hollywood, CA 90028
(213) 876-5080

Anton/Bauer
One Controls Drive
Shelton, CT 06484
(203) 929-1100

Bel-Air Plastics inc.
9938 Hayward Way
South El Monte, CA 91733
(818) 575-8765

Birns & Sawyer
1026 North Highland Avenue
Hollywood, CA 90038
(213) 466-8211
fax: (213) 466-7049

Calzone Case Co.
225 Black Rock Ave.
Bridgeport, CT 06605
(203) 367-5766

Camera Service Center
625 West 54th Street
New York, NY 10019
(212) 757-0906

Cartoni USA
960 Enchanted Way/unit 104
Simi Valley, CA 93065
805-520-6086
fax: 805-520-6949

CEI Technology
880 Maude Avenue
Mountain View, CA 94043
(415) 969-1910

Century Precision Optics
10713 Burbank Blvd.
North Hollywood, CA 91601
(818) 766-3715 fax:
(818) 505-9865

Chiswick Trading
(plastic bags)
31 Union Ave
Sudbury, MA 01776
800-225-8708 fax: (617) 443-8091

Chrosziel (see Alfred Chrosziel Film Technik)

Cinematography Electronics
31238 Via Colinas / suite A
Westlake Village, CA 91362
(818) 706-3334 fax: (818) 706-3335

Cine 60
630 9th Avenue
New York, NY 10036
(212) 586-8782

Cine 60
1050 Cahuenga Blvd.
Hollywood, CA 90038
(213) 461-3046

Clairmont Camera
4343 Lankershim Blvd.
N. Hollywood, CA 91602
(818) 761-4440
fax: (818) 761-0861

Continental Camera Systems
7240 Valgean Avenue
Van Nuys, CA 91406
(818) 989-5222

CP Cases
Worton Hall Industrial Estate
Worton Rd, Isleworth
Middlesex TW7 6ER England
01-568 1881/7
fax 01-568 1141

Cooke Lenses (see Rank Taylor Hobson)

dSam Ltd
David Samuelson
7, Montagu Mews West
London W1H 1TF
England
phone: 01-723-6562
fax: 01-724-4025

Denecke, Inc.
55417-B Cahuenga Blvd.
N. Hollywood, CA 91601
(818) 766-3525
(819) fax: (818) 766-0269

Denz (see Praezisions-Entwicklung Denz)

Edmund Scientific Co.
101 E. Gloucester Pike
Barrington, NJ 08007
(609) 573-6250
(610) fax: (609) 573-6295

Edmunds, Larry Bookshop
6658 Hollywood Blvd.
Hollywood, CA 90028
(213) 463-3273

The Equipment Broker
Roy Isaia
514 Live Oak Circle Dr.
Calabasas, CA 91302
(818) 888-3293

Excalibur Cases
12427 Foothill Blvd.
Lake View Terrace, CA 91342
(818) 899-2547

Fasula
178 West Houston Street
New York, NY 10014
(212) 242-2544

Fiberbilt Cases, Inc.
601 West 26th St.
New York, NY 10001-1199
(212) 675-5820
(213) (800) 847-4176

G + M Power Products, Inc.
943 N. Orange Dr.
Los Angeles, CA 90038
(213) 850-6800
fax: (213) 850-5143

Karl Horn Cinetech
719 Arroyo Ave / Unit C
San Fernando, CA 91340
(818) 365-0799
fax: (818) 365-8531

Hale Color Consultants
(grey scales)
1505 Phoenix Road
Phoenix, MD 21131
(301) 472-4850
(800) 777-1225

Harrison & Harrison Filters
677 North Plano St.
Porterville, CA 93257
(209) 782-0121
fax: (209) 782-0824

Hydroimage, Inc.
Pete Romano
4121 Redwood Avenue, #112
Los Angeles, CA 90066
(213) 301-8187

Ikonographics
Thomas Barron
945 N. Highland Ave.
Hollywood, CA 90038
(213) 461-3518 fax: (213) 461-5456

Image Devices Int'l
1825 NE 149 Street
Miami, FL 33181
(305) 945-1111
fax: (305) 945-1117

Innovision Optics
1318 Second Street suite 31
Santa Monica, CA 90401
(213) 394-5510
fax: (213) 395-2941

J.A.R. Enterprises
11100 Cumpston #22
North Hollywood, CA 91601
(818) 980-0572

Juergen's, Inc.
(video taps)
11235 East Mapleton Rd.
Mapleton, OR 97453
(503) 268-9980
fax: (503) 268-4023

Kaleidoscope Hot Head
128 Wembley Park Drive
Wembley, Middlesex, England
01-902-1262

Media Logic (speed controls)
17 West 20th Street #5E
New York, NY 10011
(212) 924-3 824
fax: (212) 924-3823

Nemenz International
870 N. Vine
Hollywood, CA 90038
(213) 469-ARRI fax: (212) 469-1217

Norris Film Products
(intervalometers)
1014 Green Lane
La Canada, CA 91011
(818) 790-1907

O'Connor Engineering Laboratories
100 Kalmus Drive
Costa Mesa, Ca 92626
(714) 979-3993

Optex
22-26 Victoria Road
New Barnet, Herts EN4 9PF
England
01-441 2199
fax: 01-449 3646

Otto Nemenz International
(see Nemenz)

Praezisions-Entwicklung Denz
Josephsburgstrasse 81-83
D-8000 Munich 80
West Germany
(089) 431-6047

Preston Cinema Systems
1621 Stanford St.
Santa Monica, CA 90404
(213) 453-1852

Rank Taylor Hobson Ltd.
P.O. Box 36, New Star Road
Thurmaston Lane
Leicester LE4 7JQ England
(533) 763771
fax: (0533) 740167

Richter Cine Equipment, Inc.
Ridge Road
Essex, NY 12936
(518) 963-7080

Ronford-Baker Eng Co Ltd
Braziers, Oxhey Lane
Watford, Herts, England
01-428-5941

Russell, John (see J.A.R. Enterprises)

Sachtler GmbH
Dieselstr. 16
D-8046 Garching/Munich, W. Germany
(89) 32 90 91 50
fax: (089) 32 90 91 27

Sachtler Corporation of America
55 N. Main Street
Freeport, NY 11520
(516) 867-4900
and
3316 W. Victory Blvd.
Burbank, CA 91505
(818) 845-4446

Samuelson Computer (see dSam)

Seitz Technical Products, Inc.
111-C Newark Road
PO Box 338
Avondale, PA 19311
(215) 268-2228
(fax) 215-268-2229

Shurco Tool Inc.
744 East Edina Pl
Covina, CA 91723
(818) 966-8606

Thomas Spencer Enterprises (Sundicator)
726 Chelham Way
Santa Barbara, CA 93108
805-969-7280

Tiffen Manufacturing Corp.
90 Oser Ave.
Hauppauge, NY 11788
(516) 273-2500

Tyler Camera Systems
14218 Aetna Street
Van Nuys, CA 91401
(818) 989-4420

Unilux, Inc.
290 Lodi St.
Hackensack, NJ 07601
(201) 489-0800 (800) 6FLASH3

Victory Battery Company
1508 West Burbank Blvd.
Burbank, CA 91506
818-840-2766

Weaver-Steadman
1646 20th Street
Santa Monica, CA 90404
(213) 829-3296

These listings do not constitute an endorsement, because I am sure I have left out many worthy sources, to whom I apologize.

AMERICAS

Argentina
Cine Center S.R.L.
Ing. Julio Fava
Lavalle 1925/1927
1051 Buenos Aires,
Argentina
ph: (54) (01) 40 69 63
(54) (01) 45 32 23
fx: (54) (01) 476 32 23
tlx: 18348 cemos ar (for +cctr+)
ta: zczc ctr

Brazil
Eurobras Film
Av. Graca Aranha 19-Gr 401
Rio de Janeiro, Brazil
ph: (55) (021) 240 33 99
fx: (55) (021) 240 64 30
tlx: 2139975 tphu
ta: Starfilm

Canada
ARRI Canada Inc.*
433 Horner Ave., Unit 11
Etobicoke, Ontario M8W 4Y4 Canada
ph: (416) 255-3335
fx: (416) 255-3399

Chile
Klaus Seeger Schweikart
Navidad 1200 Dept. 1006
Vitacura, Santiago de Chile, Chile
ph/fx: (56) (02) 206-7576

Mexico
Ulrich Bruenger F.
Callejon de Las Cruces 61
Apdo. Postal 85-097
10200 Mexico, D.F.,
Mexico
ph: (52) (05) 595-36-24
fx: (52) (05) 681 81 14

USA-head office
Arriflex Corporation*
617 Route 303
Blauvelt, NY 10913-1123
ph: (914) 353-1400
fx: (914) 425-1250
ta: Arriflex Blauvelt

USA-branch office
Arriflex Corporation*
600 North Victory Blvd.
Burbank, CA 91502-1639
ph: (818) 841-7070
fx: (818) 848-4028
ta: Arriflex Burbank

Venezuela
Cine Materiales C.A.
av. alfredo jahn
Apartado Postal 61.098
Caracas 1060-A,
Venezuela
ph: (58) (02) 284 41 44
(58) (02) 284 82 60
fx: (58) (02) 284 46 10
tlx: 25427 citve vc
ta: Cinematca

* = Service Assistance Available

ASIA, MIDDLE EAST, PACIFIC

Bangladesh
Marina Z Enterprise Ltd.
5 Mymensingh Road
Dhaka, Bangladesh
ph: (02) 50 43 23
(02) 50 31 56
fx: (02) 86 32 11
tlx: 642430 mze bj
ta: Camera

China, People's Republic of
Jebsen & Co. Ltd.*
EMO-Department
30/F, Caroline Centre
3-38 Yun-Ping Road
Causeway Bay, Hongkong
ph: (85) 29 23 87 77
fx: (85) 28 82 20 17,
(85) 28 82 20 54
tlx: hx 73221
hx 73769
ta: Jebemo Hongkong

Hongkong
Jebsen & Co. Ltd.
ARRI Section
28/F, Caroline Centre
3-38 Yun Ping Road
Causeway Bay, Hongkong
ph: (85) 29 26 22 22
fx: (85) 28 82 17 87
tlx: hx 73769
hx 73221
ta: Jebsen Hongkong

Taiwan
AE Media Technology Ltd.*
8th Floor, No. 63
Chang An E Road, Sec. 2
P.O. Box 578
Taipei, Taiwan
ph: (02) 507 10 00/3
fx: (02) 507 96 20
tlx: 25068 aecom
ta: Aecom Taipei

India-head office
Photophone Limited*
7, Saki Vihar Road
P.O. Box 8936
Bombay 400 072, India
ph: (022) 578 46 62
fx: (022) 578 43 25
tlx: 011-72129 fazl in
011-84736 plby in
ta: Photophone Bombay
Head Office

India-branch
Photophone Limited
179/5 II Cross Road
Palace Lower Orchards
Bangalore 560 003, India
ph: (0812) 36 52 10
(0812) 36 18 92
fx: (080) 334 60 51
tlx: 0845-2482 faxl in
ta: Comel Bangalore

* = Service Assistance Available

India-branch
Photophone Ltd.
4850, Ansari Road
24, Daryaganj
New Delhi 110 002, India
ph: (011) 327 40 43/4/5
(011) 327 25 62
fx: (011) 327 81 87
tlx: 031-65304 pldl in
ta: Photophone New Delhi

India-branch
Photophone Limited
B1 - 1st Floor, Parser Appt.
109, G.N. Chetty Road, T. Nagar
Madras 600 017, India
ta: Comeltron-Madras

Iran
Iran Tele Kala Co. Ltd
Meydan Enghelab
Shahre Tamasha Building
P.O. Box 13145-1314
Tehran, Iran
ph: (021) 92 92 82/3
(021) 92 25 47/8
fx: (021) 92 92 81
tlx: 212524 tlka ir
ta: Telekalaco Tehran

Japan
NAC Incorporated*
2-7, Nishiazuabu
1-Chome, Minato-ku
Tokyo 106, Japan
ph: (81) (03) 3470 13 19
fx: (81) (03) 3404 95 02
tlx: 0242-2490 camnac j

Korea, South
Sama Electronics Corporation*
KWTC P.O. Box 110
2nd Floor, Gugu Building
145-18
Samsung Dong, Kangnam-Ku,
Seoul, Korea
ph: (02) 565 86 41
fx: (02) 565 86 40

Saudi Arabia
Said Bin Saad Trading Est.
P.O. Box 2318
Riyadh 11451, Kingdom of Saudi Arabia
ph: (01) 403 68 96
(01) 401 33 08
fx: (01) 402 77 75
tlx: 401602 sautec sj
ta: Saad Riyadh

Singapore, Brunei, Philippines, Malaysia, Indonesia
Cine Equipment Pte. Ltd.*
10C Jalan Ampas
#08-02 Ho Seng Lee
Flatted Warehouse
Singapore 1232, Singapore
ph: 252 50 89
fx: 255 19 81

Sri-Lanka
Mart Group Limited
P.O. Box 1060
6, Kinross Avenue
Colombo 4, Sri Lanka
ph: (01) 58 02 98
(01) 58 36 27
fx: (01) 58 07 21
tlx: 31357 metalix ce
attn: Mart Group Arulanandam

Syria
Puzant Yacoubian & Sons
P.O. Box 3617
Damascus, Syria
ph: (11) 21 28 600
fx: (11) 21 28 611
tlx: 411986 puydam sy
411423 puysons sy
ta: Puy Damas

Australia, New Guinea, Oceania
John Barry Group Pty. Ltd.*
1, Mclachlan Avenue
Artarmon, Sydney, Australia
ph: (02) 439 69 55
fx: (02) 439 23 75

New Zealand
Film Facilities Ltd.*
P.O. Box 6698
The Production Village
26 Wright Street
Wellington, New Zealand
ph: (04) 384 41 92
fx: (04) 384 37 74
ta: Mopix

EUROPE

Austria
LB-Electronics Ges.mbH*
Doblinger Hauptstr. 95
1191 Wien, Austria
ph: (01) 36 76 60
fx: (01) 369 84 43
tlx: 133722 lind a

Belgium
ARC
Rue Dries, 167
1200 Bruxelles, Belgium
ph: (02) 770 64 44
fx: (02) 772 33 88
tlx: 22747

Denmark
Bico Professional ApS
Produktionsvej 23 A
P.O.B. 158
2600 Glostrup, Denmark
ph: (042) 84 54 45
fx: (042) 84 41 28
ta: Bicofoto Copenhagen

Finland
FOKI OY*
P.O.B. 56 /
(Takomotie 8 B)
SR-00381 Helsinki, Finland
ph: (0) 561 20 66
fx: (0) 561 24 41
ta: Geweberg Helsinki

France
Techni Cine Phot*
64 bis, Blvd. Jean-Jaures
Boite Postale 90
93402 St. Ouen-Cedex, France
ph: (01) 40 11 81 81
fx: (01) 40 10 17 27
tlx: 234959 cinphot f
ta: Technicine St Ouen

Great Britain, Rep. of Ireland
ARRI (GB) Ltd.*
1-3 The Airlinks, Spitfire Way
Heston, Middlesex TW5 9NR England
ph: (44) (81) 848 88 81
fx: (44) (81) 561 13 12
tlx: 916075 arrigb g

Greece
J. Calavitis & Co.*
11, Antinoros St.
Athens 116 34, Greece
ph: (01) 724 81 44
(01) 722 64 60
fx: (01) 729 16 13
tlx: 219850 cala gr
ta: Cinecal - Athens

Italy (Milano)
ARRI Italia S.R.L.
Via Oslavia 40/46
20099 Sesto S. Giovanni
Milano Italy
ph: (39) (02) 26 22 71 75
fx: (39) (02) 242 16 92

Italy (Rome)
ARRI Italia S.R.L.*
Via Paolo Orsi, 47
00179 Roma, Italy
ph: (06) 72 67 07 97
fx: (06) 723 15 41
tlx: 620339 arrit i

Netherlands
Fofic*
Kruyderlaan 35
3431 BM Nieuwegein, Netherlands
ph: (030) 604 44 22
fx: (030) 604 79 44
tlx: 40336 fofic ngl

Norway
Lars Farnes A/S*
Pottermakerveien 8
Postboks 34, Kalbakken
0901 Oslo, Norway
ph: (47) (22) 16 29 30
fx: (47) (22) 16 47 39
tlx: 77463 lf

Portugal
Sonofilme*
Pr, Francisco Sa Carneiro
9-2°-dto.
1000 Lisboa, Portugal
ph: (01) 848 23 00, (01) 80 75 11
fx: (01) 848 50 69
tlx: 15306 sonfil p
ta: Sonofilme

Spain
Cine Tecnico S.A.*
C/Verdaguer Garcia, 46
28027 Madrid, Spain
ph: (01) 403 64 57
fx: (01) 403 40 01

Sweden
SFL Svensk Film & Ljusteknik AB*
Norr Malarstrand 12
Box 22073
11220 Stockholm, Sweden
ph: (08) 654 18 55
fx: (08) 652 83 58

EUROPE - Switzerland
Erno Film & Video AG*
Niederhaslistrasse 12
8157 Dielsdorf, Switzerland
ph: (01) 855 53 53
fx: (01) 855 53 50
ta: Eugernerno Zuerich

* = Service Assistance Available

Index

B

C

D

E

F

N

O

P

Q

R

S

T

U

V

W

Z

Photocopy these focus targets.
Use 5 large targets for shooting
lens tests. Glue small targets
to your slate for easier focusing.

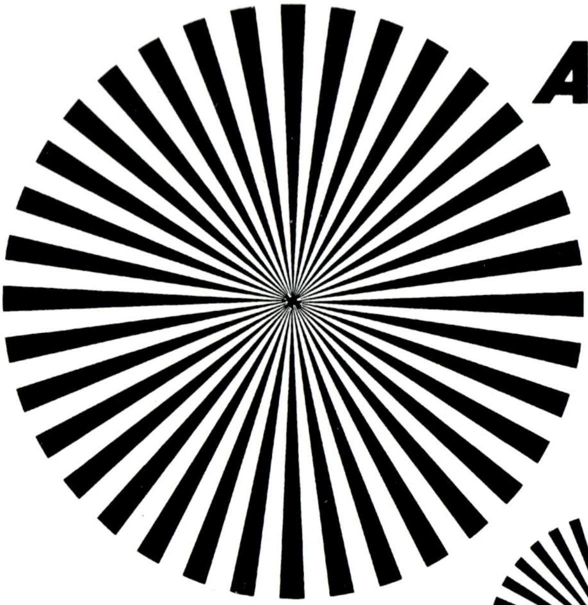

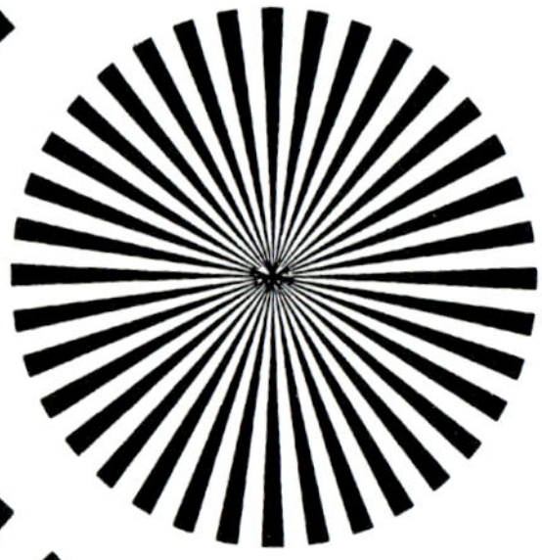

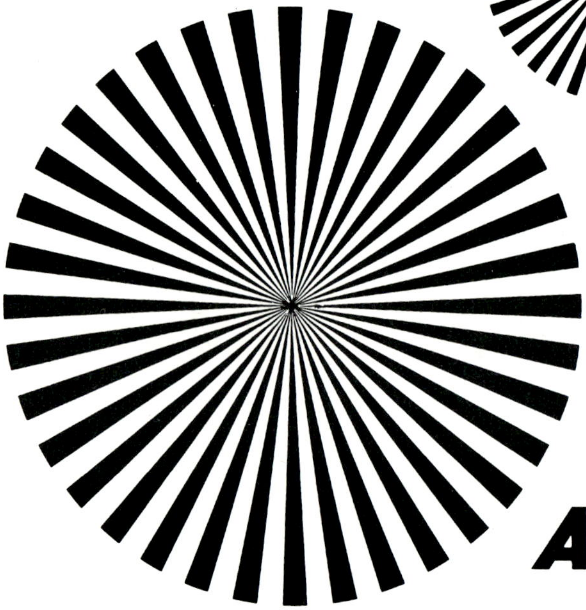

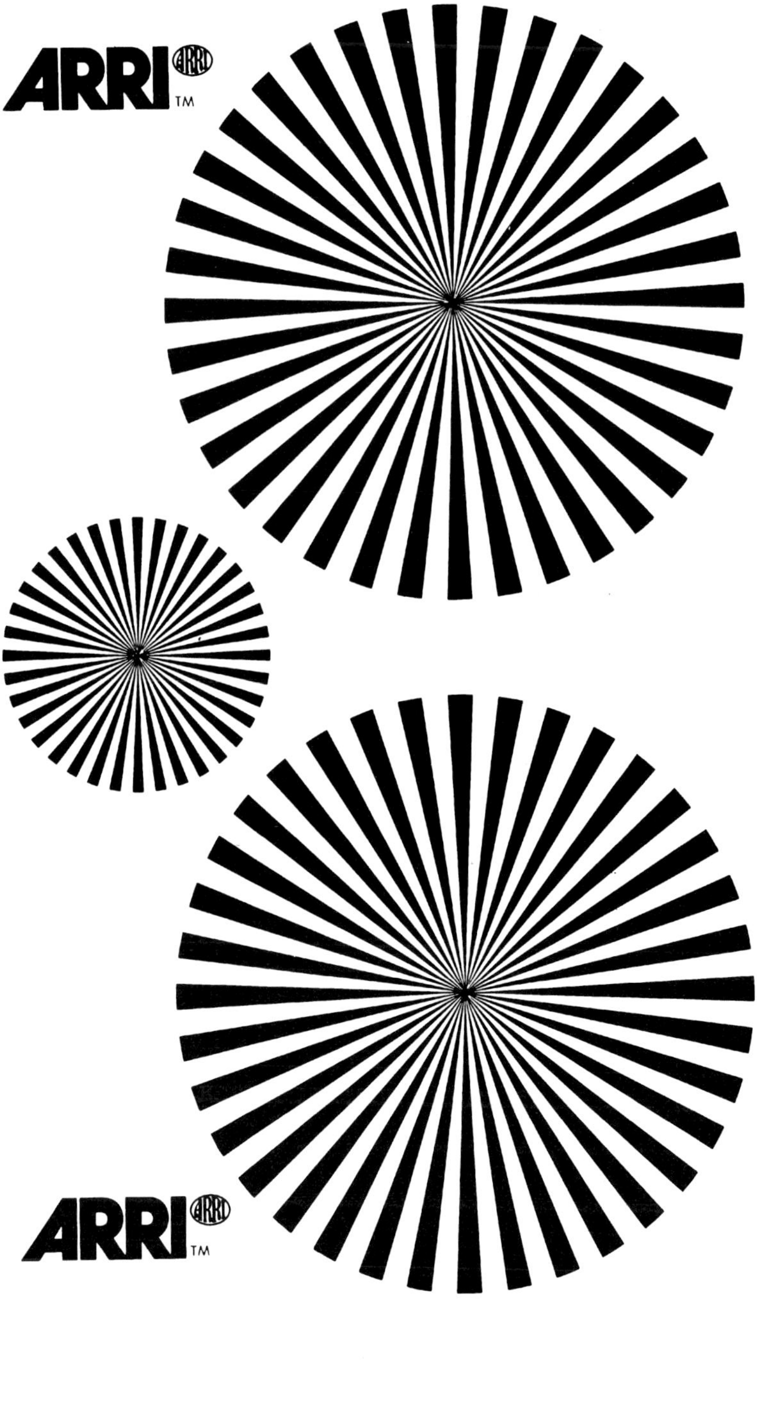